BESTIE to BEASTIE to BELGIUM

BESTIE to BEASTIE to BELGIUM

Hibs' green and white knuckle ride through the 80s

Colin Leslie

In memory of Ally 'Hector' Nicole (1972-2002),
and to the other Angels High Above,
singing Glory to the Hibees,
the team that we all love.

ACKNOWLEDGEMENTS

You touched it, you saved it...
thank you THANK YOU!

I have many people to thank for making this book a reality. My old colleagues from *The Scotsman*, Scott Coull and Paul Greaves, for putting their time, skill and creative effort into editing and typesetting this tome; Anthony Brown for showing me the self-publishing ropes – a top guy, even for a Jambo; Simon Munro at J Thomson Printers for his enthusiasm in supporting independent writers; Jim Divine for the fantastic cover design; Mr Hibs himself Paul Kane for putting me in touch with so many ex-players and for helping me to get the ball rolling when we met in the Tor; Simon Pia for his critical eye and for letting me peer into the nicotine-stained Press Box of the 80s; Steve Nicole and family for allowing me to pay tribute to my old pal Hector, who I stood alongside at some of those crazy games; Jan Williamson for her support; and finally to big captain fantastic Gordon Rae – a gentleman and a Hibbie – for the foreword.

Others to thank for their help, including all of the interviewees, are: Mike Aitken, Sean Allan, Bertie Auld, John Blackley, Andy Blance, Ally Brazil, Mike Burns, Ralph Callachan, John Campbell, Gordon Chisholm, John Collins, Steve Cowan, David Duff, Gareth Evans, Graham Ewing, Alan Hart, Stuart Hall, Keith Houchen, Ricky Hill, Mark Leech, Duncan Leslie, Jim McArthur, Kevin McKee, Jackie McNamara, Patrick McPartlin, Gary Mackay, Rod MacLeod, Sandy Macnair, Eddie May, Alex Miller, Callum Milne, Graham Mitchell, Andy O'Brien, Julie Orr, Neil Orr, Craig Paterson, Alan Pattullo, Richard Payne, George Peters, Rob Primrose, Brian Rice, Alan Rough, Bobby Sinnet, Aidan Smith, Andrew Smith, Alan Sneddon, Pat Stanton, George Stewart, Gordon Timmins, Joe Tortolano, Colin Thompson of the Royal Gazette, Steven Tweed, Mickey Weir and Alan Woodhouse. Apologies if I have missed anyone out, be sure to let me know and I'll give you a shout out. Similarly, to the players I was unable to get in touch with on this occasion – unfortunately there has to be a cut-off point when deadlines creep up on you, and I had so much great material in the bag that I couldn't get round everyone, which is a shame. I'll catch you next time! Thanks also to all the Hibbies who shared their personal memories of following the club with me, via the online survey I set up.

This is an entirely independent production, with no fancy marketing budget or department, so if you enjoy the book please spread the word on social media, and you can give me a follow or tag @Hibs80s.

Glory Glory to the Hibees.

Colin Leslie, November 2021

First published in Scotland in December 2021

A CIP catalogue record for this book
is available from the British Library

ISBN 978-1-3999-0515-2

Cover design by JimDeanPhotography.com
Front and back cover images by Mark Leech/Offside Sports Photography

Printed and bound in Scotland by
J Thomson Colour Printers Limited, Glasgow

CONTENTS

COVER STORY:

A moment in time

There were several strong contenders when it came to choosing the front cover picture for 'Bestie to Beastie to Belgium', but the one that stood out above others is the incredible image Mark Leech captured at Easter Road on 9 August 1986.

Graeme Souness – facing Hibs in his debut game as player-manager of Rangers – had just lost control and savagely sunk his studs into the leg of George McCluskey. The 1980s was never short of blood and thunder, and this snapshot covers both. As he begins his long walk to the dressing room, a shame-faced Souness is seen sheepishly surveying the damage he has done as blood seeps into the white sock of McCluskey, while physio Tom McNiven supports the stricken Hibs striker, and team-mate Billy Kirkwood hovers in the background to let the Rangers player-manager know exactly what he thought of the cowardly act.

London-based Leech, a leading football photographer since 1974 and managing director of Offside Sports Photography, had 'previous' for visiting combustible Scottish football fixtures. In a recent interview, he said: "I remember the Scottish Cup final, Celtic v Rangers in 1980. I wasn't ready for that, I thought I'd seen trouble. There were just bodies and bottles and police horses all over the pitch. This one photographer, a guy came at him, grabbed his camera and smacked him over the head with it, and then said 'that bastard's got Nikon back to front on his fucking head now'."

It didn't put Leech off returning north of the Border, however, and that hot summer's day in 86, he headed to Easter Road, unaware that he was about to cover *one of the football stories of the decade. Here is the story behind this amazing picture, told in Mark's own words...*

In the 80s you could get the BA shuttle up to Glasgow or Edinburgh. It wasn't environmentally friendly, but nor was it expensive. I turned up at Heathrow, expecting the usual core of 6-8 photographers to be going up, especially for Souness's first match as player-manager of Rangers, which I regarded as a massive story. He had been a big player and had won European Cups with Liverpool. The English clubs were out of Europe in the aftermath of Heysel, and you saw that he had taken Terry Butcher and some of the England World Cup team up with him, so it felt like there might be a shift of power. But when I turned up and looked around there was no-one there – I checked the kick-off time in case I had got it wrong! I hadn't, so I headed up to Edinburgh. I got to the game and still there were no English photographers to be seen, which I thought was amazing. There were plenty of the Scottish lads, but they mainly sat behind the goal. The light at Easter Road was coming in right above the tunnel, beautiful light, so I thought to myself: Souness is going to be in the middle of the park, I'm not really interested in goal pictures, I want to be where the midfield action is going to be and capture Souness on the ball. In my head I could imagine Terry Butcher bringing the ball out of defence with his left foot and I would be able to pick him up too.

It was a hostile start to the game and Souness got booked for a bad tackle early on. Minutes later, he kicked someone else, and I could see McCluskey heading for Souness as if to say 'Hey, what are you doing?' George wasn't a trouble-maker, but Souness went up to him and just studded him on the side of the knee. People will talk about it being 'off-the-ball', but it wasn't, it was just something he did in cold blood – incredible! With all his experience of semi-finals and finals with Liverpool, he should have been able to handle it better. But there's no two ways about it, the crowd got to him. The crowd must have been thinking 'let's get stuck into Souness and see if he loses the head' and they did their job that day.

I was in the perfect position as they came towards me: one player with blood running down his sock and the other one being sent off barely half an hour into his debut. I knew I had a big story on my hands and considered leaving and getting an earlier flight back with what I had. But I met Ken Montgomery, the chief football writer from the *Sunday Mirror*, who had flown up, and we arranged to go back to the airport together after the game, so I hung around.

With a few minutes to go I went up the tunnel to pack my gear away safely so I could hotfoot it to the airport. As you came up the tunnel at Easter Road it widened out, and there were two recesses left and right. I went into the left-hand recess to pack my gear away, and the whistle must have gone for full-time because Ally McCoist came flying up the tunnel and went into the opposite recess from me, looking wound up. I looked at him, and at first I thought he had been sent off too, but then Terry Butcher came in after him. Butcher looked first at me and half-recognised me from Ipswich and England games, and then looked across and did a double take as he saw McCoist standing there waiting, with his fist clenched shouting 'I'm gonnae kill him, I'm gonnae kill him!' Butcher just grabbed him and dragged him up the tunnel and towards the Rangers dressing room. He was the peacemaker on this occasion. McCoist was obviously after someone, who I don't know, and I was thinking to myself 'Oh my word, there's going to be even more trouble'. I'm not sure I would have taken a picture as I might have copped a right-hander myself.

I met Ken and we got the cab to the airport and I knew I had a lot of work ahead of me, to get these pictures developed and out there. It was the good old days when they brought the drink trolley up and you were able to get a couple of beers and a couple of large scotches. I sat with Ken, who was a Glasgow boy through and through, and as the plane took off he said: 'Graeme's an animal, isn't he?'

I usually did colour pictures for magazines, but I knew these would be of interest to the newspapers, and the only newspaper really doing colour pictures in England then was *Today* (a national tabloid between 1986-1995). I headed straight to their offices and told them I had something they might be interested in. They went mad on it and ran nine pictures from the game and of the Souness incident, on the back page and across a massive spread. My friend was a staff photographer, and he told me: 'They've never changed the back page for me once, and then you come along and get them to do that first time!' But it was a big story, and they saw that.

I had not gone up there as a newshound, I had gone up there to take some lovely colour pictures for magazines. I say that to younger photographers: don't go to shoot lovely pools of light and then ignore the big story if the mother of all riots breaks out. Be prepared to drop Plan A and go with Plan B. I had some great images from that game – let's just say it wasn't the calm picture of Souness with his foot on the ball, looking around, that I thought I would be getting that day!

More about the 'Souness game' in Chapter 8: The Battle of Easter Road

FOREWORD

by Gordon Rae

It was an absolute honour to play for Hibs and to stay around long enough to become captain and lead the team. They are a truly special club, and I can look back with great pride and satisfaction that I got to wear the jersey from 1977 to 1990. Most of my time was, of course, spent playing in the 1980s, and although any major trophies eluded us during that period, it's safe to say that the decade had its moments – very few of them dull! So, it's a real privilege to be asked to write the foreword for *Bestie to Beastie to Belgium: Hibs green and white knuckle ride through the 80s*, and I am sure you will enjoy many of the stories told in this book.

Looking back, the 80s was unmistakably a time of huge transition for Hibs. When I first started playing, it was towards the end of the Turnbull's Tornadoes era. I was still playing with the likes of John Brownlie, John Blackley, Erich Schaedler, Arthur Duncan and Alex Edwards, Jim McArthur, Jackie McNamara, Ally MacLeod – and plenty of other really good players that you could depend on and learn from. I'd like to think as I became an experienced player, and later a coach, that I passed down many of the good habits I learned from these guys.

As we headed into the 1980s we sadly got relegated, despite having George Best among us, and while it was tough at the time, we bounced back – as Hibs always seem to do, eventually! There were some dramas and new managers along the way, but by the time we got to 1989, the club had qualified for Europe again – something we hadn't managed in 11 years. After Eddie Turnbull, you had Willie Ormond, you had Bertie Auld, Pat Stanton John Blackley – that's a high turnover of managers – before Alex Miller steadied the ship towards the end of the decade. There was a lot of upheaval in the boardroom too – when Tom Hart died, Kenny Waugh took over, and then David Duff and Jim Gray came along.

I also had the immense privilege of being granted a testimonial by the club in 1988, and that night at Easter Road is a special memory... even if wee Joe Tortolano did his best to put a spanner in the works! It was the icing on the cake for me, and I have a lot of people to thank for the way they pulled all that together. I am humbled and grateful. We had started that season like it was a dream – we were undefeated at the top of the league and we'd beaten Celtic 3-1. The Proclaimers had got involved in the first official event of the testimonial year – the whole thing was just fantastic. Alex Ferguson brought up that great Manchester United team, which was packed top to bottom with superstars and internationals, and they never asked for a penny. It was a special night and another wee reward for the fans.

The Hibs supporters meant the world to me, and I am glad to be one myself now. You come to know what to expect of them – they are brilliant, and follow the team through good times and bad. When the rallying cry goes out, you are there! I had just left the club when the Hands off Hibs campaign started, but it was amazing how the whole thing came together and saved the club for the community and for future generations. That was in 1990, but looking back you can see that there was trouble bubbling away under the surface by the end of 1989. David Duff and Jim Gray had left the club in a vulnerable position which hopefully they will never be again. The Hibs fans all came together as you'd expect, and the 1991 Skol League Cup win proved to be a fitting reward for their loyalty.

I was a wee bit sad to miss out on that, of course, because I would have loved to have been in a Hibs team that won a cup, but I was delighted for all the lads I had left behind, as well as the supporters. It was a shame to leave, but then all good things come to an end, don't they? To be fair, I think I forced it a bit. Alex wasn't playing me. He had bought Neil Cooper and was playing him at centre-half. I thought I should have been playing, and I had been doing really well in the reserves, but you have to move on eventually I suppose. I came back out of the blue to play my first game in ages against Rangers, the day before Hogmanay in 1989 – it was 0-0 and I was man of the match. I then played against Hearts in the 1990 New Year's Day fixture and that turned out to be my last game before I moved to Partick Thistle, where I also enjoyed my time. The finish to my Hibs career was always going to be sad, Hibs was where I wanted to be, and I just loved the place.

They were special times, and any book about the club in the 80s brings those memories flooding back. I had so many great days and memories at Hibs, and the club will always mean the world to me.

I showed just how much they meant to me on 21 May 2016 – an amazing day in the life of any Hibbie. While you were at Hampden, I was sitting in a wee bar in Corfu, and it just so happened that Jimmy O'Rourke was on the other side of the island at the same time. When we won it, there was a family of Irish people next to us in the bar, and the woman turned to my wife and said: 'Your husband is crying!' My wife said: 'Yes, it's a long story!' I was standing there with my hands in the air, re-enacting my goalscoring pose from the 70s and the tears were running down my face. It was unbelievable, it really was. I got up early the next morning, with my Hibs strip still on, drinking out my Hibs mug, sitting on our balcony in glorious sunshine and under blue skies, just basking in the glory of a Hibs Scottish Cup win. Hearing of the big party in Leith Links back home set me off again. I met up with Jimmy and we had a right good bevvy to celebrate and some great laughs.

You'll get some great laughs from this book too. There were some special characters that have played, watched and been involved with the Hibs, and it's nice to see their stories get told here.

Glory Glory to the Hibees.

Gordon Rae

CHAPTER 1

ACCEPTABLE in the EIGHTIES

"The decade started and ended with a wayward superstar in the team, George Best and Steve Archibald, two players past their best but born entertainers."

The Eighties? Why would any right-minded Hibs supporter want to go and dredge up the 1980s? No frills, no trophies, precious few derby wins and an alarming slide towards near extinction.

It's a question I have been asked, with justification, as I embarked on this project. For me, and others of a similar vintage, it's simple – it was the decade my lifelong love affair with the Cabbage 'n' Ribs truly bloomed. Okay, at times it was blooming awful, but I wouldn't change it for anything. These were my formative years. The years before I became cynical and hardened to some of the grim predictability that comes with being a Hibs fan. These were my wide-eyed, innocent, coming of age years; of skiving into grounds (Douglas Park was my speciality), having illegal then legal pints before the game, getting up to and joining in the nonsense that took place on supporters' buses, going to Europe for the first time. Much of what was considered acceptable in the 80s is far from it now, and we live in more enlightened times, but if I could jump in a Tardis or – if we are being truly 80s, a DeLorean Time Machine – and go back and relive some of the grime and grit of that decade I would. It was raw and real, and completely devoid of the corporate flim-flam which somewhat sanitises football these days.

Growing up in 80s Edinburgh wasn't in the least glamorous – although growing up in any of the UK's cities was depressingly the same. Coffee shops, vegan delis and boutiques were light years away. PC was your ZX Spectrum or Commodore 64, flares were bad trousers rather than pyrotechnics at away games, Zoom was just an ice lolly and DMs were Doctor Marten boots – the skinhead's weapon of choice. Great Britain sat awkwardly at a social cross-roads, caught in a whirlwind of uncertainty, violence and political turmoil. The times might have been a changin', but not nearly quick enough for some people. Typifying the gloom and frustration that had pervaded a bitterly divided nation, Pink Floyd's *Another Brick in the Wall* was the 1979 Christmas No 1 and stayed on top of the charts as the bells rang for a new decade.

The opening message in Hibs' first programme of 1980, against Dundee, recognised that society and football both had a multitude of challenges to overcome – a realisation that would crystallise within months when pissed-up tribes of the two Old Firm teams fought running battles on the Hampden turf at the end of the Scottish Cup final. In a gloomy portent of the shame and chaos to come, written under the ominous headline 'Football Moves into the Nervous 80s', Hibs' unattributed New Year message to supporters warned: "There are various battles to win before the game in Scotland can be labelled healthy again. A decline in standards and an upsurge in hooliganism have been the major factors in the fall of attendance figures. Few fans envisaged 10 years ago that the big grounds would need to be equipped with perimeter fences to keep unruly fans in their rightful place."

Football in Scotland's capital was in the doldrums as 1980 loomed. Hearts were still shite, but then – let's face it – so were Hibs. Having been the city's dominant club in the 70s, winning admirers and silverware in a glorious spell under Eddie Turnbull, the team was now in freefall. Off the pitch, supporter-turned-chairman Tom Hart was rummaging deep into his own pockets to halt the decline. And for all it was well intentioned and tempted thousands of curious spectators through the gates, even the sensational signing of fading superstar George Best looked to all intents and purposes like a last throw of the dice.

Even the bold Bestie could not prevent Hibs from sliding to relegation in 1980 – the first time such a fate had befallen our proud club since 1931. On our way down, an extra boot was delivered to the proverbial baws in devastating fashion when Celtic dished out a 5-0 thrashing in the Scottish Cup semi-finals. It was Turnbull's 454th and final competitive game in charge of Hibs, the team he had served so significantly as part of the Famous Five forward line – a sour note for such a legendary figure to go out on.

Next into the hotseat, briefly, would be another celebrated member of the Famous Five, Willie Ormond. To emphasise how much the country's football landscape was changing, with new forces emerging as others faded, Ormond looked on with a heavy heart as Hibs limped their way to the end of that wretched relegation season with another 5-0 caning. This time it was on the Easter Road turf he had graced so majestically as a player, as Aberdeen ran riot and clinched the first of a succession of championships and trophies under Alex Ferguson.

Ormond and the deflated players could have been forgiven for wanting to immediately scuttle away on their summer break there and then, seizing the chance to lick their wounds and plan how to bounce back to the Premier League. Perversely though, they had to return to the stadium 48 hours later to fulfil one final fixture – a 1-0 defeat to Partick Thistle. The attendance was 1,191. Yes, you read it correctly: ONE THOUSAND ONE HUNDRED AND NINETY ONE!

The eminently likeable and trusted Ormond, who had taken arguably Scotland's greatest squad to the 1974 World Cup finals, had made his way back to Hibs via a three-year spell as Hearts manager. His stint as boss at Easter Road would be much more short-lived – and illness forced him to step down midway through the 1980-81 season. Ormond's departure paved the way for an altogether different character to become Hibs' third manager in six months. Enter, amid thick clouds of cigar smoke and bluster, Bertie Auld.

Bertie's claim to fame was a notable one – he had, after all, been one of the Lisbon Lions, Celtic's illustrious side who made history as the first British team to lift the European Cup in 1967. The trouble was, he made sure no-one forgot it. Ever.

Auld had already played and coached for Hibs under Turnbull, so he had a strong in-built affiliation to his second favourite team in green and white. But when he walked back through the doors at Easter Road as manager, he made the mistake of trying to replicate the style of the inimitable Eddie and, in doing so, upset a lot of people in the process. Although Bertie would ultimately lead the club back into the promised land of the Premier at the first attempt and generate a few snappy headlines and picture captions along the way for his outlandish quotes and oversized cigars, the dressing room was quickly lost. The supporters' confidence soon followed.

Brash and flamboyant his personality may have been, but Auld's brand of football was cautious and stale – an odd paradox given his undeniable flair and grit as a player. He didn't endear himself to a squad of strong person-alities, chief among them captain and team spokesman Jackie McNamara, especially by wearing his European Cup medal round his neck at training and showing it to the players at any given opportunity. John Collins flexing his six-pack to Scott Brown and Kevin Thomson 25 years later doesn't come close to Bertie's self-indulgent displays of boastfulness.

Disenchanted fans began to vote with their feet, as mediocre Hibs huffed and puffed their way through a 0-0 draw-laden 81-82 season, and the gloom around the club deepened further when chairman Hart tragically passed away after suffering a brain haemorrhage before a trip to Pittodrie. With Hart's chosen successor Kenny Waugh now running the club, Auld was allowed to linger on to the following pre-season, but a deeply uninspiring League Cup section campaign at the start of 1982-83 sealed his fate and he was finally axed – much to the relief of the group of players he had alienated. The players soon had smiles restored to their faces when they learned who was being brought in to replace him: living legends Pat Stanton and Jimmy O'Rourke, with the popular George Stewart completing a managerial trio steeped in the club's history and traditions.

They certainly looked like the Dream Team... and should have stayed in that category for quite some time, but football – as the cliché holds true to this day – is a results-driven business.

Under the calm but authoritative leadership of the revered Stanton, and the enthusiastic and nurturing assistance on the training ground of George and Jimmy, a welcome feelgood factor flooded back into the dressing room, and young players were given the chance to learn from the older pros, develop, and break through into the first team. But financially, the club was on its uppers, and there was only so long the triumvirate could paper over the widening cracks.

The harder Pat tried, the tougher it got, and the club could not drag itself out of the mire. For fuck's sake, we even got dumped out the Scottish Cup by East Fife! Having drawn 0-0 at Easter Road, in my youthful innocence I had thought the replay would be a formality. I had not long turned 12 and there was no chance of me getting a free pass to go to Methil on a midweek night. While the hardy band of Hibbies who made their way through to Bayview that night found themselves watching the drama unfold in all its live, unadulterated horror, I would learn the desperate news of the 2-0 defeat at 6.30 the next morning. I had a paper round at the local newsagent and would usually be kept waiting in the shop doorway before my old boss finally wheezed and spluttered his way into work. To while away the idle time, I would sometimes burst open the newspaper bales and devour the sports news on the back of papers like *The Scotsman, Daily Record* and *Scottish Daily Express*. I didn't so much devour as choke on the contents that morning. The headlines brutally informed me that not only had Hibs been humped by the underdogs, our star goalie Alan Rough had suffered a suspected broken ankle and faced months on the sidelines. I must have looked quite a sight huffing my way round the streets delivering papers to the posh houses that day.

The proceeds from that same paper-round (aye it WAS a heavy paper-round, before you ask!) financed my first Hibs season ticket that same season, but it didn't take long for me to regret my 'investment'. Paddy Stanton was a name which, quite properly, enjoyed protected status when uttered in my house, but after Bayview anyone could have been forgiven for questioning if his super-powers as a player carried the same weight as a manager. After the scars of the 1979-80 season, the word relegation was never far from any Hibs supporter's thoughts and lips, and the team of the Stanton era was doing little to soothe the nerves. Well, at least we had the return of the derbies to look forward to... I foolishly thought!

Like most of you reading this book, I was a Hibbie born and raised, and a crucial part of the green-tinted upbringing I followed was to be taught how evil the Jambos were. I didn't need a lot of convincing to be honest. My first derby, as a seven-year-old perched on the first row of the upper tier of the old East terrace, was the 1979 Scottish Cup quarter-final at Easter Road. A brilliant, boisterous 2-1 win for Hibs was marred by hardcore, prolonged violence from the Gorgie Aggro packed into the Dunbar End. My abiding memory, aside from the wild Hibs celebrations that followed the victory, was my old man telling me repeatedly to 'watch the game, not them' as hordes of hate-filled Hearts skinheads went to war with the Polis.

I also remember heading along to the Tom Hart Memorial Game at Easter Road – with my mate this time (I had escaped the parental shackles by then) and beating 'them' 1-0. This was in the period when either they had been relegated, or we had, and by the time we got to the beginning of the 1983-84 season, the clubs had not faced each other in a league fixture for four barren years.

The renewal of the derby in the top division was a biggie, you could feel it all around the city, and in my world that meant school. We had plenty mates who were Jambos, and our clash of allegiances had led to many a playground pagger over the years. If I'm being honest – in the same way many modern Hearts fans cling to some misguided superiority complex – back then, we thought Hibs were a class above our foes and they were just noisy neighbours who were a pest rather than a threat. That kind of entitled thinking never ends well, as the Jambos certainly found in the Scottish Cup campaign of 2016. We enjoy it when we can dish it out, but we certainly got our medicine rammed down our throat by the Jambos in the 80s, that's for sure.

I hadn't even contemplated that Hibs could lose when I made my first ever visit to Tynecastle in September 1983. I could instantly feel the malevolence towards us spewing out from the swaying masses in The Shed and we soon recognised that we were deep in enemy territory. But what was there to worry about? We were Hibs. We had spent most of the Seventies giving them a skelping, illuminated in the finest possible fashion by the Greatest Game in History, The Game on New Year's Day: Heart of Midlothian 0, Hibernian 7. These ugly upstarts may have finally clawed their way back from the bowels of the First Division, but we would soon show them who was No 1 in Edinburgh, wouldn't we?

An early goal from Ralphy Callachan took us to an even higher level of self-satisfaction and complacency. But as we prepared to saunter our way on to Easy Street, a roadblock appeared in the shape of Hearts' unheralded young striker that day – a name that would haunt us for a decade and more: John Robertson. The legend of Robbo was born on that day when he equalised, and then repeated the trick again within five minutes of Willie Irvine restoring our lead. The noise, the pressure, the tension – I remember it all. This was the other side to derbies I hadn't yet truly experienced. And then came the other thing I needed to learn. We all do eventually. You've got to experience the horrendous, gut-wrenching lows of football, to properly appreciate the highs when they come along. It's what true football fans understand – not the £80-a-game plastic Piers Morgan types you see in the 21st century, crying in a padded seat because their team has been pipped to a place in the Champions League.

People disparagingly referred to Robertson as 'wee fat Robbo', but he was positively svelte compared to the barrel-chested barbarian who delivered the sucker-punch to us Hibbies gathered in the Gorgie Road End that day. Veteran forward Jimmy Bone, with a Yosser Hughes moustache perched on his gnarled puss and legs akin to ancient oak trees, pounced to win the game for Hearts. Ahh, NOW I knew what the sickening flip-side to watching football was! We had waited four long years to cross swords with Hearts again. And we would wait four more before we beat them again. Four fucking years. Hibs' story of the 80s, warts and all, HAS to be relived and we can perhaps spare ourselves the cost of further therapy! Anyway, more of the derbies later, including the rare ones we actually won.

Pat Stanton wouldn't be the only Hibs manager to try and fail to win a derby. He had bigger problems besides trying to gain the upper hand in the capital. Seventh position wasn't a complete failure in a league containing Aberdeen and Dundee United – then respectively winning and going close in European competitions – as well as the Old Firm and a resurgent Hearts side. However, Hibs looked a team going unerringly in the wrong direction and the relegation jitters had resurfaced again by the start of the 84-85 campaign.

A derby defeat and an embarrassing League Cup exit to Meadowbank Thistle, within a few days of each other, pushed poor Pat to the precipice. When we faced the worst team in the league, Dumbarton, a couple of weeks later at Easter Road it would signal Stanton's last stand. In my head, it could have been mine too. As I watched a dismal 3-2 defeat unfold, I sat glumly on the terracing and started to ponder who else I could support. Maybe Dundee, where one half of my family hailed from? And hadn't the great Gordon Smith played for them? They had a cool programme too. What I knew was that I couldn't take much more of this. I wasn't yet a teenager and my mind and body were being ravaged by this weekly torture. As the Government warning should have said: *watching Hibs can seriously damage your health!*

I didn't even know what 'fickle' meant back then, but within 24 hours I was back to being a fully committed dyed-in-the-wool Hibbie, and I haven't wavered since. Pat resigned and, although no-one was blaming him for the deeper problems anchoring the club, optimism was somehow back on the agenda. Watching Dundee would have been shite anyway... with the obvious exception of a certain day at Dens Park in May 1986.

I was sad to see Pat go, as he was such a popular figure, and having had the privilege of meeting him many times through the years, it is not hard to fathom why. He had already earned his place in folklore for his performances and leadership in a Hibs jersey, and he speaks later in this book about the challenges he faced during his time as manager. He doesn't make excuses and he's not looking to blame anyone, but he is disappointed he could not bring back the glory days. It was a job he could not turn down when it was offered, but the timing was all wrong. Regardless, Pat is the very definition of Hibs Legend, and a lovely man with a great football brain too. Credit to Hibs for getting him back into a public-facing role where he can represent the club he loves.

After Pat came Sloop John B, promoted to manager from the coaching ranks after hanging up his boots. Like Stanton, Blackley commanded respect and admiration for his displays in the Tornadoes team. Like Stanton, he faced many obstacles to get Hibs back into the top half of the table.

The Sloop years, from late 84 to late 86, were in keeping with my whole Hibs-supporting experience. Crazy highs and depressing lows. If you are around my age or above, you will remember with fondness the breathless run to the Skol Cup final in 1985. Six-goal thrashings meted out in the early rounds to Cowdenbeath and Motherwell, an epic eight-goal thriller under the Easter Road lights against Celtic, decided by an even more dramatic penalty shootout, a two-leg ding-dong semi-final battle against Rangers, bravely won in front of 8,000 Hibs fans at a packed Ibrox. But the fairytale run would be halted by the immovable juggernaut of Fergie's Aberdeen, who ruthlessly blew us away at the final hurdle. It was my first time watching Hibs in a cup final, the first time I had seen them play at Hampden, and little did I know the contrasting emotions that would lie in store for me at the national stadium in the next 30-plus years.

The 1985-86 Scottish Cup run was also a stormer under Sloop before, predictably, the Dons stepped in and spoiled our fun at Dens. A month later, there were far saltier tears streaming through that venue! The 'Albert Kidd' game was football at its bonkers best. A day to revel in your arch-rivals' misfortune.

I was a full-on Hibs fanatic by this time, and I couldn't wait for the start of the

86-87 season – Rangers at home. And not the Rangers of old – the much-hyped Graeme Souness' version, packed with prima-donna England stars fresh from getting mastered by Maradona at the 1986 World Cup in Mexico. I've dedicated the cover and much of a chapter of this book to 'The Battle of Easter Road', so fondly and clearly it is remembered as a huge highlight for those who were lucky enough to be there. What a match and what a story to revisit – Souness sent off in the first half for a cowardly assault on George 'Beastie' McCluskey, and Hibs victorious. Bedlam has never tasted better!

That was the last notable high of Blackley's time in charge, and Sloop is another ex-manager who speaks candidly and admirably in this book about his frustration of failing to give the fans the glory that they craved. Which brings us to the polarising figure of Alex Miller, the longest-serving Hibs manager since Eddie T ruled the roost.

As creator and editor of the fanzine *Hibs Monthly* (better remembered in its next iteration *Mass Hibsteria*), I was savagely critical of 'Lexo' in the early days of his tenure, but I have to say my attitude has relaxed markedly towards him over time. Yes, I have gone soft!

In mitigation, back in the 80s I was looking at him through a prism of teenage angst, and I did not see or appreciate the hard work that he was putting in behind the scenes to bring some professionalism to the club. I do still think, looking beyond the Eighties at his entire time in charge, that he was there too long and was afforded slack by the board that others didn't get, but I'm forever grateful to him for the Skol Cup win in 1991 and the European nights he brought back to Easter Road.

It was fascinating to sit down with him for this book and chat about his time in charge, to learn what it was like to be in his shoes. He did not duck a single question. It's not that I have turned full circle and become an apologist for Alex Miller, because I still feel that not losing rather than winning was often the over-riding gameplan, but I do respect the man, what he has done in football, and he absolutely deserves his place in our affections as a trophy-winning Hibs manager.

This is no love-in with Miller though. To be honest, there were times the football under him was mind-numbingly dull and it felt like a long, occasionally arduous 10 years that he was in charge! He was more comfortable on the training ground or in the dug-out than fulfilling media duties or engaging with fans or entertaining their dreams of glory. To underline this, here is what he bluntly said, writing in the programme before one of the final home games of 1989. "We are now without a win in our last seven outings. However, there's no feeling of being despondent in the dressing room. We started the league campaign very well, but we were never going to stay up at the top of the league – let's be honest. We'll never finish first in the league. We're not equipped to win the title. We don't have the quality of player needed or the depth of pool needed."

Looking back, you can see Miller quickly improved the team, although much of that transformation was made possible by the ambition and spending spree of new chairman David Duff. Within a short time of Duff taking over, in came Andy Goram, one of the greatest goalkeepers to have played for Hibs, despite the negative connotations that swirl around his name after he nailed his colours to the mast of the Bad Ship Ibrox.

With Goram in goal, we finally beat Hearts, and got that monkey off our back (until next time), and by the end of that season we were moving purposefully in the right direction. On the very same day that a certain David Gray was born – 4 May 1988 (long before his knighthood) – Hibs were signalling better times ahead, beating Aberdeen 2-0 at Pittodrie. To put that into perspective, that was one of only two wins against the Dons in 36 league games in that decade. This win was not quite enough to end our exile from Europe, but that would follow 12 months later.

Thoughts of that taste of Europe in 1989 get me particularly misty eyed. I didn't make it to Hungary for the Videoton trip, but I was among the thousands in Liege, and that was enough to make Brussels a must a few years later when we got back to Belgium in the 1990s. What amazing times they were to be a young Hibbie, and naturally a chapter is reserved for those adventures.

A chapter also belongs to the enigmatic but hugely entertaining Steve Archibald. It remains incredible to reflect that a superstar from Barcelona, the man who followed Diego Maradona into the No 10 shirt at the Nou Camp, made Easter Road the next stop on his travels. Sadly, I got a polite reply from Stevie to say that business and personal commitments meant that unfortunately he could not fit in an interview for this book. All of the team-mates, along with his manager Miller, have their say on Archie in this book, and the legend only grows! The enduring image of the controversial striker is him standing arms aloft in front of the Hibs fans after his derby-winning strike at Tynecastle.

I did, however, manage an intriguing sit down with Duff, himself in the process of writing and publishing a book on his tumultuous time in charge of Hibs. Like Alex Miller, he answered every question, and while many will accuse him of being the man who put the club in grave danger of being put out of business by the predatory Wallace Mercer, there are many layers to the Duff story and what happened in the summer of 1990. In truth, he was ultimately able to stop that universally condemned takeover from happening, by refusing to sell out. I wish him well in his endeavours to have his story published and you can then judge for yourselves.

There is no doubting Duff brought colour and no little razzamatazz to the club. The decade started and ended with a wayward superstar in the team, Bestie and Archie, two players past their best but born entertainers. In between, many great lads served the club with distinction, and it has been an absolute pleasure to speak to them and hear their stories. Turnbull and Ormond are no longer with us, but the men who followed them into the Hibs job all gave me their time and insight into their time in charge. Bertie Auld sadly was diagnosed with dementia not long after we spoke, and I wish him and his family well.

This book has always been in me, and it has felt both cathartic and nostalgic to write. It's also been an odd experience, given that it has been put together during a pandemic, and coinciding with my 50th birthday – definitely a time to reflect! Many interviews had to be conducted remotely, using a mixture of phone calls, Facetime and Zoom, before restrictions were lifted and face-to-face meetings could resume. To a man, the interviewees were different class – engaging people from a fascinating era in football. It is not intended to be a game-by-game historical record, and anecdotal stories have been prioritised rather than hard facts and figures. I hope you enjoy reliving the 80s, told through the eyes of those who were there.

And then there's you – the supporters. While I'm worth my room on this Earth, I will be with you. You make Hibs the club that it is, and huge thanks to all of you who shared your memories of the 80s with me. I've weaved a few of these stories into the book, but here's a couple of samples. Kenny Murphy told me: "My best memory was aged 11 getting into the club in the summer holidays and helping the club groundsman Alex Kerr doing weeding at the back of the Dunbar End! I got to meet the manager Pat Stanton and all the players. I also then met the late Erich Schaedler. It was a really hot day and he took me up to the kitchen in the old main stand with his Dobermans and got me a cold pint of diluting orange juice!"

Sean Allan, who I collaborated and colluded with on *Hibs Monthly/Mass Hibsteria*, sums up how odd the decade could be. "There was a spell in the early 80s when Hibs were pish," he says. "I shared a flat with hippy types and were 'organic' yonks before it was trendy – it's the only explanation I have for taking a four-foot high Wile E Coyote in a Hibs strip on my shoulders to every game that season!

"My favourite memory of meeting a Hibs player was after an office Christmas party. Staggering alone inebriated along Queen Street, I was singing Hibs songs at the top of my voice. Nearing the National Portrait Gallery, I became aware I was part of a duet. I caught up with my staggering singing partner shortly after. It was Eddie May! I asked if he was injured. 'Naw.' I asked if he was suspended. 'Naw.' I asked if he was playing the following day. 'Aye!' I asked why he was pished so late on a Friday night then! He pulled a big bag of oranges out a carrier bag: 'It's alright, I've got these, juice and vitamins!' We accompanied each other along London Road to Hillside where we partied. Eddie shared his oranges with me, we both belted out Hibs song after Hibs song, and ripped a passing Hun a new one. The 80s weren't all bad!"

Sure, it is a green and white-knuckle ride following Hibs through thick and thin, and the 80s exemplified that. Enjoy the book, but strap yourself in, it gets a bit bumpy in places!

CHAPTER 2

(GEORGE) BEST of TIMES. WORST of TIMES

*"Imagine training and playing alongside one of the
best players who has ever walked the planet."*
– Craig Paterson

When Hibs trudged off the Hampden Park pitch on 28 May 1979 after a third cup final showdown with Rangers in 16 days, they did so with their heads bowed in disappointment but comforted by the hope that there would be plenty days like this ahead before long. They had come close, oh so close, to ending a 77-year wait to lift the Scottish Cup, only to come up agonisingly short.

Ironically, it was one of the club's great servants, Arthur Duncan, who decided the fate of this protracted final in Rangers' favour. After two mind-numbing 0-0 draws failed to separate the sides, a meagre 30,000 crowd at the second replay at least witnessed five goals and a belated injection of excitement. The last of those goals regrettably came off Arthur's napper, earning him a place in the history books not deserving of one of the most electric players of the Turnbull's Tornadoes era. Arthur at least got the recognition of a testimonial match in 1981, against an International XI.

Eddie Turnbull, in his ninth season in charge, put a brave face on the sickening cup final defeat. "What can you say about such a match?" he asked. "We can take a lot out of it, especially the young boys. It's a let-down not getting into Europe but I am sure the players will have matured after this experience."

It wasn't the time or place to challenge such optimistic words, especially when they had been voiced by a club legend, but Hibs were not a team about to mature or bounce back from this major setback – they were a fading force about to lurch dramatically in the opposite direction.

The 1979-80 season started badly, and a 5-2 win over Dundee would prove to be Hibs' only league victory before December. But Christmas came early for Hibs supporters when the incredible news broke that they planned to sign one of football's true superstars – George Best. With Hibs floundering, rumours began swirling in October that chairman Tom Hart was pondering an audacious swoop for Best, which followed a tip-off from football writer Stewart Brown of the *Evening News* that the football genius might be ready for another crack at British football, having left these shores for the glitz of the North American Soccer League.

It might seem alien to today's generation that a football reporter could hold such sway in a major transfer deal, but back then, before agents appeared on the scene, Scotland's press men did a nifty sideline in wheeling and dealing. As journalist Simon Pia explains: "Stewart Brown was eminence grise of the press box. He would dictate who would do what. He was a very tall, imposing character, but a good guy too. Stewart came from that era where reporters acted as agents almost. Stewart could get people moves and would get a few quid for doing so. The most influential at that time was Jim 'Jolly' Rodger. He was a pretty average reporter, but he had an amazing network of contacts and could make things happen. Jim had been a miner in the unions before he got into football journalism, and it was because of his contacts that the *Record* and *Mirror* employed him. He was even a pal of Harold Wilson and Jock Stein. Stewart had a very close relationship with Stein and Jock used to phone up the *Evening News* looking for Stewart, using a codename. Stewart was tight with a lot of the managers and directors."

Hart took Brown's tip-off seriously and started doing his homework to see if he really could pull off a major coup and tempt Best into a Hibs shirt. Best's reputation was forged on his early brilliance at Manchester United, but since walking out of Old Trafford for the last time in 1974, his battle with alcoholism had curbed his career. For all his faults and flaws, he remained big box office however, and it was his undoubted magnetic appeal that piqued Hart's interest when Brown alerted him to his potential availability.

Brown's colleague at North Bridge, Mike Aitken, then an up-and-coming football writer at *The Scotsman*, said: "At the time the signing of Best was painted as being Stewart Brown's idea, but I'm not convinced that was entirely the case. I think what Tom Hart did was to leak the story to Stewart and get Stewart to run it, to float whether it would be a good idea if Hibs signed George Best. And of course, the response to that – quite rightly – was OF COURSE they should sign George Best if they get a chance. Would you want one of the best players who ever lived, even at the fag-end of his career, to come and play for you? Of course you would! I liked Tom Hart. He was a builder and a straight talker, and his son Alan was involved with Hibs too. The Hart family had the best interests of Hibs at heart, I don't think there is any doubt about that."

Best was duly courted by Hibs and persuaded to fly in to watch Hibs play Kilmarnock. Even though he knew the rest of the press pack would be all over the story the moment Georgie set foot inside Easter Road, Hart had been playing his cards fairly close to his chest. His own son Alan, a director on the board, was in the dark until Best rocked up for that Killie match. "The first I knew he was turning up to watch a Hibs game to get a feel for the place," he says. "I think it was a case of weighing up whether he was going to attract the attention we needed, and he did. At the end of the day, he didn't save us from relegation, so you couldn't say it was strictly a success, but it lifted the profile and the spirits of the supporters for a while.

"It was tough to find a balance back then. You could get 25,000 at Easter Road for games against Celtic, Rangers or Hearts but it was tough to get any more than 6,000 against the rest. Season tickets were not the same as they are now. You would expect to sell between 900 to 1,100 on average in season ticket sales and it would pretty much be the same hardcore of people that bought them year after year. People would generally prefer to pay through the gate and if the weather was bad the gate could be killed. It was a real hand-to-mouth existence and the thought of borrowing fortunes and investing in a team was high risk – you'd have been as well putting the money on a horse!"

In horse-racing terms, Best was a thoroughbred, although he was not far from being put out to grass! God only knows what Best, and his model wife Angie, made of the ramshackle stand at Easter Road on a bracing autumn day. Whatever Georgie saw, it wasn't enough to dissuade him from relaunching his career in Leith – even if he was signing up for a fraught relegation battle in the depths of a Scottish winter.

There was another major problem. Forget all the positive spin the club put on the monumental move at the time, using Stewart Brown and other trusted press men to paint a picture of happiness and harmony. Turnbull's typically blunt – if private – view was that he needed Best like a hole in the head. His relationship with Tom Hart, once strong and productive, was showing distinct signs of wear and tear, and the pressure brought on by a combination of poor results and dwindling attendances put further distance between the pair. Eddie would later lament in his autobiography: "We had our occasional run-ins, including one spectacular barney in the North British Hotel, but we were still friendly enough until things started to go wrong at the start of the 1979-80 season. This man had been my friend, but now he saw me more as an under-achieving employee."

When the bugles sounded and Hibs announced their sensational transfer coup, Turnbull was left feeling excluded and exposed. "I knew absolutely nothing about it. The deal was done behind my back," said Turnbull. "George had secured a promise from Hart that he would play in every game possible.

The man who actually picked the team – me – was not even consulted. I was a huge admirer of George in his prime, but I could not see what he would bring to Hibs at that stage in his career. Everyone knew about George's boozing, and at 33, he was overweight, unfit and frankly not ready to play professional football at a high level. If men like Matt Busby and Tommy Docherty could not control him (at Manchester United), what chance did I have?"

With supporters still pinching themselves as they clicked their way through the turnstiles, living legend Best made his debut on 24 November 1979 at St Mirren, scoring and showing enough flashes of his unrivalled skill in a 2-1 defeat to pull in 20,662 for his home debut against Partick Thistle the following week. Again, he did not disappoint, and the fans went home happy after seeing a first victory since August. While Hart would have surveyed the gate and the associated income with great satisfaction, Best did not come cheap. He was on a reputed £2,000-£2,500 a game – dwarfing the manager's salary, while most players could only expect a tenth of that each week. "I knew the huge imbalance in earning was certain to cause friction in the dressing room," said Turnbull.

George Stewart, a key figure in the dressing room and lifelong Hibs supporter, reveals that Turnbull uncharacteristically confided in players that he was dissatisfied with the arrangement. "Eddie and I got on quite well, and he asked me what I thought of George Best. Eddie said: 'Tom Hart has gone behind me and his wages are £2,000 a game.' We were on about £100-a-game at the time and of course, Jackie McNamara, a big pal of mine, had to go up to Turnbull and tell him that the boys weren't happy about only getting £100 a game. It was a difficult situation. George was a lovely guy, Eddie was trying to keep us up, while Tom Hart was the greatest chairman you could ask for – they all wanted to try their best for Hibs." Best's wage may have created waves, but his personality did not. Turnbull recognised this, recalling: "Most of the players did indeed take to George, and no wonder. He did not come across as a big head."

Ralph Callachan, looking back on Best's spell at Easter Road, says: "We all got on well with George, the times we actually saw him, because he never stayed in Edinburgh most of the week and was flying up for the games from London. Sometimes he wouldn't even train with us and would fly up and go straight into the game. You didn't see that much of him, but he did come over well and was a good lad – we all thought that. I think we all understood that what he experienced from a young age would have been hard for anyone to handle.

"Reporters would love to try and stir things up by reminding us about how much he was on per game, but it didn't really bother us. We were on nowhere near the same money, but most of us understood it, and when it comes to contracts it's sometimes down to the individual to do the best they can for themselves. The money Hibs were paying him was justified in many respects by the size of the gates who would come and see him play. The first game at Easter Road against Partick was unbelievable. It was a game we might have been expected to get around 5,000, but we got four times that. It was good from our point of view because you always got a lift from playing in front of bigger crowds. Players never held anything against George. You couldn't complain, because the reality was that these extra thousands of fans that were coming to the game were paying their money to come and see George Best, not us!"

The significance of the quadrupled crowd sizes was also not lost on goal-keeper Jim McArthur, although it initially needed to be pointed out to him by the chairman. "I remember being in the dressing room before his home debut in that Partick game. Tom Hart usually popped his head in – something he was good about, just enough to wish us good luck and all the best lads, without feeling he was intruding somewhere where he shouldn't have been. When he popped his head in that day, the lads saw him come in, but they didn't let on to me... and there was me all the while spouting off, asking 'how come George Best is getting two grand a week and we're getting £80?' Then I heard Tom Hart's voice behind me: 'Come here son!' He took me into the physio's room, where there was a wee window. He asked me to stand up on the stool and look outside, where I could see all the punters streaming into the stand. 'What do you see?' he asked. I said: 'Mr Hart, I see 20,000 people coming into the stadium when usually there is 5,000.' He smiled and said: 'There you go son, there's your answer. Now have a good game.' We won 2-1 and I saved a penalty. George got paid a lot more than us, but that's because he was putting bums on seats."

Hibs fans may remember seeing one striking photograph of the great George Best – a European Cup winner and in his heyday one of the best players in the world – running out the tunnel at Easter Road, followed in technicolour con-trast by none other than Ally 'Benny' Brazil. Benny was a good, honest pro-fessional. Indeed, no-one who played with or managed him has a bad word to say about him in this book despite the uncharitable comments that were sometimes hurled in his direction from the terracing. However, this image capturing two team-mates from opposite ends of the skill spectrum illustrated just how bizarre it was where Bestie was now playing his football.

Brazil was just delighted to be in such exalted company. "It was honestly like a breath of fresh air him coming in, because we were struggling at the time," says Benny, who is still a regular sight around Edinburgh, as a driver for Lothian Buses. "We were getting just a few thousand supporters coming to the games, and then when George arrived the crowds started pouring in. It really rejuvenated us."

Craig Paterson, then a wide-eyed teenager on the verge of becoming a first-team regular, was similarly awestruck, and got stick from his pals in his hometown of Penicuik for becoming a 'Bestie Bore' whenever he joined them for a pint in the local and regaled them with tales of the illustrious Irishman. "Imagine it's your first year as a professional player and you are going to work that morning and you find out you are going to be training and playing along-side one of the best players who has ever walked the planet," asks Paterson. "It was an absolute dream come true.

"Okay, it wasn't George of 1968 and the Benfica game at Wembley in the European Cup final. He might not have had the pace by the time he came to Hibs, but he still had the vision, he still had the class, the skill. The great thing about George was that he had no airs or graces, he was just a lovely man. We always used to go down to the wee gym under the stand at Easter Road after training – Gordon Rae, Colin Campbell, Stevie Brown and myself, and we would play three-a-side as that's all there was room for. We would get the school bench and turn it on its side for goals, and George used to come down and join us. It was such a thrill in that tight environment just seeing what the guy could do, it was an education.

"During his time at Hibs, George saved his best for the big games, against Celtic and Rangers, which seemed to get the juices flowing, but when he did, you could see there was so much still there. It was just unfortunate he no longer had the pace to show what he could really do. But any Hibs fan who went along to watch went away happy to have seen him in action."

However, McArthur and some of the more senior players in the dressing room noticed that while Best possessed tremendous natural skill, he was far removed from the force of old. "People can say what they like, George was a great player, but by that stage he was only a great player on a wee pitch. He could play in the five-a-sides at training, but as soon as you got on a big pitch you could see he was not the same player. He couldn't pick up, couldn't run. He would show flashes of quality and could do things others could only dream of, but he was a luxury we couldn't really afford, especially in a relegation battle."

Jackie McNamara, club captain at the time, agrees: "He was streets ahead with his vision but even though he was only just 30, you could see that his legs had taken some beating after years of punishment and crude tackles by defenders. I had seen that at Celtic with Jimmy Johnstone as well. You look back at the old days and see some of the tackles – they were assault. It's not like now, when a player can get the wind in their eye and they're rolling about. The tackles were brutal back when talents like George and Jimmy were wingers. Tackling is an art, not when you are assassinating somebody.

"George was a lovely lad, he was not disruptive, but he was ill. George got on great with the lads, at training and socially. He would go for a pint with us, and he would go out and train after we had all finished, go out with the kids, and be taking free-kicks and corners. I didn't see a bad bone in his body to be honest with you, but he had an illness."

McArthur adds: "What an amazing guy, he was the nicest boy in the world, and I couldn't say a bad word about him. He was shy and quiet, but he just blended in, whether it was having a pint or cup of coffee with the boys. He didn't seem to have a single regret about the way things had worked out for him. You could speak to him about his drinking and other problems, and he had no regrets whatsoever. George was charismatic and a great lad in the dressing room, he was brilliant fun, and we loved having him among us."

While the affable Best had quickly integrated with his new team-mates, and was pulling in added thousands through the gate, manager Turnbull remained sceptical of his value to achieving the number one aim – namely getting Hibs up the league table and away from danger. The manager also knew a drinker when he saw one. "I knew drink was his problem and that to try and stop him would be completely useless, because Best was to all intents and purposes an alcoholic," he said in his book. "The only person who could stop George drinking was himself, and he showed no inclination to do so. When he turned up, he was thoroughly professional, training as hard as anyone, and would often stay for sessions after he finished. Often it was a pleasure just to sit and watch him training this way."

When he flew up from London, Hibs would put Best up in the North British Hotel, and Eddie insisted it was Hart not he who had their player watched to see if he was over-indulging at the bar. "A whole mythology has grown up about how I tried to tame George Best, by posting spies in various hostelries to report back to me that George had been out on the tiles. There is not a single shred of truth in those claims. I told Tom Hart that I wanted nothing to do with imposing discipline on Georgie, and in the five months I was his manager I did not do a single thing to curb his activities."

Best's initial impact had been promising, especially when he stole the show in a Christmas victory over Rangers. But the first game of the new decade, at Kilmarnock, ended in defeat and it wasn't long before Best's attention started to wander from the pitch to the pint glass. "I remember the time he went missing," says Alan Hart. "The arrangement was that he would stay in London for most of the week and come up on the Thursday to prepare for the weekend's game. Cecil Graham, the club secretary, would usually meet him at the airport and drive him to the North British Hotel and then make sure he got in there and settled. Cecil was out at the airport waiting for him and George never got off the plane. So, he got on the phone to his house and Angie Best told him: 'Oh no, he definitely got on the plane, I left him at the departure lounge.' But seemingly he met up with some of his old Manchester pals, and instead of getting on the Edinburgh flight he had gone to Manchester instead, and that was him on a bender!"

The problem deepened when he was suspended for missing a game against Morton, and then Tom Hart was pushed to the brink when Hibs hosted Ayr in the Scottish Cup on a Sunday in February. This time Best had made it off the plane and into his hotel – but the night before the cup tie, it just so happened that the North British was hosting a raucous post-match dinner for the France rugby team after they had played Scotland at Murrayfield. Best was soon invited to join the revelries and ended up in no fit state to play football the next day.

In his own autobiography, *Where Do I Go From Here*, published in 1981, George explained candidly how loneliness and boredom had led to him escaping his hotel room in search of some stimulation. "There was one almighty party going on in the North British. Players, fans, Frenchmen, Scots – it was bedlam, but it was better than sitting in my own room," he said. "The drinks were coming fast and furious. Someone introduced me to Jean-Pierre Rives, the French captain, and we talked and drank; or rather I did the drinking. He'd had enough. The main difference though, was that he'd played his game and I still had mine to play the next day. Except that I didn't. When Tom Hart came for me on Sunday I was out like a light, sleeping off a week's misery and many days' drinking."

Hart went ballistic when he learned what his expensive signing had been up to and announced that he was 'sacked'. DJ Bill Barclay, who made the announcements from the Radio Hibs box perched above the tunnel in those days, said: "I was doing the sound at the Ayr United game and the place was packed. Tom Hart wasn't very pleased, and he told me to go out and announce that George would not be appearing that day and that Willie Murray would be playing rather than George. I said 'You tell them – I'll get lynched!' But I ended up making the announcement anyway."

Best returned to London and sat out the next game against Dundee United, which saw former fans' favourite Peter Cormack return to the club as player-coach. But even his reintroduction to the team from thereon in could not prevent Hibs sliding towards the abyss. George – taking Antibuse pills to stop him drinking – was forgiven by Hart and billeted in the Caledonian Hotel at the West End for the rest of the season, this time with his wife Angie present to help keep him on the straight and narrow, and to encourage him to keep up a fitness regime which included solo training runs on Portobello beach. To further protect him from the press, public glare and French rugby stars, the couple were booked in under the alias Mr and Mrs Smith.

Meanwhile, on the pitch, the Scottish Cup was providing some respite from some dismal results in the Premier, where Hibs' relegation was all but confirmed. However, Turnbull's nadir arrived in the semi-final of the cup against

Celtic at Hampden. "For some reason, Eddie put George Best on Bobby Lennox, who was the fastest, most energetic player on the park. Eddie was a great coach and tactician, but I don't know what he was thinking by doing that – Bobby Lennox scored and ran the show," says McArthur.

Given that Turnbull himself admitted this was an "utter humiliation", he left a despairing Hart with no choice but to end the reign of one of the greatest Hibs managers of all time. "Three days after the semi-final, I went into training and was summoned upstairs into the boardroom. I knew that could only mean one thing," said Turnbull. "It was all over in seconds, Hart thanking me for my services and me getting out the door as quickly as possible. My sacking had been inevitable from the day George Best walked in the door."

McNamara believes it was only a matter of time before Eddie either jumped or would be pushed. "Obviously the end came after that 5-0 defeat to Celtic. They murdered us that day. But I remember the season before the cup final, we went on an end-of-season tour to Canada, and he was talking about packing in then. We were worried to hear that because we all had so much respect for him. He felt he wasn't getting the help he wanted from the board. We then went on and had that cup run, ending in the three cup finals against Rangers, and we thought everything was going to be okay, but I don't think he was getting the backing with investment."

Craig Paterson was very sorry to see his first manager go, particularly as he was a family friend, having played in the same title-winning Hibs team as Paterson's dad, Jock. "Eddie was a pal of my Dad's but that became awkward when I started playing myself because he couldn't show me any favouritism. He was a hard taskmaster, but a great tactician, just one of these people that was way ahead of his time – anyone who knew him or worked with him realised that. He had been a hard player and could be a hard man. It was a good grounding in the game that you knew if you did well you got a pat on the back, but if you performed poorly you were going to get it with both barrels. You knew where you stood with Eddie Turnbull at any given time. I think the fact that he lost his job at a time I was there, it's one of these things you look back on with a sense of real sadness and disappointment."

Hart immediately turned to Willie Ormond, like Eddie a former Famous Five icon, to come in and try to steady the sinking ship. "Out went Eddie and in came Willie," says Jim McArthur. "It was really sad to see Eddie go. There were times, during his days as a manager, that he wasn't a very nice man – although he became a great man later in his life – but what a great coach. For me, he was unbeatable. People who were at Dundee United might say it was Jim McLean and those at Celtic would say Jock Stein, but Eddie was the best in my eyes. It was really sad the way it ended for him at Hibs."

Incredibly, Hibs, with Ormond in charge for the first time, picked themselves up from their Hampden humbling and somehow managed to go to champions-in-waiting Aberdeen and come away with a draw, a game that involved a flare-up between Best and the opposition captain. "We were fighting for our lives at Pittodrie, and George Best got the ball on the halfway line and he turned and passed the ball back. Willie Miller started having a go at him, saying that kind of thing would get the game stopped. Willie wasn't fit to lace his boots. It was a horrible thing to say," says McNamara.

With Turnbull gone, Best's exit soon followed – for the 1979/80 season at least. Hibs were forced to play seven league games in 17 days, a result of a fixture pile-up brought on by the cold winter and their cup run, and relegation was grimly confirmed when Hibs hosted Kilmarnock, with Best there only as a spectator to say his goodbyes. Some of the 2,659 fans who joined him adopted a defiant stance at full-time and invaded the pitch. Radio Hibs man Barclay recalled: "I went into the dressing room and said George will you come out and say something to the fans because they are all on the pitch. He said no problem and just came out and apologised to the fans because the team were going down – it was quite an emotional night." Best's words to the fans were: "I'm a little sad to be leaving when the team is doing so badly but I am sure with the tradition Hibs have they will soon be back in the Premier League."

The realisation that the team had been relegated hit the other players hard, but those who had been around the club long enough, knew deep down that it had been coming. Skipper McNamara recalls: "We lost a few key players and once we lost the engine of the team, which was Des Bremner, it left us short. I don't want to be disrespectful to the boys who replaced him, but they weren't Des. He was a terrific player as he proved when he went on to win the league with Aston Villa, and then the European Cup. I don't think Eddie was ever going to be able to replace someone like Dessie. Whatever Aston Villa paid for him, Eddie should have got that money to work with, to rebuild the squad, but I don't think he did.

"After the three cup finals we should have gone on to have a great season but alas it didn't happen. We made inferior signings. When you are a football club and you are getting beaten, and losing games, there is a depression around the place, and it can be really hard to shake off. It wasn't Eddie's fault because he was a fabulous manager and coach. He swapped me for The King (Pat Stanton) and I was getting booed when I first came through, but I didn't know what I was walking into – I thought I was signing for a good team capable of competing with the best."

Ally Brazil says: "I was especially sorry for Eddie, and he always did right by me. He knew the game inside out and was a fantastic coach. It was maybe too little too late (signing Best), which was a real pity, because we still went down that season. Relegation was really tough. It was a hard one to take, because up until that season we had been doing quite well and feeling comfortable within the league. Then that season, results never went our way, and it dawns on you that you are sinking down."

Ralph Callachan also bristles at the memory of relegation. "It was a shock to the system, especially having got to the Scottish Cup final the season before and coming so close to winning it. You can't put your finger on why things changed so dramatically. It was a really difficult season. Nobody likes to get relegated, but there's no hiding the fact that we got relegated because we weren't good enough, we weren't consistent enough and we didn't get the results we needed in the crunch games. We just couldn't do it, and once you get in a spiral like that it can be hard to break. If you don't get the result in a big game, then the next one becomes even bigger, and we just couldn't stop that slide and that's why we went down."

Gordon Rae was another who found the experience hard to take. "You always hoped you were going to win games and stay up. I was still one of the younger players in the team, but the more senior guys like Jackie, Ralphie and Ally MacLeod maybe felt the inevitability of our situation a bit more – there were too many defeats. Us younger guys had the mindset that we might put a run together and win a few games, and get ourselves out of it, but the reality was there was no chance. In a ten-team league there was very little margin for error, and there were some good sides in it, especially with Aberdeen and Dundee United starting to emerge as great teams. We still were capable of playing really well, especially in the big games and when Bestie was in the team – against Celtic and Rangers in particular. There were glimmers of hope but, ultimately, we were in decline. Eddie ruled with an iron fist, that was his style of management, but he was still a great coach and a great man."

Director Alan Hart agrees: "It was pretty dire for us back then. We had been so good in the early 70s under Eddie Turnbull, when everyone he signed seemed to play fantastic football for us. Then by 1975 to 1977, we began to wane, and the people we were bringing in were just not able to sustain that top quality of a few years earlier. It was sad to see the demise and although we still had some occasional good moments, including that trip to the Scottish Cup final in 1979, it was a period of decline."

Before Hibs headed down to the First Division, they had to experience further indignity by hosting Aberdeen's title party as Alex Ferguson clinched the first of his many championships. To emphasise the gulf between top and bottom in the league that season, the Dons romped to a 5-0 victory, with future Hibs players Steve Archibald and Andy Watson on the scoresheet.

Jim McArthur is keen to get something on the record. "Everyone thinks I played in the Aberdeen 5-0 thrashing, but I didn't! It's the only game I ever missed with a hamstring injury. George McNeill used to come in and do sprint training with us and before that game I was flying by my standards – especially for a goalie – but then my hamstring went. I remember before the game, Fergie was walking past and asked me if I was playing, and he looked pleased to hear that I wasn't, which I took as a big compliment. It was Davie Huggins who was in goal for that one. He only played three times for Hibs and then got freed. The funny thing about the 1979/80 season was that I got the player of the year award, probably because I had so much to do!"

If there was one saving grace among the wreckage of the nightmare 1979-80 campaign, it was the fact that several young players were coming through the ranks, and the club would need that mix of youthful energy and hardened pros to make their escape from the First Division. Paterson was among the youngsters who were signalling that the future wasn't as bleak as it appeared at first glance. "That was my breakthrough year and I got into the team on a regular basis, but unfortunately the club got relegated," he says. "Towards the end of the season, when the team was struggling, they did tend to play the younger players more, figuring that they had to plan for the future so it meant maybe I got more games than I would have done in normal circumstances. It was good from that point of view to be in there, getting that experience. I had Jim McArthur behind me, Jim Brown at right-back, Jackie or George Stewart and Arthur Duncan next to me – guys with loads of experience, which was just great for a young player still learning the game. They were great lads who were keen to help you. They could be hard on you if you did things wrong, but it was a good learning curve for me with them in the team."

Paterson's future looked promising, even though ultimately it would not be in a Hibs shirt. Best, meanwhile, headed back to California to recharge his batteries and – sadly – to recharge his glass. But he would be back, we had not seen the last of Georgie boy.

CHAPTER 3

KILBOWIE to the CARIBBEAN

"I thought Haiti was a Caribbean country full of hula skirts and coconut trees. But when we got there the reality was so different. Oh My God!" – Craig Paterson

What a difference five years and an extra 'n' can make. 1975: Hibs head to Anfield in their centenary year defending a first-leg lead against Bill Shankly's luminaries Liverpool, the second time in five years the team has visited the world-famous arena to face off in European competition. 1980: Hibs head to Annfield, Stirling, in the second tier of Scottish football, without a point to their name, and watched by a crowd little more than 2,000. How the mighty had fallen!

The raging hangover from the 1979-80 relegation season had unfortunately lingered into the new season, and Hibs – perhaps still trying to get their bearings in the First Division – had opened their bid to bounce back up with a dispiriting 1-0 defeat at home to Raith Rovers. "The 80s didn't start well for Hibs," says 'Hibstorian' and author John Campbell. "They had been relegated the previous season and got off to the worst possible start in the new season by losing at home to Raith. I was gutted because I still hadn't really come to terms with the relegation. Willie Ormond was the manager and I recall being in a crowd of less than 5,000 to witness this losing start. Thankfully, it was a blip."

The following week's trip to Stirling Albion's windswept old ground was the first road trip of the season, and thankfully Hibs came to their senses and won 2-0, featuring the last of veteran Peter Cormack's 106 goals in his two spells with the Cabbage. Coincidentally, he was in the Liverpool side that put Hibs to the sword in the aforementioned 1975 encounter at the 'other' Anfield.

"For those of us lucky enough to have our formative teenage years immeasurably enhanced by Turnbull's Tornadoes going all for goals and glory, it was disheartening to see our team plying their trade in the second tier come the start of the new decade," explains Sandy Macnair, author of several Hibs books and the mane behind the man who is the 'Hibbie Hibbie' of fanzine fame. "My first away trip of 1980-81 was at Annfield – Stirling, not Liverpool! This game was enlivened by the old changing ends at half-time tradition. But what sticks in the mind is that rather than walk round the terracing as usual, my side-kick – a certain Irvine Welsh – chose to stroll directly across the pitch instead. However, no-one seemed to bat an eye and happily Hibs went on to win."

Winning ugly was a phrase well suited to grounds like Kilbowie and Boghead, and trips to these glamourless grounds were now part of Hibs' new world... although these venues would seem like the San Siro compared to the dusty field the team would later find themselves playing on at the end of the season, 4,000 miles away in the Caribbean! We will come to that later in this chapter. With promotion the singular aim, the most important thing was just winning, ugly or not! Not that Hibs would have faced the hairdryer treatment if they lost in those early months of the campaign. The iron regime of Eddie Turnbull was over, and the genteel Willie Ormond had an altogether different approach. "Even though we lost our first game against Raith, wee Willie didn't panic or make us worry," says captain that season, Jackie McNamara. "He was a lovely man, but he wasn't in the same class as Eddie as a coach or tactically.

"I remember during pre-season training, Willie had us up at Keith and I thought we were going to get hammered. Why else were we there – up in the Highlands, with plenty of hills and mountains to run up? It was a scorching day too, and we went out and did the warm-up, jogging a couple of circuits, before I heard Willie shouting on us to stop. 'Oh aye... here we go... here's where the battering starts, we are going to get run into the ground now', I thought. But, instead, Willie asked us to gather into a circle and then told us: 'You're the best bunch of boys I have ever worked with. Let's just go into the social club for a wee drink now.' After the Raith game we played Stirling Albion and Willie sat us down and again told us what a great bunch of lads we were and told us to go out there and enjoy ourselves. That was it – team talk over! He didn't concentrate on formation or any set plays. But we went on a good run after that."

Jackie's team-mate and close pal Ralph Callachan concurs: "Willie Ormond was a different type of manager to Eddie, a bit more easy-going. He was a bit more relaxed, but both had a lot of respect. I got to know him quite well not just through football, but when Jackie and I later went into the pub business. We had our pub in Musselburgh, as did Willie, so I got to know him and his son."

Jim McArthur has fond memories of Ormond's time in charge: "The thing about Willie is that he was really skilful at blending a team. He had done the same when he was Scotland manager – he could bring boys in and create the perfect balance. He had been sacked by Hearts when they were top of the league, and then he left Hibs when they were top of the league. I had a lot of time for Willie."

Ormond was always accessible and obliging with the press too, and Mike Aitken, a football reporter with *The Scotsman*, says: "I had worked with Willie when he was Scotland manager and he was a completely different character to Eddie. A very nice man, and he knew a player. But, in truth, it was a stop-gap appointment and Willie was brought in to put a sticking plaster on the club at that time. Willie was a bit of a throwback. We (football writers) always used to go in for a drink at Easter Road to speak to the manager afterwards. There would be a table with a whole load of different drinks set out on it and maybe a sandwich or two, it was all very civilised, and there was a girl that Hibs employed to serve everybody. Most clubs did the same. At Aberdeen, for example, Fergie had the 'on-the-record room' and 'off-the-record room' where you got the real story! But I remember the girl going round during Ormond's time as Hibs manager, making sure everyone had a drink. She asked Willie what he wanted and he replied: "Naw, nothing for me hen, just a wee sherry!" That was Willie's idea of not having alcohol, to just have a 'wee sherry' rather than something a bit stronger. He was a nice man, but he didn't last long in the job and didn't have time to accomplish much."

George Stewart lived out his childhood dream by joining Hibs after years of success with his first professional club, Dundee, but the change of manager, combined with the advancing of years and the realisation that there were young players coming through behind him, led to Big Geordie asking himself – and the new manager – some searching questions about the future. "When Eddie got fired, I went to see Willie Ormond," he says. "We got on well. He was a Musselburgh man and a real Hibs man, so I trusted him and asked him if it might be time for me to go. He asked me where I wanted to go, and when I told him it was to go and join Pat (Stanton) at Cowdenbeath, he said: 'George, no problem, it's been a pleasure. If you'd said you were going to join the Hearts it might not have been the same answer!'"

Stewart, as well as Pat and Jimmy O'Rourke, would make a future return to Easter Road, and although Ormond's time in charge lasted only seven months and 30-odd games, he had the foresight to bring in some new faces to freshen up the club. Not many were fresher than that of skinny teenager Brian Rice, a stand-out straight away by virtue of his bright ginger hair. "Yes, it was Willie Ormond who signed me and I'm forever grateful for that," says Ricey 40 years on, speaking to me on a Zoom call, wearing his Hamilton Accies manager's jacket (before he hung it up for the last time in August) and wrestling with a new puppy he has bought during lockdown. "I had been at Celtic as a teenager and I was meant to go to West Brom, but my Mum didn't want me to leave home. When I left school Hibs offered me a full-time contract, but my mum wanted me to get a job and go part-time instead. I actually applied for a job at a bank in Edinburgh in Queen Street and got the job, so the decision I had to make was: do I go and work in the bank or do I go and try to become a football player? I should have stuck with my Ma's idea I think! I had to beg her a bit, but she came round eventually and I joined Hibs."

There was an early thrill for Rice, as well as some silverware, when Hibs produced a storming comeback to beat Hearts on penalties at Tynie in the 1980 East of Scotland Shield. "I made my debut at 16 and the first wee taste I got was the East of Scotland Shield final at Tynecastle. Because both teams had managed to pass each other in the league again, with Hearts getting promoted and Hibs getting relegated, there was a big crowd and both teams had decided to make the team up of seven first-team players and some reserve and youth players. I think I had just left school, and I was on the bench, watching as we went 2-0 down, before I got the shout, 'Get ready, you are going on!' And from my first ever touch in a Hibs shirt I scored from 25 yards into the top corner! We then went on and equalised and won on penalties."

Supporter Macnair says: "That unlikely extra-time and penalties triumph over the Jambos at Tynecastle did gladden the Hibbie heart, especially since we had been two down. In those days it was still treated as a serious game between two first-choice sides, rather than the largely reserve team sideshow it later became."

Rice, meanwhile, had a thirst for more action. "Soon after that game I came on against Ayr United in the League Cup in extra-time for my first competitive game for the first team, and I made my full debut against Motherwell on a frozen pitch – I had to wear Adidas Kicks trainers – and we won 1-0. There were only two subs in those days, so your chances of getting involved were limited a wee bit. But when the first team were playing, the reserves were playing the reverse fixture. Those games were fantastic, and I still say to this day that it was these games where we learned football properly, because you would get first-team players alongside you if they were coming back from injury or suspension. I remember playing alongside Alex Cropley when he came back to the club and Bobby Smith, as well as guys like Jackie and Ralphy. The experience we got from playing alongside them was unbelievable."

Ormond had started the job of getting Hibs promoted, but it would be another manager who finished it. Ormond's health was creating concerns in the boardroom, and they agreed to part ways in mid-November. Out went the courteous, uncomplicated Ormond, and in came the loud and brash Bertie Auld, who had played for Hibs and coached under Eddie Turnbull.

When I contacted Bertie for this book, he was polite and helpful, as he had been when I interviewed him back in 2013 for the *Shades* biography I wrote about the late Erich Schaedler. I had been impressed by Auld's powers of recall and the razor-wit he displayed during that first conversation, but this time it was apparent that his memory was starting to fade. Within a couple of months of us chatting, it was made public by his family that poor Bertie had been diagnosed with dementia, something that has engulfed many football men of his generation. My thoughts and good wishes immediately went out to Bertie and those around him, particularly as this cruel disease is something that has affected my own family. It may appear harsh, given what he is living with, that there are accounts later in this book from players severely criticising Bertie's management style and behaviour, but history should not be rewritten out of sympathy, and it would be wrong and disrespectful to sugar-coat people's honest opinions.

Although Bertie was unable to be as expansive as he had been in 2013, he still reflected with pride that he had been able to return to Easter Road to manage the club. "After Eddie, Willie had a spell as manager before me," says Auld. "They were two well experienced managers, with great knowledge and a great attitude towards the game, so they were hard acts to follow. Ned, as far as I'm concerned, was one of the best coaches I ever played under – a man I always admired. He was a hardy man, but he was level-hearted. If you had a job to do and you didn't do it right, you were told, and you learned. It was a real education learning under him. He was great at bringing on the young players – those who were clever enough to listen to him. I felt I was well equipped to be a manager and it was a great thing for me to have the knowledge that I had working under and playing under Jock Stein too. He was a tremendous person and different entirely from Eddie Turnbull, but the two of them could have ruled the world! I was lucky enough to know and work under them both."

"When Bertie then came in, I found him very strict," says Rice. "I found it hard because he was hard on me, but I think he saw something in me that he liked, because he and Pat Quinn used to take me out for extra training sessions in the afternoon and they would work me on certain passes they wanted me to play. Those two and John Lambie would do that with us young boys, they would play against us 3 v 3 in the wee gym and absolutely kick hell out of us! We never saw it at the time, we thought they were just being rough with us, but they were trying to toughen us up – trying to show us what it took to make it. Bertie knew the game inside out. He wasn't everyone's cup of tea, I'm the first to admit that, and he had a lot of fall-outs in the dressing room, but he knew the game inside out."

"Where do I start with Bertie?" says Ralph Callachan, not his No 1 fan. "We had heard some of the stories about him during his time at Partick Thistle, but then we experienced him first-hand. He could be nicey-nicey, but behind the scenes the way he would talk to people and treat people could be poor. I think it would often be to the younger guys too, rather than older experienced players, and I don't think that says much about the guy. He would pick and choose certain things he would say. Personally, I felt he was a great football player, who played in a great team, so it was a surprise to find as a manager that he was so defensively-minded. I thought he would be far more attacking in his style, but quite often he seemed to be willing to settle for a draw. His excuse would be that he couldn't do what he wanted to do with the players he had at that time, but I thought we still had enough good players to be a bit more adventurous and attack-minded. It was more about him than the team and the club to be honest. Bertie was always the man who was showing off with the big cigar and holding court with the press – he loved being the centre of attention. I'm not saying the players should be the centre of attention either, there should be a balance, but most of the time it was all about Bertie."

One thing Auld was sure of was the reason he had been hired – to get Hibs promoted, and to keep the players focused. Gordon Rae says the rocky start to the season had already left the team in no doubt they had to stop feeling sorry for themselves and get their minds on the job in hand. They had to have the mindset to go to no-frills venues like Annfield, Boghead and Kilbowie and do whatever was required to win. "Relegation felt bad enough, but when we actually lost the first game of the season to Raith Rovers at Easter Road, it was a jolt for us all. I was suspended for that one, it was a carry-over from the season before, and I missed the Aberdeen game at home when they beat us 5-0. I had to sit in the stand watching that – it was terrible, they absolutely humped us. But we soon found our feet in the First Division and went on a run that was incredible.

"We just picked up the winning habit – even when they changed the manager and Willie was replaced by Bertie Auld. He brought big Snoddy and Mike Conroy from Celtic. Snoddy's first game was at Raith Rovers and we got beat off them again, 2-0 this time. Apart from that, we barely lost a game. We were by far the best team in the league, but we still had to go and prove that."

Alan Sneddon, who had a winner's medal from the shameful 1980 Scottish Cup final when fans had rioted after Celtic won the cup against Rangers, did not enjoy an auspicious start to what would prove to be a long and loyal Hibs career, but he was just grateful at the time to have a new lease of life. "To say Hibs went through a few ups and downs in the Eighties would be putting it mildly. It was not the most stable of times," he says. "We had just won the cup with Celtic and I found myself out the team and thinking I would probably be moving on at some stage. But I wasn't expecting wee Bertie to come in for me at that particular time. When I saw it was Hibs who were interested in me, it was a no-brainer as far as I was concerned because I knew they would come straight back up. Hibs had always been a top team and I thought if I'm not likely to be playing every week at Celtic then I'm as well taking my chance at Hibs. I was impressed straight away with the chairman Tom Hart – he did anything and everything to help the club and was probably a supporter first before he was a director. He was probably the last of that era of chairmen. Nothing was too good for Tom, everything had to be the best for Hibs.

"I remember that first game. I hadn't even trained with the boys and I met them that first morning and we went up to Raith and we got beat 2-0. I gave away a penalty, which I deny to this day – it was never a penalty! It wasn't a great start for myself, coming into the club, because you always want to start off well and with a win. So, I just had to take it on the chin. But it was just good to get back playing. The players that were at Hibs, guys like Jackie Mac, Ally MacLeod and Ralph had all played in the top flight, so we had lots of experience running through the team. I had played against these guys and knew they had lots of ability, so it was nice to find myself being part of a team with them. It brought it home how big the club was."

Rice agrees: "Ralphy especially was a big influence and a big hero of mine. He was a gentleman and still is, I met him in Tenerife on holiday last year. I admired the way he played football – he was cool on the ball and was fit and looked after himself. He had a good athletic build, for me he just looked like a real footballer."

Callachan's poise and composure on the ball certainly helped, but he was under no illusions that the results came first that season. "We needed to get back up, not to look too far ahead and just win games," he says. "I think we did well enough and played some good football, but with no disrespect to the teams we were up against, we were the biggest team in the league and we were expected to win most games, so there was pressure that came with that. It was great that we bounced straight back and it gave the club the lift we all needed."

The title was effectively clinched when Hibs beat Clydebank 3-0 and then three days later, the trophy was hoisted by Jackie Mac amid wild scenes and a good old-fashioned pitch invasion as the title was celebrated in style with a 2-0 win over Raith. Even the TV cameras were there to record it, unheard of for a First Division fixture in those days! "It was good for me that it came against Raith," says Sneddon, who exorcised the demons of his debut. "I also remember that day as clear as anything, because the place was packed and we were expected to get the result. We were going up anyway, but we wanted to make sure we won and went up in style. It was a great atmosphere and a great feeling to know that we had got the job done and would be back in the big time." Craig Paterson also savoured the occasion. "Winning the league and promotion was a thrill for me because it was the first thing in senior football that I had won – a championship medal," he says. "It didn't quite match up to my Dad's championship medal but I enjoyed it nonetheless."

However, director Alan Hart recalls how he viewed that particular piece of silverware with mixed emotions. "After the game, the visiting directors come down and have a drink, but after they'd left and there was just Hibs people left there was the championship trophy sitting there taking pride of place on the boardroom table. I picked it up and pretended to throw it out the window, saying that's the last time I ever want us to be in the First Division competing for that!"

One mystery I have frustratingly tried and failed to get to the bottom of for this book is: was Bertie away on holiday for that championship party against Raith? I've asked many Hibbies older (and wiser) than me, from Australia to Leith, whether they can confirm or deny that Auld had excused himself pre-maturely and was actually away on a sunshine break by the time the trophy was finally lifted that day. Certainly, the grainy TV coverage that exists on YouTube of the Raith game shows John Lambie and Pat Quinn in charge of the team, with Auld nowhere to be seen. The closing credits and music, as the players sup champagne from the trophy in the directors' box in the Centre Stand, also make a cryptic nod to Auld's absence. The newspapers didn't tend to make much of a fuss back then of such matters, and I can find no report making reference one way or the other to whether Bertie hung around for all the pomp and ceremony. For years, it's rattled away in the back of my mind somewhere that he was stretched out on a sun lounger that afternoon rather than celebrating with his players in Leith, so I will go with Jackie McNamara's take on the question: "Aye he was away on holiday, copying someone from down south, trying to be extrovert."

If Bertie was indeed away, perhaps he was getting himself a base tan for another trip which was about to happen. Tom Hart's reward for Bertie Auld and the squad was an end-of-season tour to California for a friendly against George Best's new team San Jose Earthquakes, and then on to Haiti in the Caribbean. Sounds good... but it would prove very much to be a trip of two halves!

Before Hibs even boarded the plane, Auld managed to cause resentment within his team, when he vetoed the trip for Ralph Callachan and Jim McArthur, because they had both not yet committed to new contracts for the following season. It still irks them both to this day that they were left behind, especially as they had every intention of signing, and had merely been negotiating the best possible deal they could to provide security for their families.

"Basically, they had said we would get the trip if we got promotion," says McArthur. "We did that, so we assumed we would be going. But then Bertie said: 'If you are not signed players then you are not getting to go.' I was due a testimonial by that time and was hoping to get a new contract that put that in writing, while Ralphy was also trying to work out the best deal for him. We both wanted to stay at Hibs, it's just we were holding out to get the terms we thought we deserved. For me, they were two separate things – the trip was a reward for what we had just achieved, not an added condition for us to sign contracts there and then. The deals didn't have to be done before we went, we could still talk when we got back. Then Jackie (McNamara) got involved as the shop steward and declared 'All for one, and one for all. If you're no going we're no going'. Aye right... Jackie and the rest were in California before you knew it! So we got left behind, and Davie Huggins got my place, even though Ralph and I had been pretty much ever-presents during the season we won promotion. In the end, I got my testimonial and Ralphy got his deal too, but only after they came back."

Callachan recalls: "I was disappointed, getting rejected by Bertie in that way. We were promised that if we got promoted we would get taken away on a holiday at the end of the season, it was supposed to be a thank you from the club. I reminded Bertie that the trip was a thank you and had nothing to do with contracts, but he said: 'Well, sorry son, if you're not prepared to sign then I can't see any reason why I should take you on a trip like this.' I thought he was totally out of order doing that, but he got away with it because he was Bertie Auld. It was a disgrace really and I had a big-time falling out with him about it. He did the same with Jim McArthur, so we were both left behind, and it left a sour taste in my mouth. To be honest, that summed Bertie up. We did eventually sign contracts anyway, monthly to begin with, and then something more permanent. I was actually a bit disappointed in myself because after that happened I had vowed never to sign for Bertie Auld again, but circumstances changed, I wanted to stay with Hibs, and I did sign."

McNamara reveals he did his best to intervene on his team-mates' behalf and force the club into a change of heart. Indeed, chairman Hart had sympathy for the rebel two, and left it to Auld to hopefully acquiesce and let Callachan and McArthur come on the trip. "But this is how evil he could be," says Jackie. "When I tried to plead on their behalf, Bertie said 'naw, they're not going for not signing'. So I phoned up Mr Hart and pointed out to him that this trip was promised as a bonus for winning the league. Tom listened and said to leave it with him, then gave me a call back and told me: 'The manager will meet you son, and you're not to be late.' I was living in the West at the time, so I went through on the train and got a taxi down to Easter Road in plenty time for our meeting. But as I was arriving in the taxi, just on the corner of Easter Road, there was Bertie coming out in his big Mercedes, driving away. He even smiled at me! 'You bastard,' I thought. He could be a horrible man, I was not a fan of Bertie."

Ralphy's loss turned out to be Brian Rice's gain, as the teenage midfielder was told to get suited and booted, and to get himself ready for the trip of a life-time. "Ralph and Jim McArthur got left behind and myself and Davie Huggins got called into the squad. I had never even been outside of Scotland so there was a frantic rush to get me a passport. I got told to go up town to Austin Reed's. At first, I asked: 'Whae's Austin Reed?' They sent me up to this big shop in Princes Street to collect a suit, with a camel collar. I think I got the one that was meant for Bimbo (Jim McArthur)! It was short and wide on me. I had never worn or owned a suit in my life – I was fae Whitburn! What an experience that trip was!"

Also missing from the tour party was the unfortunate Benny Brazil, who was fighting to save his career. "During the promotion season I only played five or six league games because I had a cartilage operation," he says. "I didn't warrant enough to get a medal and I didn't go on the trip to Haiti because I was injured then as well. I got two cartilages taken out of my left knee around that time. It's a bit of a mess now and I need a new knee. But back then they would just take it out and Tam McNiven actually got my cartilage and kept it in a wee jar so he could show people what a cartilage looked like!"

Meanwhile, the rest of the able-bodied, signed and sealed Hibs players were California dreamin' and the Land of Milk and Honey lived up to their expectations. Director Alan Hart was present with his Dad and took some great pictures chronicling this trip – even ones of Bertie Auld strutting about by the side of the pool wearing nothing but his Speedos and, of course, his prized possession, his Lisbon Lions medal from 1967! Alan Sneddon laughs at the memory: "Wee Bertie would walk about with his shirt open showing off his European Cup medal. We hardly saw the manager and the directors on that trip because they would be away doing their own thing, but every so often Bertie would reappear with a Desperate Dan growth on his chin and start barking out his orders."

Hart says the American leg of the trip was a great chance for players and directors to relax, and have some fun, although there were a couple of fixtures thrown in – including the chance to catch up with George Best, in a friendly against San Jose Earthquakes. "We beat them 4-2. I scored a hat-trick for Hibs and George scored the two for them. I outscored George Best!" laughs Gordon Rae. "Bestie was such a nice man, a great guy, and he came and chatted to all the guys. When we were on the training ground before the game Bertie was doing his usual – it was about 80 degrees and we were getting run to death on the pitch training. Bestie came along to a have a chat with some of the guys and we saw him again when we played the game a day or two later."

Hibs would return the favour to the Earthquakes, by hosting a friendly the following year at Easter Road, and in between, Best would be back for another brief stint in green and white. Relationships between club and player remained strong. "George had gone off to the States because we couldn't realistically keep him in the First Division with those wages and those crowds," explains Alan Hart, still a Hibs season-ticket holder in the Lower West. "The agreement was that he went off to San Jose Earthquakes and they would pay for a trip for us if we won the league. It was more a holiday and a reward for the players.

"Before we played San Jose, we stayed in this place Visalia down the southern end of the Californian valley and played a Fresno University team sponsored by a local guy of Portuguese descent and very keen on football. He was a really nice guy and took all the team and directors back to his house, and we got to sit around his pool. We were in a small town of about 10,000 with a university complex on it, and we were happy for the players able to go out and enjoy themselves. There was a typical American bar 100 yards away from the place we were staying, with music on and a couple of pool tables. I remember Jackie was on the table and this local lass went up and said to Jackie with a smile on her face 'Could you show me how to play pool?' Jackie said no problem and was showing her how to hold the cue, while all the time she was pretending she couldn't play. She eventually turned the conversation round and said 'I bet you 20 bucks I could beat you'. They set the balls up and she cleared up – Jackie had been hustled!"

With spirits high and the players tanned and relaxed, they headed off blissfully unaware what lay in store for them in Haiti. The second stage of their May 1980 expedition would turn into a terrifying nightmare, leaving the Scots fleeing the poverty-stricken island before they were lynched.

"I thought I was going to Tahiti – what a let-down that was," laughs Craig Paterson. "I thought Haiti was a Caribbean country full of hula skirts and coconut trees. But when we got there the reality was so different. Oh My God, the people were so poor. We were told not to leave the hotel and to not go out under any circumstances because if you're white, they will think you have got money and they will chase you and try and sell you anything they can."

Gordon Rae agrees: "Aye Haiti was a bit mental. We went there to play their national team twice in a week. I mean, who would take you to Haiti? Only Hibs could do that! We actually arrived in the country in the week Bob Marley died and there was a crazy atmosphere. It was pretty volatile. It was the kind of place where you were constantly on edge and feeling that anything could happen. But we were all young and saw it as one big adventure. It's been a country hit with a lot of problems – it was a shame to see how poor they were."

Hart picks up the story: "We flew from San Francisco via Miami to Port-au-Prince and the place wasn't even third world – nearer fourth or fifth! We got driven to our hotel in a clapped-out bus and the hotel was a wreck and we refused to stay there. We got told of an American-styled hotel a few miles away and after a bit of hassle managed to get transferred there.

"Locals had got word that there were tourists staying so they descended on the hotel trying to flog us their souvenirs. The local currency was the Gourde, which was practically worthless and you couldn't change it. I bought a couple of things, wood carvings and so on, but Jackie McNamara was down at the gate and saw something he wanted and handed over a fifty-dollar US note. He expected to get change, but they just kept giving him more souvenirs and loading him up with plates and carved faces that he didn't want and pretending they didn't understand him. I don't think he was even able to get his suitcase shut because he had bought so much tat!"

Hibs might at least have expected to find some sanctuary on the football pitch from the chaotic scenes they were witnessing all around them, but their two 'friendlies' with Haiti was anything but. Hart continues: "We played the games in a ruinous stadium on a bare, stone-strewed pitch. One of the games didn't last long before it developed into a huge punch-up. The local ref was turning a blind eye to all sorts of sneaky trips, pulls and handballs by the Haitians and it came to a head when one of their players punched Arthur Duncan in the gut and winded him. By the time Arthur got up, the ball was at the other end of the pitch and he took a 30-yard run at the offending Haiti player and hit him with a two-footed drop kick between the shoulder blades! All hell broke loose, but we were fortunate to have guys like Gordon Rae and Billy McLaren in the side and they brought any afters to an end very quickly.

"I remember the country was in a terrible state but the people (apart from the Haiti footballers) were very friendly and seemed happy. Also, voodoo was very real over there. Before the game, a tall, thin guy went round the pitch in all his voodoo regalia and any locals he approached looked genuinely terrified."

The youngest member of the Hibs party knew that he was a long way from Whitburn! "Haiti was just plain scary," says Brian Rice. "There were snakes around and the poverty I saw there was a real eye-opener. It was a trip you'll never forget. They were kicking hell out of Ally MacLeod and he picked the ball up as if he was going to retaliate and kick it against him, but flicked it up in the air instead. Then all hell broke loose. The next thing I know we are all in the dressing room, barricaded in. The games themselves turned into an absolute shambles. The second game was about 25 minutes in when a full-scale melee broke out and the referee just blew the whistle and said that's enough of that!"

Craig Paterson adds: "It was nice to say that I have been to Haiti but I won't be rushing back. Half the island was like the Dominican Republic, but the other was steeped in voodoo. The worry was that after the game had turned into such a riot and the referee had abandoned it, people would have a go at us. We got back on to this rickety bus and I was thinking to myself 'this could be an interesting journey' – said he, brave as a lion, trying to hide! But I think the lad who was organising the trip assured us there wouldn't be any more trouble because it would be viewed as a national disgrace. The president Baby Doc and his secret police, the Tonton Macoute, would make sure nothing would happen that would embarrass the country. So that eased my mind just a little, but when we took off I was a lot happier when I could see Haiti in the rear-view mirror of the aeroplane!"

The First Division was also in the rear-view mirror and was preparing to welcome Hearts back into its clutches after they had once again been relegated. Hibs were Edinburgh's Premier team again, and the top-flight beckoned for Bertie's boys for the 1981-82 season.

CHAPTER 4

CIGAR SMOKE and MIRRORS

*"I am adamant that that period was the most
united a Hibs squad has ever been – because every
single person hated Bertie." – Gordon Rae*

With his dazzling grin and trademark giant cigar, Bertie Auld cultivated a cheery persona in the press that implied to the outside world that he was loving life at Hibs – and that his players loved him back. He had achieved what he had been tasked to do by the Hibs hierarchy: to restore the club immediately to the Premier League, and he entered the new campaign armed with a solid squad rich in experience and emerging talent. But beneath this veneer, there was trouble brewing. To be blunt, while respecting Auld's standing in the game, the majority of the dressing room could not stand their manager or his style of football.

Auld had already upset senior pros Ralph Callachan and Jim McArthur by leaving them at home while the rest of the promotion-winning team jetted off to California at the end of the 80-81 season. In Auld's eyes, it was punishment for them not yet having signed new contracts. Both players ultimately opted to put pen to paper and stay, and while the pair would always put Hibs first and give 100 per cent for the jersey, they would neither forgive not forget their manager's petulant intervention. Not that it would have bothered Auld, who appeared to have no appetite for diplomacy or reconciliation

Worse than that – he had a major beef with the club captain, the hugely influential Jackie McNamara. A Glasgow man and ex-Celtic player just like Auld, you might have expected the two men to get along swimmingly. But McNamara had developed a reputation as an outspoken firebrand, who was no stranger to the referee's book or the manager's office. He championed social justice and workers' rights and was labelled 'Red Jackie' for his links to the Union and his role as shop steward of his team-mates. With an ego to rival the size of his Cuban cigars, an envious Bertie seemed unnerved by the deep respect the skipper had earned from his team-mates, and it seems that he took an instant dislike to McNamara the moment he became Hibs manager. It wouldn't be long before such a toxic relationship became unsustainable.

The friction came to a head when McNamara walked off the training ground (if you can call the Jack Kane Centre an authentic training ground!), with Auld shouting after him that he was barred from taking the team minibus back and better make his own way back to Easter Road. Jackie explains: "He took the captaincy off me and gave it to Billy McLaren and then Alan Sneddon. He also tried to make an example of me at training. We were training up at Hunter's Hall at the Jack Kane Centre in the winter and it had frozen over. There was dug-shit, needles, boot-prints still on the pitch from the amateur games on the Saturday, it was a real mess. It wasn't conducive to playing passing football. I was playing at the back and got the ball and there was nobody near me, so I moved into midfield. Straight away, Bertie was shouting 'Stop the fuckin game! You think you are a prima donna, superstar bastard, do you?' I replied 'Sorry, what did you say?' and then I just walked off. As I walked away, he shouted after me: 'And you'll be walking back to Easter Road!' Our director Alan Hart turned up in the car dropping Erik Sørensen, the goalkeeping coach, off to do a session, and he asked me what was up. I told him I wasn't taking that kind of abuse, and he told me to jump in and he'd give me a run back to the ground."

With McNamara already on his way back to Easter Road in the comfort of Alan Hart's car, Auld's paranoia bubbled to the fore when he ordered the minibus to be searched in case the captain had sneaked in and was hiding. "Bertie got the bus searched because he thought Jackie was hiding on the bus when they fell out at training," says goalkeeper Jim McArthur, who admits "relationships were not great" between the manager and the squad. "There was another time when we had gone to train at the Jack Kane in the morning, but the pitch was rutted and frozen. He took us back and told us we would be going back to train in the afternoon. A lot of the boys had things on, including me as I was a PE teacher at the time. You would have arrangements made, because you expected to have the afternoon off. Bertie knew that, but he cancelled our time off in a heartbeat. So, we went back there in the afternoon and he set up a circuit, 30 seconds at each station. We finished the first 30 seconds only for him to say: 'Right, you can go now.' He just wanted to knacker up your afternoon. It was frustrating."

Journalist Simon Pia laughs at the absurdity of Bertie ordering his assistant Pat Quinn to search the bus for a stow-away McNamara, and says it was well known that animosity was escalating fast between the manager and his players. "When Bertie came to Easter Road people were quite excited by that, a

Lisbon Lion and great footballer," says Pia, "but it became very quickly obviously obvious that his management style did not match the way he played. He played a very defensive, dour, unpopular style of football. I got to know some of the guys, and they would say that Derek Rodier in particular would be getting a hard time. Gordon Rae told me he had never seen a guy massacred so badly by a manager. Bertie picked on Derek because he had been a university student, but him and Jackie McNamara was the main clash."

This collision of personalities intensified after the training ground spat at the Jack Kane, and the captain was not for backing down – especially when he discovered later that week that his wages had been docked. "Wednesday was always pay-day, and our trainer and physio Tam McNiven would read people's names and hand out the wage packets in alphabetical order," says Jackie. "When Tam skipped past M for McNamara, I asked him: 'Hey Tam, where's mine?' He said: 'I've been told not to give it to you Jackie.' I said: 'Just get my wages out here.' Tom said apologetically: 'I can't give you them Jackie. The manager's asked to see you.' I said: 'Aye, I'll be going up to see him, don't you worry!' I went straight up to see him in his office, and he was waiting for me. He put his hand out to shake it and congratulated me for standing up to him. I said to him I wasn't going to shake his hand and said: 'Make sure when I come out of here that my wages are waiting for me. Don't be messing about with my wages. You are not entitled by law to do that. I don't care who you are.' I got my wages in the end, but they soon had me out for extra training in the afternoons. Bertie had Pat Quinn, John Lambie and John Fraser all working me, while he stood in the stand watching. He told me: 'I was watching you against Falkirk and you kept breaking into the midfield. You're my valve.' I had never been called a VALVE in my life! I didn't know what he was on about. He then said 'your job is to get the ball and lift and lay.' He wanted me to sidestep across the 18-yard line, and as the coaches were getting the ball and rolling it to me, I had to control it then kick it as far away from our goals as possible – that was his definition of 'lift and lay', something else I had also never heard of. It was basically just pumping it into corners! I was doing this no problem because I could ping a ball, but eventually I got fed up and started deliberately punting them into the terracing. The three coaches ended up having to climb over the fence to get all the balls I was aiming there. Then we had to stop it because the coaches got too tired retrieving balls."

The harsh treatment meted out to McNamara and others still rankles. "In my opinion, he was not a very nice person," says Jackie. "Another time, I had been recovering from a broken ankle and had just come out of the shower when he started an inquest into us losing cheap goals at Ibrox. Wee Derek Rodier had played in that game and Bertie had been slaughtering him. I had been in the dug-out so heard it all. So, we had had this inquest and Derek, who had been sitting there with his head down, eventually challenged Bertie, saying: 'I don't think you saying all these personal things about me is going to help my game or my confidence.' Bertie claimed he hadn't said all these things, but I'd heard them myself. He was saying to all the players, 'Come on, we are all in this together. Feel free to speak your mind.' They were all looking at their bootlaces, and naebody was saying a word. I was sitting there in my towel, having come out the shower, so I piped up 'well boss...' when he cut me off and said 'McNamara... I don't give a fuck what you think!' I just put a towel in my mouth and shut up, there was no point."

Results in that first season back in the Premier League were steady, if unspectacular, and under Auld Hibs developed a reputation for being bland, safe and unadventurous – not at all in keeping with the club's traditions for attacking football. "I'm not just trying to make excuses for the players and how we played, but I felt the system Bertie was relying on and the negativity was holding us back. It was not the best for Hibs the way he was trying to play the game," says Ralph Callachan.

While Hibs were lacking in certain areas, one thing they could not be accused of was a shortage of team spirit. "I've said it before, but I am adamant that that period was the most united a Hibs squad has ever been – because every single person hated Bertie," says Gordon Rae. "He certainly succeeded in so much as he had us pulling in the same direction. What a man Bertie was – Christ! Obviously, he had been a great player, no doubt about it, but as a manager he had his faults. I just think he was really old school, similar to Eddie, but he didn't have the same air of authority or respect."

The perception that Auld was modelling himself on Turnbull was accurate enough, as Bertie confirms himself. "Eddie Turnbull was one of the best coaches ever," says Auld now. "He didn't mess about with his words. He was a true professional. He had a great knowledge in the game, particularly when it came to tactics. When I took over at Firhill and then other places, I would say to myself: 'I'm speaking a bit like Ned.' His influence had rubbed off on me and I believed in him – I was a great listener as a player and I learned from him. Eddie wasn't always everyone's favourite because he just told people how he felt. He also didn't mind if that upset linesmen and referees. People would call him a growler, but he would only growl at you if you weren't prepared to listen to him. You would be a fool to shut your ears and not take the advice Eddie Turnbull had to offer."

Football writer Mike Aitken believes that trying to follow the old-school approach of Turnbull was a mistake on Auld's part and questions whether Bertie was ever a good fit for Hibs. "What Bertie had achieved at Partick Thistle was hugely admirable and it was quite right he got a chance to try and replicate that somewhere else. But truthfully, at Partick, he had players who were a cut above. I was never entirely convinced that Bertie was a great fit for Hibs. He should have been, but he only lasted a couple of years. Bertie was a character who was not always easy to get on with. He had been a Lisbon Lion and had achieved a lot in his own career and I don't think he transferred that to being a coach. I don't think he was able to get the best out of players. It was that era where bullying and challenging players was starting to be seen as less and less acceptable to top players or good players, and players who in the past didn't have any option but to lie down and take it, were less likely to take it by then. It was before Bosman, and the power hadn't quite shifted in players' favour, but there was that feeling by then that players were at least entitled to stand up for themselves, especially the more senior ones like Jackie: a terrific player – better for Hibs than he was for Celtic. I liked him a lot. He was versatile and a very good Hibs servant and contributed a lot to the club."

The ill-feeling towards Auld was not entirely unanimous and Craig Paterson, for one, feels that his game developed further under his management and strict code of discipline. He also believes Auld needed to put safety first to ensure Hibs consolidated their Premier League status. "Like Eddie, Bertie was another hard, old-school man. He kept on top of everybody and nobody got a free ride," says Paterson. "Coming back into the Premier, first and foremost we had to make sure we stayed there and Bertie – as an organiser – was really good at making sure his teams didn't get in any bother. I knew the Hibs fans would have liked to have seen a bit more flair and a bit more style, but when you've just been promoted people are looking at you and posing the question 'can you hack it in the top league?' Bertie got the team organised to make sure we were never going to get anywhere near the relegation spots. It was a pragmatic approach.

"I do remember him upsetting the team and the fans from time to time. We had just beaten Celtic at Easter Road, and he was on *Scotsport* on the Sunday, and he said something like, 'I can walk around my beloved Glasgow with my head held high.' I think Hibs fans weren't happy and would have thought to themselves, 'What's all this Glasgow nonsense?' Sometimes you've got to watch what you say. Bertie did a job which might not have been great to watch, but from the point of view of ensuring Hibs stayed safe, it was what was needed at the time. He made sure Hibs got in the league, got players who made sure we stayed there, and then tried to move forward."

Kevin McKee, a youth player at the time, is another who had no qualms with Auld's austere approach. "Bertie was my first manager, and my main memory is of him standing on top of the dugout when we were doing our running exercises, with his big cigar, shouting the odds. He was a character to say the least. I was only a kid and it was a tough upbringing, but it didn't do you any harm. You had to deal with it if you wanted to survive in the professional game back then." Auld kept a close eye on the young players coming through and he reflects: "I always believed in trying to give young players a chance. I felt that the reserve team today would be the first team tomorrow. You don't see that in the game now, and young players are getting starved of that opportunity."

As December 1981 approached, Hibs had become draw specialists and had won only three league games. A fierce cold snap threatened the fixture list and made training difficult, but no-one at Easter Road felt the icy temperatures chill their bones more than a young trialist, Ricky Hill, who was flown 3,200 miles from the sun-kissed island of Bermuda for a trial period in the hope that he would make history by becoming the first black player to represent Hibs in the first team.

Free-scoring forward Hill had been starring on the Atlantic island for leading local team Hotels International, where one of his team-mates was Denis McQuade – the former Hearts and Partick Thistle winger who had moved to the island with his work. McQuade was impressed enough to get word back to Auld that he had unearthed an incredible talent in Bermuda and implored his old Firhill boss to take a chance on the pacy and athletic striker before someone else did.

Acting on McQuade's tip-off, Bertie sent director Alan Hart and coach Pat Quinn out to Bermuda to watch Hill at close quarters, and when they liked what they saw, they invited him to join them on the return flight to Edinburgh for a three-game trial. There was one small problem as Hill, speaking to me on a Zoom call from the island, explains. "They reckon it was the coldest winter it had been for a century in Scotland so that obviously had a psychological effect on me, coming from Bermuda. It didn't help that it was December, so it was absolutely freezing. I was only 21 and it was my first trip to anywhere in Europe. I didn't know what to expect but the first thing I remember is the cold."

Hibs had arranged for their trialist to stay with reserve player Carlo Crolla and his family at a flat in Windsor Street, and it wasn't long before they were answering the door to journalists and photographers intrigued at the back-story of such an exotic trialist. "The reporters in Scotland got hold of the story that I was into cricket and had played for the international team back home in Bermuda, and I can remember the reporter showing up at Windsor Street with a whole load of cricket gear and getting me to pose in the pads. I was young, and I never really knew the history of Hibernian at that stage, I just knew that they played in green and white. It was all a very quick process, a bit of a whirlwind, so it didn't give me any time to do any research on Hibernian.

"I took part in three trial games with the reserve team and I remember playing against Hearts at Easter Road. However, I didn't play as well as I knew I could. Something was missing, I was struggling to adapt. I was having trouble getting acclimatised to the conditions and I just felt a bit sluggish. Although

I was fit, there was something lacking, and I was just feeling kinda tired. I then had a reserve-team game against Queen's Park on the pitch right next to Hampden Park where I played better and scored a goal. They got that news back in Bermuda that I had scored and there was a lot of excitement at home. My other game was against Dundee United, but it's not the matches I remember so much, it was the cold!

"Easter Road was the first stadium in Scotland that had installed an underground heating system, using pipes to keep the pitch from freezing – but it didn't stop me from freezing! It worked to an extent as the ground was slightly thawed out, but the other pitches I played on during that time were very icy. The rest of the boys were good to me, very welcoming and kind, and they could see I was suffering because of the conditions. For the games, I used to wear two or three jerseys and gloves, and I remember it was so cold that it hurt me to put my foot into the bath after the game – I felt a burning sensation, like fire. It was really painful. I had to thaw out for a while, and the lads used to tease me because I couldn't stand it."

Gordon Rae, who played alongside Ricky in a couple of those trial games as he worked his way back to fitness after an injury, recalls: "He was a nice lad, but what a shame. I can remember him standing in a bath of hot water to try and warm his feet up, with his socks and boots on, the whole lot – he was absolutely freezing. Hibs were trying to be innovative, and often they were, but that one backfired a little bit. It was the coldest winter in years."

Not to be confused with the Ricky Hill who would play later in the Eighties for Luton Town and England, this Ricky Hill returned to Bermuda with the club's best wishes, and a notional offer of a potential second trial the following summer, when the weather would be more to his liking. That invitation was never actioned, and Ricky got on with his life and sporting career in his homeland, excelling as a footballer and cricketer in a dual international career, and working in insurance. He also got a brief taste of pro football in the USA and is philosophical about his experience in Edinburgh.

"Sure, I was a little disappointed that it didn't work out, but at the same time it was so very, very cold and I just didn't acclimatise," says Hill, still looking as fit as a fiddle... and considerably warmer than he did in the press picture he posed for on a frost-pocked pitch back in 1981. "I'm not saying I wasn't good enough, I just think the cold weather meant I wasn't able to adapt quick enough. Over a period of time I might have got more used to it, and maybe I would have adapted. But we were going into the mountains and running on ice, going to the beach and running on ice, playing games on ice... oh my God it was a nightmare! I can clearly remember people telling me it had been the coldest winter in a century. Players these days adapt pretty quickly to playing abroad, but back in that day it was much harder to do, especially coming from

Bermuda – a tropical island. But I am very thankful for my life and the fact that I have been able to perform in both sports at a pretty high level."

Ricky may have missed out on becoming the first black player in Hibs' first team 40 years ago, a distinction which Kevin Harper would claim in 1993, but he is pleased and relieved to see that the club and Scottish football has made giant strides in embracing diversity since then. He was also delighted to rekindle his connection with Hibs by participating in an interview for this book, and to take delivery of a Hibees top I sent him to wear with pride. Ricky Hill, you're one of our own!

As Ricky pointed out, Hibs had not only made a pioneering move for him, but had broken new ground in 1980 by becoming the first club in the country to wisen up to the fact that advances in technology made it possible to protect their playing surface from the elements. State-of-the-art undersoil heating was installed at Easter Road, and most clubs would soon follow Hibs' lead.

Director Alan Hart, who helped oversee the project, remembers: "We had missed out on two big Sunday games, one of them was a cup tie, and because I was in the building industry, I was tasked with trying to find a solution. First, we tried big braziers round the pitch to heat it up and, when that never worked, we tried another method of giant industrial polythene sheets with hot-air blowers underneath, which didn't work either. We then heard that Coventry City had put in undersoil heating. So, I went down with one of the Celtic directors to see the system and it was quite impressive – it did seem to work. It was like a giant radiator with hot water through plastic pipes a foot down below the pitch. We eventually went with a similar Swedish system, and they agreed to do it for £50,000 – about a third of the price that the other supplier who had done the Coventry system wanted. All we had to do was build a boiler house for the system. It worked a treat and we were able to get games on throughout the winter months, which included the Manchester United game which was a good early success for us."

The visit of Manchester United was hastily arranged for Boxing Day 1981, when the fixture list was wiped out north and south of the Border. The 1-1 draw is remembered for two things mainly – first, the 'welcome to Scotland' bodycheck Erich Schaedler executed on a startled Bryan Robson; and second, the peacocking contest between two extravagantly-dressed managers, Bertie Auld and Ron Atkinson, who each looked determined to outdo each other.

"Ron Atkinson also liked to be seen and heard and show off, so with him and Bertie it was the perfect competition," laughs Ralph Callachan. "But it was great for the fans to get a game like that. The Bryan Robson incident showed that both teams were taking it seriously, but Erich put a few boys on their erse in his career, didn't he? He did more damage to his own players than he did to the opposition sometimes. He broke my cheekbone in training one day! Erich didn't have a scratch on him but I got carted off to the hospital. I had played against him when I was at Hearts, but Erich wasn't just a hard-man, he had a lot to offer going up and down that wing, and played in a great Hibs team."

Auld, who had played briefly alongside Erich in the early 70s, says: "Erich Schaedler was magnificent – he had pace, determination and I'll tell you this much… nobody wanted to play against him. When we had been younger, he was left-back and I was outside left at Easter Road and you could not have got a nicer man. But whoever he tackled would count how many toes they had left afterwards!"

While Big Ron preened and puffed out his chest in a sheepskin jacket, taking umbrage at Erich's assault on his up-and-coming midfield general, a sanguine Bertie blew clouds of smoke into the winter air from a giant cigar under the shadow of his comically enormous bunnet. "The cigars became something I did at Partick Thistle, when a couple of supporters from Maryhill had been away abroad and handed me some cigars they had brought back from their holidays," Auld tells me. "I never had smoked cigarettes or anything like that and I never inhaled them."

Another notable friendly that season was the welcome return of George Best in October, this time as a San Jose Earthquakes player. Hibs, wearing their sparkling yellow change kit, won this glamour game under the lights 3-1, and George was given a rapturous reception from the fans and his former team-mates. It was around this time, that the man who had first brought Best to Hibs – Tom Hart – had started to put his succession plan into place.

Edinburgh bookmaker Kenny Waugh, who had lost out to Wallace Mercer in an attempt to buy Hearts, had instead decided to pursue his dream of controlling a football club with Hibs. After an introductory spell as a director, he agreed financial terms with Hart to acquire the 300,000 shares he needed to become the new chairman. To recognise his outstanding contribution to the club, which had started in 1970 when he took over from Bill Harrower, the plan was that Hart would become the club president.

Tragically, as this transfer of power was taking place, Hart suffered a brain haemorrhage on his way up to a midweek league game at Aberdeen in March 1982, and passed away that night. His son Alan remembers: "I was not going to the game because I had a meeting, and I then got the phone call from the club doctor Jimmy Ledingham to let me know that my Dad was seriously ill and that I should come up as quick as I could. We arranged a car for my mum, me and my wife to go up, and by the time we got there he was unconscious but alive. It had been a brain haemorrhage and there was nothing they could do for him. He had just turned 60. I suppose he had been hard living and a heavy smoker, and it had taken its toll."

Among those devastated at the loss was Bertie Auld. "I loved Tom Hart, what a chairman," says Auld. "He had tremendous passion for Hibs. He was a very hard grafter himself and his son Alan was a lovely big guy. They would both come and speak to you openly, and both were very approachable and supportive. I always had a huge amount of respect for Mr Hart – he gave me that wonderful opportunity to come and manage Hibs and I wanted for nothing. He was naebody's mug – he spoke the way he thought was right. Tom Hart was not a miserable man, he would often go into his own pocket to help the club. He was tremendous."

Waugh would, as planned, become the chairman of a club numbed by the sudden loss of Hart. It was not the only tragedy to affect Hibs that season – a month before Hart's death, an 18-year-old Hibbie Mark McGhee was killed in a bus crash near Perth on the way to our Scottish Cup tie at Dundee United. "I was in the Liberton Branch A9 bus crash en route to Tannadice in 1982, in which a teenage Hibbie tragically lost his life," remembers supporter Sandy Macnair. "I was carted off to hospital for a fortnight, finally being forced to leave in protest, when a loud-mouthed Hun wearing a ludicrously embroidered dressing gown was admitted to the ward. As the medics had shaved random segments of my head to insert a patchwork of stitches, I was obliged to attend the upcoming games at Easter Road sporting a sort of lopsided hippie Mohican mullet."

Rangers, as per usual, were not flavour of the month with Hibbies. The rivalry had just kept ratcheting up notch by notch after the 1979 Scottish Cup final trilogy, and relations plumbed new depths when an outrageous dive by John MacDonald in the November clash at Easter Road conned referee Louis Thow into awarding Rangers a penalty. It was the first Hibs v Rangers game I remember attending, and I can still feel the tremors of rage threatening to splinter the wooden floor of the old North Stand as the home fans went berserk! Tom Hart would be fined by the SFA in the aftermath of the game for speaking on behalf of all present and calling a cheat a cheat.

The other three Hibs-Rangers meetings would end up all square that season, in line with the Bertie's draw specialism, and we also fared well in matches against champions Celtic... up until a point. "For some reason we did well in the big games that season," says Craig Paterson. "I think that was the last time that Hibs won both league games at home to Celtic in the same season. We beat them 1-0 both times and at Parkhead we drew 0-0. And then in the final game they beat us 6-0! Celtic had already won the title and Hibs were the only team they hadn't beaten that season and hadn't scored a goal against, so they came at us with a point to prove and that was the worst defeat I can remember in my career."

The season finished with Hibs sixth in the 10-team league, and just four points off a place in Europe. On the face of it, Auld had done a decent job in re-establishing the team in the top flight, but with Waugh now in control, and aware of the acrimony festering behind the scenes, his days would be numbered. So too would Paterson's. As one of the emerging talents in the squad, his saleable value was evident to opportunistic Waugh, and when an offer came in that matched his valuation, there was only one outcome. The problem was that the offer had come from Rangers!

"It was more or less down to money," says Paterson, who has endured a lifetime of stick as a result of that £200,000 move along the M8. "Kenny Waugh spoke to me and said Rangers had offered Hibs money that they didn't want to turn down. And that was it – you are told you are being sold. Genuinely, you were owned by the club. If you didn't sign a contract then that was you finished, you were out the game. The rule was when they offered you a contract, they had to offer you either the same terms or better, they couldn't offer you less, so it was just one of those things that came along and gave me the chance to play for a huge club. I later captained Rangers to a League Cup victory at Hampden and played in a cup-winning team against Celtic, which were fantastic memories. But Hibs were my team, and I would have gladly played for them the rest of my days. Whenever I signed a contract, I told Tom Hart: 'You know me and you know my Dad… if any club ever came in and made me an offer, and Hibs were able to match it, I would never leave.' But that's not the way football works out.

"I got pelters when I left, but then I had done the same thing when Colin Stein left, dishing the pelters out. I understood the fans – I had left their team and joined another team, and it was Rangers. I knew I was going to come back and play against Hibs and that obviously it's not going to go down well. Hibs was the dream club to play for but I've no regrets about playing for Rangers and then to go on and win the cup with Motherwell in 1991."

Paterson is the dream interviewee, very personable with a quick wit and a great memory of the era, but you can feel that the abuse he received cut deep. So, what was it really like to run the gauntlet anytime he turned up at Easter Road in a Rangers strip?

"It's no fun! These were people that I knew from supporters' clubs. They had been great with me and I knew a lot of them. But I fully understood how they felt. My first game for Rangers was a League Cup tie at Easter Road in the old group stage and you are running out the tunnel thinking to yourself 'Oh dear, here we go… this could be a long afternoon.' The song was 'Craigy Paterson, Craigy Paterson, what's it like to be a Hun?' It wasn't unexpected. I had moved on and I just had to get on with my job. Hibs were the team I had supported as a kid, but I had moved on to a new team and when you are playing against your boyhood team you are sometimes even more determined to make sure you play well and don't lose. If you are going to get stick it's better walking off the park at the end having won the game."

A commanding central defender, Paterson had broad shoulders, and manfully decided he would don his flak jacket and honour an invitation to collect his Player of the Year trophy at the Hibs Supporters' Club in person, even though he was now a Rangers player. "That was an odd night," he laughs. "I was absolutely delighted to win it and was really proud of it, especially when you saw some of the names that had won it before. I turned up, and although it was a little awkward, no-one gave me stick and it was good-hearted stuff. I think if I remember correctly when I arrived there was a TV there – which I thought would be a lovely prize. But when it came to the presentation, I got a trophy and Ally MacLeod got the telly for services to the club. I had my eye on the 36-inch Hitachi, but it's a trophy I still have and treasure, I am pleased to say. I didn't want to disrespect them by not turning up, it was worth risking a bit of stick."

The curtain-raising League Cup section of the 1982-83 season produced only a solitary win from six games, which yielded yet another two draws against Rangers. A 3-1 defeat at Airdrie in the last of this tortuous sequence was the final straw for Waugh and Bertie was shown the door.

He did at least get the chance of leading Hibs to some silverware – the Tom Hart Memorial Trophy which had been commissioned as a tribute to the chairman the club had recently lost. Hearts, who faced another season in the First Division after missing out on promotion by a single point, were chosen as the opposition and Jock Stein – fresh from taking Scotland to the 1982 World Cup finals in Spain – was invited to Easter Road to present the trophy. "I scored the winner with my shoulder, and it flew past Henry Smith," says Jackie McNamara. "The Hearts fans vandalised some shops in Easter Road and carried on into Princes Street that night. It was only a charity game – I couldn't understand it."

The repairs on those shop windows hadn't long been completed before Auld's aspirations for the season were well and truly out the window. Waugh had taken decisive action to put his own plans into place at Easter Road, and Bertie wasn't part of them. Poor Bertie has taken a bit of a panning in this chapter, so the least I can do is give him the final say, and it's a nice say at that. "I must admit I loved managing Hibs," he reflects warmly. "The players were honest pros, and the club always had the reputation of bringing through new young talent every season. They were and are a marvellous club, well respected throughout Scotland."

CHAPTER 5

S.O.S (Stanton, O'Rourke, Stewart)

"It's different if you feel things are going to change for the better, but I didn't see that at all. It was time to go, as gut-wrenching as it was." – Pat Stanton

The Dream Team. The Three Amigos. SOS – Stanton, O'Rourke and Stewart. Whatever way you referred to them, Hibs' new three-pronged management team reinvigorated a squad mentally weary from their petty squabbles with Bertie Auld and gave supporters a renewed sense of optimism. King Pat was Easter Road royalty, and his two trusted assistants Jimmy and George, were also Hibs men through and through. Sadly, as their reign would show, they were the right men at the wrong time.

Hibs had undergone change in the boardroom as well as the dug-out. While Tom Hart had been the type of philanthropic chairman who would dig deep into his own pockets to fund his dreams as an avid Hibs supporter, his successor, the amateur boxer-turned-bookmaker Kenny Waugh did not always hold such romantic beliefs, especially when it came to finances. As corners were cut and purse-strings were tightened, the club soon started to stagnate at a time when Aberdeen and Dundee United had streaked ahead as the 'best of the rest', upsetting the traditional Old Firm powerbase in Scottish football by regularly challenging for honours.

The erosion of resources was exemplified when the players, on their way to one of the random pic'n'mix of public parks in the city they used for training, had to stop the club minibus to buy a couple of cut-price footballs from a sports shop because the club had none to offer. Things would get so bad, that when two-thirds of the coaching team had to be let go to balance the books, their back-dated wages were paid in cases of vodka and whisky for them to use in the pubs they ran in their spare time. We'll come to that, but let's start at the beginning of the Stanton era, when the 1982-83 league season was about to begin. It began with a change of captain. Or, rather, the reinstatement of the true leader in the dressing room – Jackie McNamara – who had been unceremoniously removed from the venerable position by Auld.

"The first thing Pat did was pull me into his office," explains Alan Sneddon, who had just worn the armband for the pre-season Tom Hart Memorial Trophy win over Hearts, and who knew Stanton well having played alongside him at Celtic. "Bertie had made me captain, having taken the armband off Jackie because they had been at loggerheads. Pat told me he wanted me to focus on my game and concentrate on that, and not being captain. In a very diplomatic way, he was restoring Jackie as captain and doing the best to spare my feelings. That was his way of dealing with it. At the end of the day, I had never been a captain before, and that was my first experience of it. I enjoyed it while it lasted, but when you have a senior pro like Jackie who had been there, done it, and was so respected by everyone at Hibs, it was the right call from Pat. It was no big deal to me, I accepted it completely. As a player, Pat was so cultured, and as a manager he was so laid back. But he was no soft touch either. He knew how to put his message across, and if you weren't doing something right then he would tell you."

Stanton arrived at Hibs with management experience already under his belt, following his illustrious playing career, which saw him play 617 games in 14 years with Hibs before he was jettisoned by Eddie Turnbull in a controversial swap deal with McNamara. After his surprise exit from the club he supported and loved, the classy Stanton immediately went on play a key role in winning the championship with Jock Stein's Celtic – clinching the 1977 title at Easter Road, in front of Turnbull. Although relations between Turnbull and Stanton would never recover from their parting of ways, Hibs at least had the decency to invite the great man back for a star-studded testimonial in 1978, with international guests playing for the Hibs and Celtic select sides. This, incidentally, was the first match I remember being taken to as a kid!

With his competitive playing days behind him, Stanton first worked as an assistant under Alex Ferguson at Aberdeen, then cut his teeth as a manager during spells with Cowdenbeath and Dunfermline. When the call came from Hibs, he felt he had little option but to seize what he considered to be the chance of a lifetime. "Sometimes people tell you that you shouldn't retrace your steps, but when you get asked – being a Hibs man – how can you say no?" says Pat, nearly 40 years later. "I thought at the time I wouldn't be asked again if I refused. I couldn't say no. I have many happy memories and it was a good place to be, full of good Hibs people.

"If players were seeking a bit of advice, as well as me they could go to Jim, George or Tom McNiven – these backroom people were all Hibs supporters through and through. Big George and Jimmy were just terrific, smashing characters, and I could trust them, which is really important when you're the manager. It was reassuring to know these guys always had your back, and that they wanted the same as you. With Jimmy and George helping me, I went out of my way to create a good atmosphere at Easter Road, as the last thing we wanted was for it to be like a dentist's waiting room. The players stuck together and so did the staff. They had one aim – to get a result on a Saturday. It's fine if you have the players to work with, and they respond, and looking back at what we had to work with, we were lucky – we had people like McNamara, Callachan and Sneddon. I also found myself managing old team-mates from my playing days like Erich Schaedler and Arthur Duncan. But I got a great response from these guys, they were so professional and had no problem in respecting that I was the manager. Players like that didn't need anyone to motivate them to try their hardest for Hibs, they just played the way they always played, and that was a big help to me. With players like that you don't need to take them by the hand and nurse them along, they just knew what was required. We were lucky to have these guys because they were real professionals. They had so much pride in themselves and the club. There were a few strong individuals, but we were a tight group and were all in it together. It was a good environment to be in, but it was just hard to get out of the decline the club were in."

George Stewart had not long left the club as a player, but he was back in a flash when the opportunity arose to return with Stanton. "I remember the punters saying 'Here they come, SOS – Stanton O'Rourke Stewart.' Very clever! The punters were always good to me, and I felt part of the family. But we soon found out that the training facilities were not the best. We had just had to make do as best we could, but it was hard. Pat was great and the boys had a lot of respect for him, and Rourkey and I would take certain players and mix about, to keep it interesting. I would look after the central defenders and spend a lot of time with them trying to help them win balls in the air, and Gordon Rae as well. I got a lot out of that personally, I felt it was good to be passing that knowledge on, and I remember how I was treated as a young professional myself at Dundee by guys like Gordon Smith and Alan Gilzean. It was what we did in those days – passed on what we knew. I used to pick Gordon Strachan up on the way to Dens Park, a great talent, and it didn't take him long to break into the first team. He was a Hibs supporter too, so we clicked. I remember him running in when we were in the bath after we'd played up at Aberdeen for Dundee and he was saying: 'Where's the big man, where's Big Stewarty? Seven-nothing, Hibs have just beaten Hearts 7-0!' It was brilliant. I had been an experienced pro and felt I could help Gordon and the other young guys around me, and I took that into coaching too."

Gordon Rae, still only 24 at the time the trio arrived, says: "When Pat came in it was brilliant. With him, George and Jimmy it was great times, great memories, great people. That was probably the happiest times at Hibs – it was a great place to be. I know the results weren't always what we wanted them to be, and finances were tight at the time, but there was a really good feel about the place. Finances in football were very tough at that time, not just at Hibs, and you just had to scramble along, but we were still happy to come in and work together and I have very fond memories of that period. The workplace environment was fantastic. You would give 100 per cent for them every week, something that should probably go without saying as a professional but, for that particular group of people, you would be willing to dig as deep as is humanly possible to try and squeeze out that little bit extra for them. They were just great people.

"Although I could play at the back or up front, and flitted between the two, it was really when Pat came that I moved back to centre-half. George and Jimmy had done a bit of coaching when Eddie was the manager, and George – having been a centre-half himself – saw that I had the potential to make an impact playing there.

"It was actually Jimmy who was the first man to play me at centre-half in a reserve game at Ibrox. We used to have alternating fixtures, so when the first team were playing Rangers at Easter Road, we would be playing their reserves through there. I was just coming back from a knee injury and Jimmy told me I was playing centre-half. Jimmy tells the story that when we came back to Easter Road, he bumped into Eddie in the ground after the first-team game. Eddie would hang back at the stadium to wait for the reserves to come back so he could ask who had played well and how the young boys had done. When Turnbull had asked who had played well that day, Jimmy told him: 'Gordon Rae was unbelievable at centre-half.' Turnbull says: 'Centre-half? I always knew he was going to be a centre-half!' I would play there now and again under Eddie, but sometimes he would use me at centre forward. During his time there, we would go back and do extra training on other positions, so we could slot in and play two or three positions if circumstances meant we had to shuffle the team. I could play midfield too. It was if anyone was suspended, I could slot it. Benny was the same, so could Snoddy and big Craig Paterson. You learned the basics of the positions. It was when George came back with Pat and Jimmy that he suggested, 'What about playing permanently at centre-half?' So, I stayed there from that point on."

The faces of the new management team may have been familiar, but their ideas were fresh, and Ralph Callachan also welcomed the positive change of mood and approach around Easter Road: "Pat, George and Jimmy gave the place a huge lift," he says. "The three of them coming in was just what we needed, and I would give them 10 out of 10 for their training and the way they wanted to play the game – they couldn't do enough for the players. Wee Jimmy was different class in the training, big George too, and the three of them did work very well together."

Brian Rice agrees: "It was just laugh-a-minute with those three around. Pat was the gentleman and Mr Hibs and an absolute legend at the club. I remembered having watched him as a kid when my Dad used to take me to the games. I learned a lot from Pat. People earn respect and in the case of Pat, he gets 100 per cent from me. When somebody has been such a good player, you can learn from them, and I definitely took a lot out of what Pat taught me, and to a lesser extent Bertie too."

There may have been smiles back on faces, but the bulk of the squad had been around long enough to know that there could and should have been more quality and a more expansive budget for a club of Hibs' standing. "Things were not too clever, and you saw players you thought you could bring in and make a change, but there wasn't the money to do that," sighs Stanton. "It was a difficult time for everybody. Things were on a down, and it was hard to get us back up again and moving in the right direction. That took time before we got back to doing that – the club and the players. It was also hard trying to find places to train. You sometimes had to play on the sand at Portobello beach, which wasn't ideal, and then if you went up to Holyrood Park to train up there and it was wet the parkie would chase you off the grass. It was a poor situation to be in – we were meant to be a professional club, and you didn't have anywhere to train when the weather was bad. At least we had a core of players who just got on with it."

Callachan agrees: "For a big club like us it was embarrassing. I can remember us driving around looking for spare ground to train on. It was difficult for Pat, trying to get the team playing the way he wanted to play and behind the scenes it was difficult. You could tell money was tight and we were even lacking the basics like training gear and footballs. I can remember us using balls out the shop to do some training, it was like playing with balloons – it might sound far-fetched now, but that's how bad it was."

The removal of Auld did not give Hibs instant impetus and results remained iffy. It would take Stanton and his coaches until their seventh league game in charge to record a win, and only one more would follow before the New Year. Hibs' problems were mounting, and another was added to the pile in a 3-2 defeat at Ibrox when Jim McArthur took a blow to the face and had to leave the field, to be replaced in goal by Arthur Duncan. An own goal from Jackie Mac and a missed penalty from Callachan compounded a miserable day in Govan.

A fortnight later, captain McNamara was handed a triple red card at Love Street. Although he's mellowed with the years, and is enjoying his retirement in Spain, it's an injustice that still simmers with McNamara. "A lot of people thought I was dirty, but I honestly don't think I was," he says. "I sometimes mistimed tackles, but as you get older you get slower. The triple sending off happened after I tackled Doug Somner at St Mirren. It was a typical Renfrewshire day, pissing with rain, and you have to allow for the conditions. I sent big Doug sprawling, but he got up right away. But the referee – who was a novice – Thomas Timmons, sent me off three times in the one game. My opponent was pleading my case, saying that I hadn't really touched him, but as Timmons was giving me a second booking, I said to him: 'You must have been a milk monitor or a prefect at school, behaving like this...' so he sent me off again. I was going to punch him but stopped myself and took my shirt off and threw it at him instead. That was red card number three. I've got photos of Ralph pulling me away. I was raging and, of course, there was no right to appeal. The SFA fined me, and I told them they were not taking money out my wages, that it was against employment law. Then, when I heard that the Hibs supporters were willing to have a whip-round and pay my fine, I couldn't have them doing that, so I bit the bullet and stumped up."

Stanton must have already been cursing his luck, and he could see his depleted squad beginning to get stretched. They were leaking points, goals and not scoring many either. Pat even had to bring in ex-Hearts winger Malky Robertson for a couple of games in the twilight of his career, and sign Ormiston Primrose forward Graham Harvey straight from the Juniors. In fairness to Harvey, he did well, and established himself in professional football, but more when he left Easter Road. At that time, Stanton needed something – or someone – special to turn it around. The Scotland keeper Alan Rough, linked with a move to Hibs throughout Auld's time in charge, would answer the call. "When we mentioned that we were interested in signing him people questioned us, saying that we shouldn't be looking at bringing in a goalkeeper as a priority, saying he doesn't score goals," recalls Stanton. "But just by having Roughie there he would give you 10-15 points a season."

Just five months before signing for Hibs, Rough had faced one of the great Brazil teams of the modern era at the World Cup in Spain, watching on in awe – like the rest of us – as Zico, Eder and Falcao pinged sublime goals past him in retaliation for Davie Narey's world-class 'toe-poke'. The 2-2 draw with the old USSR confirmed our exit from the finals – again at the group stage – and by the time Scotland faced East Germany in European Championship qualifying, Jock Stein had decided to replace Rough with Jim Leighton.

Realising that it was finally time to consider a move from Partick Thistle in search of a new challenge, the easy-to-please Rough was willing to keep an open mind as to whether he should stay or go, but when the move happened it came out of the blue. "I remember clearly how the move came about," laughs Rough. "I got a phone call from Thistle's secretary Molly Stallan to say I was to

come in to Firhill at 5pm. When I got there, she told me to head to the manager's office. Peter Cormack was manager at the time and he looked surprised
to see me. In fact, his exact words to me were: 'What is it that you want?' I
replied: 'I'm not wanting anything, I've just been told to come in and see YOU.'
He asked me to give him a minute and went away out, leaving me in the office.
When he came back in again, he told me: 'We've sold you to Hibs!' He obviously didn't know anything about it. I was told to go through to Edinburgh to
meet their chairman, Kenny Waugh. Kenny was at a boxing do, sponsoring an
event in a hotel, so I was told to go into a room somewhere on the second floor.
Kenny eventually came in and sat down on the bed. He said, 'I'm sponsoring the next fight so I can't stay long. I'm glad you are joining us, here's your
wages, here's your signing-on fee, I'll catch you later on,' and away he went! I
hadn't even had time to ask him about expenses or anything else really.

"I was happy to sign for Pat Stanton though. I had played in his testimonial,
and he had spoken to me back then about how I was doing at Thistle. I had
been at Thistle a long time and I was thinking it was maybe time for a move.
I don't know whether that had planted the seed and triggered it, but it was
Pat who made the move to sign me. Wee Bertie had tried to sign me for Hibs
a year or two before, when Tom Hart was the chairman. I don't know what
happened, but it fell through that time. To be honest, if Hibs hadn't put the
bid in, I would have probably just stayed at Thistle. I wasn't the kind of player
that looked for a move or was banging down doors. It just so happened that it
happened when it happened. In fact, about two or three months before that, I
could have been at Middlesbrough, but there was a mess-up and that one fell
through.

"When I met Pat, Rourkey and George, it was just a great environment, full
of absolutely great guys, like Jackie Mac, Ralphy and wee Bobby (Smith). The
unfortunate thing was that the club was going through some tough times
financially. Honestly, the first day's training I took part in we had two balls and
naewhere to train. I'm not saying Thistle were the greatest organisation in the
world, but I thought coming through to Hibs would be a lot better. We used to
come in early in the morning, and someone would ask: 'Does anyone know of
anywhere we can train today?' One of the funniest ones was when we went up
to train at Holyrood during pre-season. We'd just started a first team v second
team game and the next minute the park warden appears, looking angry and
blowing his whistle and telling us to get aff the park! You know Pat... he just
used to shrug his shoulders or shake his head, and say: 'Ach well, we'll just
have to go somewhere else.'"

Rough quickly made a big impression on his team-mates, who knew a true
professional when they saw one. While Rough was languid, laid-back and
droll off the pitch, he was switched on and focused the moment he crossed

the white line. "Aye, that comes with experience," says Rough. "I remember one of my first games for Hibs, at Morton. It had been absolutely pouring with rain and I came in half an hour early, got my gear on and got out on the pitch before anyone else to find out where the ball was skidding and where it was sticking in the mud. Half the players were looking at me, wondering what the hell I was doing, but I was finding out where I was going to be slipping, what boots I should be wearing. It just came from experience, it had been etched into you. I think when you've been in the game a long time you learn from a lot of people."

Stanton also remembers that game at Cappielow, in which Rough was rewarded for his preparation by keeping a clean-sheet and helping Hibs win a vital point. "When you look back at the way he played and what he brought to the place, he kept Hibs in the league," says Stanton. "Roughie is a big easy-going character, but at training and in matches he was really first class. He was such a good trainer and full of good advice for the young players around him. He was a great signing for us. I remember that day we went to Cappielow – there had been a lot of rain and the pitch was saturated, the water just stayed on the park. Before the game we were out on the park and he was getting people to play balls into him along the ground from different angles, and he was able to judge where the ball was holding up in the mud and rain. When it came to the crunch, he was a real professional."

Journalist Simon Pia was another admirer of the composed keeper. "Roughie was one of the coolest footballers you could meet – he was smart, clever and very droll," says Pia. "I don't know whether Alan Rough has ever raised his voice in anger. He was unflappable. One time, we were playing Rangers and a guy ran on to the pitch wearing a Santa outfit – just before Christmas – and Rough grabbed the guy and walked him into the net. Roughie managed to intercept him before he took a swing at anyone, and then the police came and took him away. I also remember coming out of a Hearts game at Tynecastle – Jackie McNamara, Ralph Callachan and Alan Rough were standing outside the Tynecastle Arms and this big gang of Hearts fans appeared from under the bridge and saw them and starting shouting abuse at them. It was a night game and I had been there reporting and Jackie wasn't for budging – and neither was Roughie. I remember them saying: 'Have you boys got a fuckin problem? Come ahead then.' There were dozens of them, but the three of them stood their ground with their hands in their pockets. I wasn't sure what to do myself... should I run for it or do I have to stand and jump in for them?"

Rough remained a big presence on the pitch, but he could not inspire Hibs to make any kind of meaningful headway in the league. The only bright spot was a freakish 8-1 demolition of Kilmarnock at Easter Road – one of only two occasions Hibs would score three goals or more in their 43 competitive games that season. Blink, and you would have missed their cup campaigns too. After the dismal League Cup campaign under Bertie, Stanton's Scottish Cup run fell at the first hurdle against the outstanding Aberdeen team who would go on to win the trophy, as well as the European Cup-Winners' Cup. Indeed, Hibs travelled to Pittodrie just days after the Dons' famous win in Gothenburg, and gave them a guard of honour, before leaving their net largely unguarded – even with Roughie in goal – to end their season with a 5-0 thrashing. We had finished seventh, and were the second lowest goalscorers in the league.

The team's travails were understandable because, behind the scenes, there was turmoil, and tension between the manager and chairman came to a head towards the end of that season. "Despite any progress we were making I was feeling continually frustrated and didn't think the board had the same will to put Hibs back on top as I had," Stanton recalled in his 1989 book, *The Quiet Man*. "There were many aspects of the way things were being run that I did not agree with. Things came to a head just before we played Motherwell at the end of the 1982-83 season and I told Kenny Waugh I was resigning."

Stanton, always an honourable man, had been upset that he had been denied the opportunity to speak face-to-face with a player who was not being offered a new contract, and to wish him the best of luck for the future. "A young player just got a note out of the blue telling him he was freed. The first I knew of it was when he came to me with the letter in his hand. I was really angry it had been done in this way. I got hold of Kenny Waugh and told him I was not going to Motherwell. Jimmy and George took the team and Stewart Brown, who knew something was up, carried the story that night in the *Evening News*. Meanwhile, I was taking in a game at Craigmillar Crossroads. There was a big reaction to this and on Sunday Kenny Waugh phoned me up and asked me to reconsider. I spoke to my father about my resignation and listened to his advice. I decided to reconsider, but with hindsight it was maybe the wrong decision."

Yet again, Stewart Brown – who covered the club for the *News* for decades, before David Hardie picked up the Hibs beat – had been the reporter to land a major scoop. Using his trusted network of sources, the exclusives Brown broke in the *Evening News*, the *Evening Despatch* then *The Pink News*, could usually be soundly relied upon. "Stewart was the main man in the press box," says Simon Pia. "There were other guys like Glenn Gibbons, Ray Hepburn and Ron Scott, but Stewart was the voice of authority. I remember one occasion, when I didn't know better, some of the other guys had asked Stewart who had played a particular pass for a goal. I spoke up and corrected him and said: 'No, I don't think so Stewart...' then said whoever it was. Stewart turned round and gave this glare that could have cut me in two. Afterwards, he took me aside, and said: 'Eh Simon, I know you were right there, but in future you do not show me up in front of the boys like that, okay?' Point made, and I apologised. We got on well from that point on. Stewart had a really good football brain and understood the game, while Mike Aitken was one of the best I ever saw at putting a match report together on the spot."

Shoe-horned into the end of the 1982-83 season was the testimonial match promised to loyal keeper Jim McArthur, who had lost his place to Rough and even had to suffer the awkwardness of being subbed off for the new Hibs No 1 in his own big game. Hearts, who had finally succeeded in escaping the First Division, were invited to provide the opposition and while a low-key encounter ended in a 4-2 win for Hibs, ANY taste of victory against their rivals would soon become a rare vintage! "I've never been in a losing team against the Hearts mind!" McArthur points out. "It was actually Wallace Mercer of all people who helped arrange for Hearts to come. The police tried to put it off because they were worried they would need helicopters and police dogs to stop any violence, and it was far more trouble and money than it was worth. They were worried there would be mayhem. The game was on the Sunday, and on the Thursday it was all still hanging in the balance with a chance it might get called off. In the end, it was Alistair Darling – then on the council – who stepped in and gave the green light for the game to go ahead. There was a deluge, thunder and lightning, but the crowd was big enough considering the weather and the late notice. There was never a programme because they didn't want to take the risk of printing one. There were a lot of guest players, and then Rough came on to replace me with 10 minutes to go. That was nice... hooked in my own testimonial!"

Stanton may have been persuaded to stay, but with the wage bill about to be put through Waugh's wringer once again, it was decided that George Stewart and Jimmy O'Rourke should move on. "Aye, we got paid off in drink," laughs George Stewart. "I was the one with the big mouth. Pat wasn't like that and neither was Jimmy, so when we found out we were being punted I went to see Kenny Waugh about the money we were due. He said he'd give us what was due in cases of whisky, vodka and cans, because a drink company had just sponsored one of our matches. I thought 'okay then, might as well'. I had the Chesser Inn and Jimmy had the Corstorphine Inn at the time. Rourkey wasn't too happy and didn't want to take it at first, and he was wanting cash instead, as he was entitled to. But wee Kano was about the place, so I shouted him over and said 'Come and give me a hand son, take that drink and stick it in my van – the one with the Chesser Inn on the side.' Kano got one or two of the young apprentices, stuck it in my van and away I went. Then Rourkey phoned me a couple of hours later to say he had changed his mind. So that's how we ended up our time with Hibs – paid off in vodka!"

Mike Aitken, *The Scotsman's* football writer, watched on with interest as

Stanton and his lieutenants struggled to make an impact at Hibs, and remains of the view that he would have gone further in his post-playing career in a secondary role. "Stanton, O'Rourke and Stewart had all been terrific Hibs players, but I still say the role that suited Pat most was working with Alex Ferguson at Aberdeen. When Alex got the Manchester United job, I thought Pat would have been the perfect person to go with him. They were a great team together – they were a contrast to one another. Pat was probably too nice, and that would have been part of the problem. He was quietly spoken but hugely knowledgeable about the game, no question. He was a great foil to Alex Ferguson, who was at the other end of the spectrum. Pat knew the game inside out and was a great Hibs man, but it's very rare you get an ex-player of that calibre who makes the transfer to become one of the greatest managers at a club. Giving top jobs to ex-players, simply because they were a top player for that club, is a big gamble. That one didn't work for me."

Another great player was about to the return to the club, first as assistant to Stanton, and later his successor. John Blackley, like his fellow Hibs great Pat, felt this was an offer he could not refuse, such was the allure of his former club. "I was treading on old ground, which isn't always the wise thing to do, but it was always nice to go back to Easter Road, as it is to this day," says Blackley. "I had been player-manager at Hamilton and Pat Stanton got on the phone and invited me to be his assistant manager, which was brilliant. Pat was excellent with me, and I got a really good start in my coaching and managerial life. It was good to be back."

Blackley was principally there to further his coaching career, but such was the dearth of experience in the squad, the veteran former Scotland international was encouraged to keep donning the boots and playing for the first team. "I only played as an emergency measure," he explains. "Jackie McNamara was injured and unavailable and was out for two or three weeks and that's the only reason I went back to playing. I was reasonably fit and playing at the back was more a case of reading the game anyway than running about, so I got away with it. I still enjoyed playing, but at the same time I didn't want to deny any young player the opportunity to come in. Jackie was a great player for Hibs at that time, but sadly he was getting knocked down by repeating injuries, particularly his knee, so Pat was keen to replace that experience in the team and turned to me. One day, I remember we were playing at St Mirren, and during the warm-up I pulled up and I had to tell Pat I was out. That helped make my mind up to stop playing as I felt terrible that I had let the team down and Pat, because he had to change the team at the last minute. I had to be honest with myself. I think my last game was actually a 0-0 draw against Rangers towards the end of the season."

The 1983-84 season would prove to be similar to the previous campaign –

another seventh-placed finish and a stinging Scottish Cup defeat, this time to East Fife! "Aye that was a big disappointment," Paddy reflects now. "Things just took a turn for the worse. That was a game we really should have won. We had chances to put them away but full marks to East Fife, they got stuck in, and we didn't respond as we should. You go into these games against teams in the lower leagues, and they have that incentive to do something, but you do have to step it up as well and respond to that. No disrespect to teams like that, but you should be able to play the game at a higher tempo than them and dictate the game. But if you allow the pace of the game to drop... and we fell into that trap against East Fife. There were no excuses. It's a horrible feeling, you are sitting there in the dressing room after the game, wishing you can go out there again and rectify it, but you can't – it's gone and you have to learn from it. You've had your chance, there's no point talking about it and what you would and should have done after the event."

The humiliation was compounded by Alan Rough breaking his ankle. "There's a story that goes with that," remembers Rough. "I was out for two months and Robin Rae came in. My ankle was getting a bit better, I was training, but I was still struggling to generate any power when I was kicking a dead ball. The reserves were playing against Dundee, as were the first team, and I asked Pat 'let me play and I'll get someone to take the bye-kicks.' But Pat said he had spoken to the doctor and that he had recommended I leave it for another couple of weeks, just to be on the safe side. I said fair enough. I was sitting in the house on the Friday night before the Dundee game and the phone went, and it was Pat. He asked me how my ankle was and I told him it was just the same as it had been two days ago when we had our chat. Pat then said: 'We're going to take a chance, you can play for the first team tomorrow.' I asked him why there had been the big change of heart and, anyway, why couldn't Robin play? 'Robin's in the jail!' Pat replied."

Some of back-up goalkeeper Robin 'Basher' Rae's extra-curricular escapades are the stuff of legend, and most fans remember him for the immense promise the Scotland youth international failed to fulfil. The Musselburgh man had a habit of getting into off-field scrapes, such as that night in the cells, and consequentially his first-team appearances for Hibs were limited to just 14 before he re-emerged in the Junior ranks as an effective outfield player. Now living in Kent and an active member of the Hibs Former Players' network, I had been hoping to hear some of his stories from the past, but Robin politely declined, saying he wanted to leave his past in the past, which I fully respect.

Robin was not the only player who had a wild streak that had the usually serene Stanton tearing his hair out. Powerful forward Bobby Thomson, who signed when Auld was still around, was proving to be a useful, hard-working player who had struck up an excellent strike partnership with the prolific

Willie Irvine. But Bobby was well-known to match officials, who had him pegged as a villain, and he was wired on the shortest of fuses. As Stanton would later rue in his autobiography, "Bobby's needle went to red" the day Hibs hosted St Johnstone in November 1983.

Despite being on the way to a resounding 4-1 win, Thomson raged at a linesman's flag and went flying into him in front of the old South Enclosure. In his match report for *The Scotsman*, wordsmith Ian Wood wonderfully described the flashpoint by observing: "He jostled the unfortunate official and struck the sort of belligerent attitude which, if exhibited by an adult male gorilla, would have had David Attenborough groping for the tranquilising darts."

While it was an outrageous act, which brought him the 10th red card of his career and the heftiest of punishments from the SFA (a six-month ban), Thomson feels it was exaggerated at the time, and is now sick hearing about it. In an attempt to address the urban myth once and for all, the Glaswegian – whose daughter Hollie went on to play for Hibs women's team – gave an illuminating interview to Stephen Halliday of *The Scotsman* in 2014. "I always remember it, because people never let me forget it," said Thomson. "So many come up to me and say 'Oh, you're the guy that punched that linesman'. I can remember the incident clearly. The linesman put his flag up but the ref didn't see it. John Brogan ran through and scored. I ran across to the linesman. At that time, there was a kind of six-inch step from the turf to the trackside at Easter Road. I was shouting at the linesman, asking him why he didn't keep his flag up, then I pushed him with an open hand. Because of that wee step, he fell backwards and made a big issue of it, as if I'd really assaulted him. He made a meal of it, there was nothing malicious in it. Listen, you could have pushed a two-year-old kid the way I pushed that linesman and the kid wouldn't have moved. It was a stupid thing for me to do, but the linesman made more of it than it was. It was a bit like what happened years later with Paolo Di Canio and the English ref Paul Alcock, who stumbled back about 10 paces and then fell down."

Stanton has vivid memories of the incident, and says he was fond of Thomson, despite the temper that lurked beneath his thick black locks. "I would describe Bobby as a character," chuckles Pat. "He was very wholehearted – a nice big chap and good player. He knew the game and you didn't have to tell him much. He wasn't a shirker and went about his business and he was well liked by the rest of the squad. He was really good alongside Willie Irvine. Willie was a real competitor who got stuck in when he was on the park, but he was also a really nice laddie, a smashing fella and very pleasant to talk to. He was quiet off the park, that was his nature, but on the pitch he knew where the goals were. He was an easy person to manage, no problems with him. Bobby was the same, you knew exactly what he was going to give you... well, maybe apart from the game against St Johnstone! It was all over in a flash, there was nothing you could do about it. We won the game, but that was just him, he got worked up about it. You couldn't give Bobby a hard time – he was so plausible and pleasant off the park!"

Simon Pia remembers Stanton's typically calm demeanour when he faced the press after Thomson's tornado had been unleashed. "After Bobby Thomson had banjoed the linesman, I was upstairs in the press room afterwards and Pat was sitting there with his wee Hamlet cigar. Somebody asked about another player who had picked up a knock. Pat said: 'Aye, he'll be seeing a specialist. And as for Thomson... he'll be seeing a psychiatrist!'"

Bizarrely, it would take nearly fourth months before Thomson was finally summoned to the SFA's headquarters at Park Gardens and slapped with his six-month suspension. He was not the only enforced change of personnel. Veteran Arthur Duncan, the flying winger who lit up Turnbull's Tornadoes and played 626 games for Hibs, broke his collarbone in the East of Scotland Shield final against Meadowbank, and would be transferred to the same near neighbours at the end of the season.

Also on his way was keeper McArthur, who still feels let down by the manner of his departure. "Pat and I were pals when he was a player, but I respected the fact he was now the manager. I said to him, 'I'm moving home, and I have a bigger family so I need a bigger house, am I getting a contract?' He told me I was, but it never materialised. I wasn't too chuffed I can tell you. I had been injured when Roughie came, but I would have even been happy with being second goalie. I had sustained an eye injury, which took three months to get over, and Roughie came and played well so I had absolutely no complaints about him being in the team ahead of me at that time. Fair dos."

Pat was now entering his third season at the helm, but relations with him and Kenny Waugh remained fragile, and while he had changed his mind following his 'resignation' in 1983, this time there would no going back when he quit early in the 1984-85 season, a 3-2 defeat to Dumbarton proving to be the final straw. Looking back on it now, Stanton says: "You were trying your best, the players were trying their best, but I just felt 'No, enough is enough'. At times like that you have got your pride. It's different if you can see a way out of it and you feel things are going to change for the better, but I didn't see that at all. It was time to go, as gut-wrenching as it was. One thing sure in football is that you are guaranteed to experience disappointment at some stage, and that was one of the biggest disappointments for me. When I go to games now, I try not to be too critical. I don't mind, if I'm asked, offering an opinion, but I never go too far in terms of criticising anyone because I have been there myself."

Was it a case of him getting a job he coveted and cherished at the worst possible time? "Yes, maybe it was the wrong time to be there," he admits. "If you are there, in that job, then you are held responsible for what happens. When I went there, I think there was a nagging doubt at the back of my mind that this wasn't such a clever move. There was no way I could say no to Hibs because I knew I wouldn't be asked again. I had been in the game long enough to know that you need half a chance to succeed, but when things turned, it justified my doubts."

Simon Pia reflects: "It was a big disappointment for everyone, because these guys were Hibs through and through and club legends. Everyone had such high hopes. You didn't like to see Pat's reputation getting tarnished in any way, he didn't deserve that. I don't think people really knew what a difficult job it was for him and how tightly the purse-strings were being held by Kenny Waugh."

Waugh didn't have to look far for his new manager, with a man of John Blackley's calibre and Hibs heritage already on the payroll. It wouldn't be long before Sloop was having the same doubts Stanton had experienced when he was offered the job. He says: "When Pat decided to pack in, I thought it was only right and fair that I should do the same, but Pat said 'No, you remain here. I'm out but if you get the chance, you stay'. They turned to me and asked me to become manager. I couldn't refuse it because Hibs are my club. But looking back on it, I lacked a bit of the experience needed of a managerial set-up. It was great to get the opportunity, even if they had no money to spend and I was the easy option."

CHAPTER 6

DIG the NEW BREED

"They were magical times. Every time I drive near Easter Road, I'll get the tingle down the back of the spine at the thought of these memories. It was one big happy family." – John Collins

Being put in a fierce arm-lock, frog-marched across the room, then having your ear placed within a millimetre or two of a red-hot water pipe, may sound more like a brutal Army initiation ceremony than some hi-jinks within a professional football club. But the owner of the young lug, Brian Rice, would not change it for the world.

Ricey, or 'Chipper' as he's known in football circles, was a precocious young apprentice at the club in the early 80s, and found himself in an environment where respect, discipline and good habits were imparted by the older professionals and where talent could take you all the way to the first team if you had the right attitude and willingness to learn. With resources limited, if you were good enough, you were old enough. The formidable figure behind the threats of a burnt lobe was respected Hibs veteran Erich Schaedler, and while he was never going to fry Rice on that drying room pipe, he knew that he was teaching him that standards had to be exceptionally high at the club – on and off the pitch.

Disappointing is the best word to describe the 80s as far as results and glory are concerned, but in terms of bringing through home-grown talent it was a resounding success. To borrow the title of The Jam's farewell album in 1982, Hibs fans were ready to *Dig The New Breed*. Brian Rice (98 appearances for Hibs), Mickey Weir (247), Gordon Hunter (409), John Collins (195), Paul Kane (292), Callum Milne (87) and Kevin McKee (46) were among those to make the grade, and all of them are eternally grateful for the hard but invaluable grounding they were given as a foundation to enjoy long careers. While Pat

Stanton and John Blackley deserve great credit as managers willing to recognise the value of allowing talent to flourish, Schaedler was just one of a band of willing senior professionals at Easter Road prepared to dutifully pass down their knowledge and guidance to an eager bunch of young players – who would listen (if their ears weren't burn to a crisp) and learn.

"Shades was some man, a real professional, ahead of his time in terms of his preparation and fitness," recalls Rice. "I was on the groundstaff and I had to look after Shades' gear – the short straw some would say. Everything had to be immaculate with Shades. He always looked the part. His trousers were pressed, shirt was pressed, he was just immaculate in everything he did – he always looked a million dollars. When I was put in charge of his kit, it meant I would have to fold his top right, the shorts right, and when it came to the socks, the tabs had to be the exact same length on each one. But if I was in a rush, and I was doing two or three players' kit, there were times I didn't get it right. And that meant getting called through to the first-team dressing room. In those days, us young lads would all be in the away dressing room, the young lads – me, Carlo Crolla, Davie Anderson, Gordon Byrne, Tam Aitchison, big 'Treacle' Gordon Wilson, a brilliant squad of us.

"We used to have to chap the door to get into the first-team dressing room after you had been summoned. You knew as you were going in that you were in trouble – either that or they were going to take the piss out of you or do something to you. When I opened the door, I would look up, see who was waiting for me and say to myself 'Aw naw, it's Shades!' You would be shaking sometimes before you even went in there. Shades would beckon you in, then grab you by the ear, say 'look at these socks!' and then take you through to the drying room and hold your ear close to the hot pipes – it was mental torture. I was just a wee skinny boy and he was this big powerful man, all rippling muscles! But honestly it was all good fun, it was part of the learning process, and getting the discipline of making sure everything I did was right. He was a really top man."

Mickey Weir, a couple of years younger than Rice, also found himself paired with a tough task-master, and he had to make damn sure the kit he was tending to was spic n span – particularly when training gear was scarce and there was not limitless pairs of boots to go round like there is now. "The apprentices had to do a string of jobs as well as training – we would be painting, cutting the grass, you name it," says Mickey. "You would clean the boots first, do your training, come back and then do boots again for the next day, washing and helping with the kit. I never looked on it as a chore, I just loved doing it and being part of the day-to-day activity at the club. It was part of our apprenticeship, but it was hard, tiring work – I don't think people now would appreciate just how hard we had to work.

"You were in there early in the morning and didn't finish until late at night sometimes, or even go and play a game for the reserves that night having been in there all day. It was hard, but I wouldn't change anything. I was given Ally MacLeod's boots to clean, and he was a hard man to please! Shades was a great man, a real star, and had a lot of time for the younger players, he would always pass on his wisdom to us. But Ally was a different character. I used to be terrified of him to be honest, because he would tell you the way it was – always. He would not mince his words or shy away from any confrontation. If you were picked in his team for the five-a-sides, he would moan all the time. I used to dread being in his team because he used to go mad at you if you made the slightest mistake. I maybe didn't appreciate it at the time, but it was all part of the learning curve, and you needed guys like that to be tough on you and harden you for the professional game. It might have seemed like really hard work, but it prepared me well for the rest of my life, having that strong work ethic.

"When we first joined Hibs, it was on the YTS Scheme. Everyone was in the same boat – you knew if you were going to have any chance of making it as a player then you were going to have to graft really hard to get there. But the biggest and fondest memory for me was the camaraderie. We loved our work. The older guys were a big part of that too – people like Erich, Gordon Rae, Alan Sneddon, Arthur Duncan – they all helped to make us become good professionals and good people first, more than simply becoming a good footballer. Their professionalism was a huge influence on my career."

The apprentices also proved useful to a thrifty chairman whenever he needed jobs doing on the cheap and wanted to save a few bob... which in Kenny Waugh's case was pretty much all the time. Paul Kane, an apprentice alongside Weir, remembers: "I was brought in as a professional football player, but my first day's work was more like a builder's apprentice. I was sent by the chairman to do some work on the wee sponsors' lounge they were building in the stand, and I managed to stand on a nail that went right through my trainers. I went through to see our trainer and physio, Tam McNiven, to show him my cut foot and get it patched up. He shook his head and asked what the hell I was doing trying to masquerade as a joiner, and I just blurted out 'It was Mr Waugh who asked me to do it!'"

Callum Milne, who like Kane had joined the club from Salvesen Boys Club, would go on to become a player admired for his courage and aggressive style of play – and he also names Schaedler as the man he looked up to as a youngster. "When I first joined the club in 1983, part-time at first then full-time, Erich Schaedler was already a hero of mine, so I looked up to him and wanted to be like him," says Milne who initially joined as a part-timer before getting a full-time deal at 17. "My game wasn't dissimilar, although I didn't have the big throw-in that was Shades' trademark. He always gave 100 per cent in every single thing he did, so I watched and learned. Even though he was a bit older than most of the lads, he still won all his races at training, and was just striving for perfection in everything he did. I'm grateful for the time he took helping me to develop. We had a wee gym at Easter Road and me and Erich would sometimes go down there after training. He would get a medicine ball, then lie flat on his back and throw it the length of the hall. He was unbelievable."

While some of the lads like Kano, Callum and Mickey Weir came from live-wire places in Edinburgh like Leith, Sighthill and Clermiston, a young lad was brought in alongside them from the Borders. And the way this Galashiels youngster integrated with the city boys and his new surroundings suggested that he had the right temperament and a big future ahead of him. "It was exciting times for me, leaving school and starting my apprenticeship with Hibs, with Pat Stanton as the manager," says John Collins. "It was a full-on routine, with a lot of travelling up and down the road from Gala, and it took a lot of dedication, but it was well worth it. There were plenty early rises, getting up for that 7.10 bus to Edinburgh. Nobody got dropped off and picked up by their mum and dad in those days, you were in the big bad world yourself and you just jumped on public transport and got on with it. It was a bit of character building, all part of the journey."

Rice also remembers those early rises and dependence on old boneshaker buses, wheezing their way through a number of staging posts in West Lothian before eventually making it to the St Andrew Square station. "I stayed in Whitburn, and I used to get the bus at 6.30 and it would go through West Calder and all these places, and I would get to St Andrew Square just before 8. I then had to get a bus from Queen Street to the top of Easter Road and be there by 8.30. What made it even worse is that I would see the managers Bertie Auld and his assistants John Lambie and Pat Quinn driving past me in the car, even though John stayed in Whitburn too."

Post-Bertie, Rice went on to make further progress in the first team under the guidance of Stanton, and he thrived on the action and the competitive nature of the league, although he admits his slender frame made it physically challenging. "It was tough in the Scottish Premier in those days," he says. "Nowadays there are big gaps between the top two and the rest, the top four and the rest, but in those days you had Celtic and Rangers, Aberdeen and Dundee United. There were lots of really good teams and really good players. It could be a struggle and it was hard for me coming into the team. I got a good run at it though, and it was great for me because I was playing with Shades at left-back and Flyer (Arthur Duncan) at outside left, and you also had Ralphy, Jackie, Snoddy, Gordon Rae, Ally MacLeod all around me – brilliant lads. Lots of good players, but it was tough to get the ball at my feet and make an impact at times. To be fair to the managers, they kept playing me, sometimes maybe when I deserved to be dropped, and it was a brilliant grounding for me. I was getting battered about the place, but the supporters were patient with me. Fans are the same everywhere you play – they just want the best, they just want their team to win and enjoy their Saturday. The best way to enjoy it is by winning. Unfortunately, we weren't winning as much as we should have been. What the fans did appreciate was young players coming through in the team and I felt the fans encouraged me when I broke through.

"I absolutely loved my time at Hibs. Even when we started playing in the reserves, the standard of the league was fantastic. I used to play in the reserve league on a Saturday and the youth league on a Sunday. We would play two games at the weekend. We actually won the youth league. We needed to get a point against Celtic in the last game of the season at Easter Road and we got the job done. But out of that squad of 15 or 16 of us, only three of us got kept on – myself, Gordon Byrne and Robin Rae. Me and Robin were in the Scotland youth squad that went to the World Cup. He was some goalkeeper and had a heart of gold, but he should have done better – he should have played for Hibs for a lot of seasons, he was fantastic. Another lad I played with was Kevin McKee, who went to school with me, and he had a rough time of it at Ibrox when a fan came on the pitch and took a swing at him."

McKee, who would soon be breaking into the side behind Rice, works in financial services now, and would probably be comfortably retired if he had a pound for every time he had heard that he "wasn't the same" after the shocking Ibrox incident in September 1984. Right-back McKee had worked hard to establish himself in the Hibs team since making his debut in 1983, also at Ibrox, and was putting together a consistent run of games, when he was inexplicably punched by a Rangers fan as he prepared to defend a corner.

"My memories are quite vague to be honest, because I was just a young kid at the time," he says now. "I vaguely remember tackling Davie Cooper, God rest his soul, and the ball going out for a corner. My job was to go on the post, so I was running towards the post and I just remember, out of nowhere, getting smacked from behind. I didn't really know anything about it, and when I came to my senses and got up, I could see that Alan Rough and Erich Schaedler had a hold of the guy. I think Pat [Stanton] has said in the past that I was never really the same after that, but I don't think I really agree with that. It didn't really affect me as such in that I was scared. For most of my professional career I think I played my best football away from Hibs unfortunately. I had never actually played full-back in my life before I went to Hibs. I had been a midfielder all the way through. So, learning a new position at the same time as trying to bed yourself into professional football as a young boy, was quite difficult, especially playing against players like Davie Cooper and Peter Weir – there were lots of good wingers around in the Scottish game then. The change in position came about because I had been on the bench for the reserves and the right-back got injured and I had to go on, and that's where I stayed during my time at Hibs, with a couple of exceptions where I played wide right. I went on, did my best and it seemed to be that they saw something in me as a full-back."

McKee played 46 times for Hibs before going on to do consistently well at Hamilton Accies then Partick Thistle, and while he regrets not making more of an impact at Easter Road, he is philosophical about the way it worked out and grateful for the football education he received. "There was a group of us all coming through together in a short period," he says. "It was a good environment to learn in and some fantastic players you could learn from. I used to travel with Arthur because I was too young to drive. It was a great club to grow up in and for myself it probably happened a bit too early for me – and probably why I left Hibs, having not made that many appearances for them, which was disappointing with me being a Hibs supporter. You just have to move on, and not dwell on it, and I still had a good grounding in the game by being in that environment. Jackie McNamara and Gordon Rae were great to play alongside, with all the experience they had to share – Ally Brazil and Willie Jamieson too – all of them were a big help."

Like McKee, Paul Kane signed while Bertie Auld was still the boss, but he admits: "I just had one month under Bertie and I'll always be grateful to him for being the man who made my dream come true and signed me for Hibs. His love for Celtic was the same as mine is for Hibs. But then came the Dream Team for me, the three lieutenants – Pat, George and Jimmy – all coming in together and I couldn't have asked for anything better than that. As well as those three there was Erich, big Roughie, Jackie, Gordon Rae, Ralph – all strong characters who had been a long time at Hibs. They were absolutely committed to the club and its history. They were good professionals who looked after all the young players and taught them good habits, which would stand them in good stead for the rest of their careers. It was up to us to take these habits and pass them on to the next generation of players. That was the way it worked back then and what it meant to be a professional."

The arrival of the 'Dream Team' had a profoundly positive effect on the apprentices at Easter Road, and the lack of a transfer kitty meant that many found themselves on a fast-track to the first team – so long as they first proved their worth. "It was lucky in a way that Hibs weren't doing so well (early 80s) because all us young lads got a chance – myself, Kevin McKee, Gordon Hunter, Mickey Weir, Callum Milne, wee Johnny Collins," adds Kane. "But clearly you still need to have ability to take that chance and Johnny was always going to be a top player, there was never going to be any holding someone like that back."

Collins lights up at mention of his first-team debut in a Hibs shirt in 1984 – a Friday night friendly against Manchester City (0-0) – which he followed up 48 hours later by taking part in Jackie McNamara's testimonial against Newcastle

United, rubbing shoulders with the likes of George Best, and Geordie legends Peter Beardsley and Chris Waddle.

"I remember being told just a few hours before the game that I was playing," says JC. "It was Friday morning and, as one of the groundstaff, I was up cleaning the stand. I was cleaning the seats, which had been dusty from the summer, and getting them in good nick in time for the game. In those days we were the cleaners! I got a shout up that the manager wanted to speak to me in his office and when I got there he was sitting there with his wee cigar. He said: 'Is your Dad coming the night, son?' I said no, he wasn't and told Pat that he normally just came and watched me if I was playing.' Pat said: 'Oh aye, is that right? Well you better give him a call son, because he'll be watching you play tonight.' I walked out, thinking it was a bit strange. When I went to see the rest of the groundstaff boys they asked me what Pat had wanted to speak to me about. When I told them he said I was playing, I started to have doubts and wondered if he might be joking, so I went back down and chapped his door again and said: 'Boss, were you serious?' He said: 'Aye I am serious son, you're playing!' I was only 16 and it was incredible, Pat gave me a wee taste of what it was like to play first-team football. I was just a nine-and-a-half-stone skinny wee laddie and I had just joined in January of that year, but he must have seen something in me to give me a chance at such a young age. It was so exciting."

"I played him at left-back," explains Stanton. "He had a great attitude, he was willing to listen and I remember after we played Man City, coming down the stairs and walking alongside me was Jock Stein, who had been through watching the game. We were just blethering away and without any prompting he turned to me and said: 'You'll be happy with HIM!' It dawned on me he was talking about John. You could already see that John had all the qualities and skill to make the grade as a midfield player and a lot of players would have balked at the thought of playing out of position at left-back, but he never said a word – he played left-back and played well. I thought to myself we've got a good one here – although I couldn't bloody understand his accent half the time, coming from Galashiels! There was a group of players at that time who worked hard, big Ricey too, and they were all willing to listen if you were wanting to point something out. They were anxious to do well."

Weir had a similar introduction to first-team football, understated Stanton-style. "For my debut I remember being told while we were just finishing up our jobs for the day. The manager pulled me aside and asked if I could play at left-back! I said, 'aye, I'll play anywhere!' It was a wee chance for me to go on and get a taste of first-team football. It was a chance I wasn't going to turn down, you didn't worry about positions, you just wanted to get out there and play for the first team," he says.

Stanton adds: "There was no margin for error with so many good sides around. When you bring these young players in, they brought something fresh with them. You could only tell them so much – you are only guiding the talent and the attitude they already have. If their attitude was good from the outset, then you knew you had half a chance of improving and developing them further. They all came through at the one time, it wasn't just an accident, because these older professionals would bring them on. For Hearts, when Alex MacDonald and Sandy Jardine took over, it was a similar scenario and not an accident either that they had a crop of younger players who flourished from learning the game from them. These people were learning off influential guys.

"It was uplifting to see all of these young players' talent and attitude. There was not a lot of money flying around, but there was still a good vibe at the club, Paul Kane, Michael Weir, Gordon Hunter started to push themselves in. When they were coming into Easter Road, the environment that was created by the senior players and the backroom staff, including Tom McNiven, they created a great atmosphere. It was excellent surroundings for them to learn and develop. They took a lot of encouragement from the fact they were working with people who wanted them to do well, and that was a big part of their successful step up from the reserves to the first team. They all got what the club was about and the traditions. They worked hard for one another, and it wasn't an accident that they all started to push through, John Collins and so on. It was very satisfying to see them go on to have good careers. They were good lads, determined people, willing to listen and a good level of ability to begin with. You meet them now and they are still pleasant and chat away, they are good people.

"The senior professionals were a great example to them. The way they conducted themselves before and during a game, the young players would see that and try to emulate that. You need that mix, the older professionals know what is required."

An appreciative Rice agrees: "These guys used to be fantastic. I used to travel with Alan Sneddon, and every day after training they would get together in this wee coffee shop up Easter Road called Meals – there would be Jackie, Ralph, Ally McLeod, Alan Sneddon, John Connolly when he was there, there was quite a few. They would sit there and talk about anything and everything and get their football coupons and betting slips out and drink coffee after coffee. For me, just being a young kid sitting and listening to them was a big influence. Then you had that lunatic Roughie when he came – he was something else! In those days the squad was full of characters: Ally McLeod was a real talent, Craig Paterson was an excellent defender, big Gordon Rae too. Just a great squad of boys – a brilliant place to be and Hibs were a great club to be part of."

One of the older heads in the dressing room, Alan Sneddon, says that the number of youngsters pushing for a place gave the team much-need impetus.

"All the young players came through at roughly the same time and Pat wasn't slow at giving them their debut because they were showing that they were good enough," he says. "Nowadays, they all go on about experience being the big thing, but how do you get that experience in the first place? You have to blood them sometimes and that was Pat's approach – he had the trust and confidence in those young guys to be able to perform at that level. We had Mickey Weir, Paul Kane, John Collins, Gordon Hunter, Callum Milne all coming through at the one time and it was a great crop of young lads. At that age they don't play with any fear because they don't realise the enormity of it sometimes, but you've got to handle them in the right way – if they get too much exposure and pressure too early then it can burn them out, especially the situation we were in as well, with results being up and down. You don't want to expose the younger players to that kind of pressure. Like all football fans, the Hibs fans can be quite – shall I say – demanding! When you are doing well they are right behind you, but if you are struggling then they are going to have their say. Especially if you are an out-of-towner and not a local lad then you tend to get the brunt of it. It's not easy if you are a full-back, because you are right on the touchline and you can hear a quip or two – and usually they didn't miss you, that's for sure."

Collins, still on a high from his debut, played in front of a noisier stadium on the Sunday in McNamara's testimonial, a game Hibs lost 3-0 – not that he was particularly upset. "It was unbelievable, to be sitting in the dressing room in the presence of the great George Best was the stuff of dreams," says Collins. "He played inside left and I played outside left, so it was an incredible experience. There was a big crowd in for that game too, and a good Newcastle team with Waddle and Beardsley. It was a Scotland v England game, so it was really competitive. Even though I went back to the reserves for the year, it had whet my appetite and given me a feel for it. It gave me that added incentive to work hard and wait for my chance again, and I'm sure Pat knew that. We would play for the reserves, but train every day with the first team. It was just one group, so we were lucky as young boys to get to train with the first team and learn the ropes. We had a great group of young players all knocking on the door for a place in the first team. It was pretty remarkable, but it's the way it should be."

Collins' career trajectory, as we now know, was quick and impressive, and back then he did everything with a smile on his face. "I have no regrets and nothing but fabulous memories of my time with Hibs," he says. "Leaving school and joining Hibs was a dream come true. It had been my dream to become a professional football player and I will never forget coming up for the week's trial when Pat Stanton was manager – then taking me into the office and asking me to bring my Dad the next day because they were going to offer me a two-year apprenticeship, which felt to me like winning the Lottery. £29 a week! £5 win bonus in the reserves, £2.50 for a draw. And there was me think-ing 'This is it... this is the big time!' We never had fancy training grounds or training kit, and everything was very basic and minimal. We would get changed at the stadium and then jump in the minibus to places like Wardie, Letham Park and Jock's Lodge and wherever we could get a pitch really.

"I got my full debut at Pittodrie away to Aberdeen in the first game of the 1985 season against the likes of Miller and McLeish. We lost some late goals, but we had a young team and acquitted ourselves well, it certainly wasn't a 3-0 game. I also came on as a sub against them in the Skol Cup final later that season, when John Blackley and Tommy Craig were in charge – it was really nice of them to give me that opportunity to play in a cup final.

"It was exciting times for a young boy for a Gala. The atmosphere at the club was amazing then, particularly for us as young apprentices – we were there morning, noon and night. We would start in the morning cleaning the dress-ing rooms, shower and kit, then trained and then stuck around the ground. We would play three-a-sides in the wee gym under the stand and we had the wee multi-gym, doing our sprints and circuits with John Stirling, the profes-sional sprint coach who used to come in three times a week. That would give you the strength and power you needed as a young player to compete with the seasoned pros who were much bigger and stronger than us. We just buckled down and got right into it.

"Looking back, that was absolutely the way it should be – we were all very fortunate to be around that culture. There was a real bond between the coach-ing staff and all of us young players. They put a lot of faith in us, and I suppose we responded. They were fun and memorable years, that is for sure."

Pat Stanton says: "I was very proud to see how far John went in the game. What a tremendous career he had. His whole attitude got him there – the way he trained, his ability to listen, the way he learned – it wasn't a surprise to see him develop into such a top player. He had that determination built into him. I would see John clatter into some tackles, he was certainly prepared to embrace the physical side of the game too. He had all that skill and ability but if there was a 50-50 you could bet your boots that John would get in there and win the ball. Jock Stein saw it that night of his debut and John proved him to be right."

Collins chuckles at some of his fledgling days in football, and of the camara-derie that existed between the ground-staff boys. "It was one big happy family, all of us young boys – we spent a lot of time together and it was a special time in our lives. I'll never forget these days, they were magical moments and every time I drive near Easter Road, I'll get the tingle down the back of the spine at the thought of these memories. I used to get the bus to St Andrew Square and then walk down London Road and Easter Road and across the wee bridge and back to the ground. It was happy days – we had nae money but lots of ambition and excitement and it was a brilliant foundation for my career. We never wanted to leave, and we were at the ground all day. We would just hang about. We would while away hours in that tiny wee gym under the stand. There was a goal painted up on the wall with numbers and we would play the numbers game. One touch, two-touch, play for Mars Bars – that's why we were all good passers because we would be in that gym every day pinging passes and working on our accuracy. Nothing fancy, completely basic facilities, but all of us committed to being better players. We made the most of it.

"I remember our lunches at the ground. There would be a massive pot for the tea, and you'd get a cheese roll with it – that was our lunch. A cheese roll every day and you had to cut the cheese and butter the roll yourself – no dieticians then! That, of course, was the chance for the old entrepreneur Kano to make his first step into the business world and he started his own tuck shop, selling crisps, Mars Bars and fizzy juice on the side up in the canteen to the first-team players. They'd be saying to him, 'I've nae money Kano I'll give you it tomorrow' and Kano would be saying, 'Nae Tic and nae chance. Cash up front or your no' getting your juice and crisps!' Another thing I remember is cleaning the stands with a broom on a Monday morning, clearing up all the rubbish from the game at the weekend, and there would be wee Mickey, chirpy as you like, singing his Bob Marley songs. He saw himself as a pop star with his broom as a microphone! He loved his Bob Marley and we would all be joining in."

"Aye, I liked a chant and a wee song to myself," laughs Mickey. "The days were great, we would have a smile on our faces. We used to have so much respect for the older players – you never just walked into the first-team changing room. People don't believe that – you had to knock on the door to even ask if you could go and get a shower. But when they had changed and left for the day, we used to sneak in there and feel like we were kings. You had to earn respect and give respect. Me and Kano used to sit in the bath for ages just singing Hibs songs, because you loved the club. I did like a chant to myself, even though some of them might say I was a terrible singer right enough. Back then I was Bob Marley daft. When I first went to the club when I was 16-17, Madness was my music, and then I started moving on to Bob Marley. The thing about it was, from a young age, I just couldn't get my head round racism – I just couldn't understand why people would have a major problem with black people, because I was brought up to like that music and Northern Soul. I got hooked on Bob Marley for years, to this day even."

While I've got Mickey on the subject of his musical taste, I seize the opportunity to grill him on one of the more questionable bands he had an interest in. Hibs supporter Mark Scally, who helped come up with the new name *Mass*

Hibsteria for the fanzine when we ran a competition, explains: "I was working in Virgin in Princes Street when Mickey Weir came in wearing a sheepskin jacket and asked me for the latest cassette by The Pasadenas. I remember thinking to myself that he has neither style nor music taste, thank fuck he can kick a ball! The album hadn't been released yet, so he went away empty handed."

When I run this past Mickey, he fesses up: "That's right, I actually remember that! I think they only had one decent song... they weren't the best. I also used to go to the wee record shop at Haymarket, Golden Oldies it was called, I used to go in there and it was always full of Jambos. The guys that used to sell the records were all Hearts supporters, so I used to have a good craic with them about the football. They'd recommend new tunes to me. I can remember Sweet Inspirations in Lothian Road as well. I would quite often wander into Princes Street after training and go browsing for records. It was my town in those days, I never thought anything of it or getting hassled walking along, and I was always happy to stop and chat to Hibs and Hearts fans and have a blether about the football."

Like Collins, Weir's voice crackles with emotion when he looks back on those salad days as young apprentices. "First and foremost, being brought up as a Hibs supporter it was a privilege to get involved with the club. I was very fortunate to go there as a young man. Arriving at the club, I ended up with lifelong friends – we were all young guys, most of us Hibs fans, and we were living the dream, especially with Pat Stanton as the manager, which was unbelievable for us. My Dad's hero was Paddy Stanton, so to play for Hibs and have him as the manager was surreal. It was great times. Jimmy and George too – the three of them all played a massive part in my development and my upbringing at the club, and the other young guys too like Kano and Johnny Collins. They knew what the club was about, and they knew what was needed and they just loved the club – they were Hibs men through and through. With them to guide you, you learned things very quickly, and they were great with the young players in terms of the atmosphere they generated and the encouragement and support that they gave us. You could feel how much the club meant to them and they all upheld the values of the club. They had all played at European level and knew the history, they made sure you knew what it meant to play for Hibs and pull on that shirt.

"Alex Edwards was the player I had always looked up to as a young man – the way he went about the game and the way he played. Obviously, there were so many other great players like Pat Stanton and Jimmy O'Rourke in that generation, and Jimmy was a big help to me – he always encouraged me. He was small himself so he would give me some great advice. He always said talent was not about your physical size, it was more about the size of your heart. He knew I would face an uphill battle, because of my size, but he thought I would be good enough to play for the first team and made me believe that myself."

Callum Milne is another who benefited from the encouragement of Stanton, O'Rourke and Stewart. "Pat Stanton was my first manager and I absolutely loved him – what an absolute gentleman. Too nice to be a manager!" he says. "Blackley was brilliant with me too. He was one of these players I absolutely idolised growing up watching Hibs, although you couldn't tackle now how he tackled back then. John Blackley's favourite saying to me was, 'Hey son, I would take you to the trenches with me.' I felt brilliant hearing that.

"I grew up with Kano, Mickey Weir, Johnny, Gordon Hunter – all of us used to go on holiday together. We were all Hibs supporters and got on brilliantly. I grew up in Leith and every member of my family was Hibs daft, my mum, Dad, aunties, uncles you name it. I was at the 7-0 game when I was only 8. That was the only team for me. I loved them – to be approached and to hear that Hibs wanted to sign me, what a feeling!

"For my debut Jackie McNamara got injured and I got to come in and play sweeper, against Dundee at Easter Road, we got beat 1-0 and Erich was left-back that day. Sweeper is where I wanted to play, but it was usually the more experienced players who dominated that position, and other managers started to play me at left-back and midfield, but I'd play anywhere I was asked to play for Hibs. I was in one game, two games, then dropped and I used to ask myself: I know I've played well, so why am I not keeping my place? I never played enough games, I know I should have, I don't know if it was my fault or not. I'm still hard on myself now, that's the kind of guy I am."

Milne is hard on himself, no doubt about it, and it wasn't just the supporters who admired his commitment to the cause and were sorry to see him not play considerably more than the 87 games he managed for Hibs. Mickey Weir says: "Callum Milne was an excellent player for Hibs and was very under-rated. You ask anyone who played with him at Hibs and they will tell you how good a player he was. He was a Hibs man through and through."

There is also a ringing endorsement from his old captain Gordon Rae, who says: "I don't know why Callum never got a better run of games. Alex Miller never really took to him and John Blackley only called on him now and again too. It's weird, when you saw what a great player he was. Hibs had lots of guys in the team that would kick their own granny to win a game. Things have changed now, but you could do with four or five of these type of players in the team now. Their attitude was brilliant. The one thing you were guaranteed every week was 100 per cent effort, total commitment. Now, in some people's eyes, there might be better players in the team, but for me you couldn't match the commitment, application and attitude we had from guys like Callum back then."

There are striking similarities in the careers of Milne and McKee and it is no surprise that they were – and are – good pals. Which presents me with the chance to end this chapter on a lighter note, a highlighted note even, and ask them about their infamous 80s hair-dos.

"The old mullet, that was a beauty wasn't it?" laughs McKee, who rocked a mean 'wedge' cut, a bit like Damon from *Brookside* or the lassies out of The Human League! "I had all the latest styles because my wife – my girlfriend at the time – was a hairdresser. Me and Callum used to go and see her at the hairdressers just about every week. Callum used to get his hair streaked every week, that's why he's not got any hair left now, it's all fallen out! Callum was my pal and we were very close, and we also played together at Partick. Any of the guys I played with I could phone up and they would call me right back, we made friends for life and had great team spirit. There was a lot of very successful Scottish teams at that time, it was a period to be proud of in Scottish football and we had a great togetherness at Hibs. I have nothing but great memories of being there. I am a Hibbie through and through and for me it was a great achievement just to be able to pull that jersey on. The fact it didn't work out is a different conversation, but I still enjoyed every minute I was there."

CHAPTER 7

HOIST up the JOHN B's SAIL

"You know Celtic are going to come at you, and be expected to pump you, but we had a go right back at them. It was a great night, and the atmosphere was brilliant." – Steve Cowan

If you want a football season packaged to cover the entire range of emotions, look no further than 1985-86. This was the season that Hibs managed to put the ball in Celtic's net 15 times, knock them out of both domestic cups, and then celebrate the 'Lesser Greens' winning the league title like it was us that had won it, not them. This was the season Hibs romped their way to a cup final. This was the season of Jukebox Durie and Stevie Cowan's prolific goalscoring partnership. The season they put a roof over the East Terrace. The season of Alan Rough re-emerging a Scotland hero and the nation mourning the tragic death of Jock Stein. The season of Pierce O'Leary. The season of Albert Kidd!

It was also another season that Hibs languished and laboured for prolonged periods, and the highs of the Skol Cup and Scottish Cup projected only temporary laser-beams on to a backdrop of general gloom. When the trophies were handed out in May, our name wasn't on any of them, but thankfully neither was that of Hearts – who, as we will never forget, were seven minutes away from winning the Premier League before Sir Albert's noble intervention, then collapsed to a 3-0 defeat to Aberdeen in the Scottish Cup final seven days later. While we ridiculed our arch-rivals' torment and tears, and the hordes of Hibbies that had fled the city were able to return safe in the knowledge that there was a God after all, it didn't mask the problems that were mounting on our own doorstep.

The final 85-86 league table shows that for the second season in succession Hibs finished just one uncomfortable place above the relegation spots, and shipped more than 60 goals, while our star striker and prized asset Durie was sold to Chelsea. Manager John Blackley appeared to be fighting the same losing battle that had ended the ambitions of his recent predecessors, and the supporters remained restless. Before we get to the twists and turns of that crazy 85-86 campaign, let's remind ourselves of the task Sloop John B faced from the moment he accepted the job.

After the managerial stability Hibs had enjoyed in the Seventies, with the great Eddie Turnbull in charge from 1971 onwards, the Eighties was a different story, requiring Easter Road to be installed with the proverbial revolving door. As the summer of 1984 faded, Blackley became the fourth boss of the decade, continuing the tradition of entrusting the job to former Hibs players. However, it was clear from the moment he made the step up that he had a major job on his hands simply to prevent the club from being relegated.

Pat Stanton had lasted only six games of the 1984-85 season before deciding enough was enough. For parsimonious chairman Kenny Waugh, Blackley was conveniently and cheaply placed to take on the job. Blackley may have been somewhat bounced into the job, but there was no managerial bounce effect on a squad low on morale and quality, and in his first 16 league matches in charge, he won only two. Among the defeats was a demoralising 4-0 gubbing at Morton. This is a game most of those present have purged from their memories, but not supporter Gordon Timmins! "I remember returning from Cappielow after that humiliation when I met the whole team," he explains. "The engine of our bus wouldn't start and a few of us approached Sloop to explain our predicament and he allowed us to cadge a lift back to Easter Road on the players' bus. This was my first experience of a 'quiet coach'! The Team was: Rough, Brazil, Sneddon, Kane, Rae, Jamieson, Callaghan, Durie, Irvine Craig and Rice. No autographs were requested!"

The fans were at least lifted by the arrival of teenage sensation Gordon Durie from East Fife. Although only 18, the youngster was blessed with power and pace and clearly had a big future ahead of him. When Hibs headed to Ibrox on 12 January 1985, they were fighting history as well as relegation, and not many gave them a chance of ending their winless run against Rangers, stretching back to 1979. But goals from Brian Rice and Colin Harris secured an unimaginable 2-1 victory. "That was an exceptional game," Blackley recalls. "I always felt when I was a player that, whenever we faced Rangers, we always had a shout. I think we won more against them than we lost, and it was the same for me when I was a manager – I always felt Hibs stood up against Rangers and made like difficult for them."

Buoyed by this, Hibs claimed a crucial home win against fellow strugglers Dumbarton, and then something very special happened to end the month on a high – a phenomenon rarer than Halley's Comet. I'm talking, of course, about Benny's Hat-Trick! Forget that it came in a friendly, this was a day to remember for the 6,000 who were there to witness it, and particularly for old twinkle-toes himself, Ally Brazil.

When the entire Scottish Cup fixture list was wiped out by a cold snap, quick-thinking Hibs turned their undersoil heating up full blast and hatched a plan with Celtic to put on a friendly at implausibly short notice. There were no message boards or Twitter to share breaking news in those days, and although my memory is hazy, I have a vague recollection of hearing about the game on the lunchtime *Saint & Greavsie* show. Word of mouth had done the trick, and those that were there were treated to a nine-goal bonanza, three of them from the much-maligned Benny. "Ally Brazil is the hero, for once" *The Scotsman* headline read the next day, emphasising that this would likely never be repeated. "We won 6-3 and it is something I will never forget," says Benny. "There had been a whiteout in Britain and with us having the underground heating we arranged a friendly with Celtic. I managed to get three goals, one of them a diving header and the third a penalty, and I have still got the match ball."

Benny's goal glut aside, the whole occasion bordered on the bizarre. The terracing remained shut, and most Hibs fans congregated in The Cowshed, while the Celtic supporters at the other end waited behind to boo their team off for conceding six goals. As one report described it: "The sun shone brightly at the start. Both teams lined up in summer gear. And Mo Johnston even came complete with a suntan. Add to that the amazing scoreline and you'd a match more resembling a beach bounce game at Troon at times than a winter friendly."

Back to league business, Hibs still had work to do to beat the drop, and they remained infuriatingly inconsistent during Blackley's first season at the helm. However, another hat-trick, this time from Durie, gave them a much-needed win at home to doomed Morton and – perhaps inspired by the 6-3 friendly win – a shock 1-0 win at Celtic Park meant it was down to a straight fight between Hibs and Dumbarton to stay up. When Hibs went 2-0 down against Hearts inside 20 minutes of an April midweek derby at Tynecastle, our survival chances seemed to be ebbing away. Quite a few Hibbies had left by the time the clock had ticked on to the 84th minute, but then up popped Joe McBride to score a sensational late double to salvage a draw, which felt like a victory and was wildly celebrated in the Gorgie Road end. Wild slavering conspiracy theories swept the capital for weeks after that this had been a 'fix', and that Hearts had caved to help their city rivals stay up and preserve Premier League derbies. Absolute nonsense – there was nothing remotely crooked about this comeback, and it gave me a taster of what it might be like to leave Tynecastle with a smile on my face for once! "The 2-2 game at Tynecastle was a turning point for us that season," says Blackley. "Joe McBride was a good player for us and I was glad for him, scoring those two important goals, because until then we hadn't played particularly well that night and things were running through my head (about relegation), before he turned it round for us."

Football writer and lifelong Hibs supporter Simon Pia has another reason to remember that topsy-turvy game. "I remember getting reprimanded at Tynecastle after Joe had just scored those two late goals. I jumped up in the Press Box and shouted with delight, and this stony-faced Hearts official came up to me and told me: 'Your behaviour is outrageous and we're going to ban you.' I also remember going into Tynecastle for a game at the height of the miners' strike. There were miners outside the ground, collecting money and distributing leaflets. I put a bit of cash into their bucket and was given a 'Support the Miners' badge which I stuck on my lapel on the way in. When I went into the press conference after the game, Wallace Mercer made a beeline for me and marched up to me and asked me what badge I was wearing. When I told him what it was representing, he said: 'We can't have that! No politics in here – you're barred!' I told him I was entitled to my say and was pleading my case when big John Fairgrieve from the *Daily Mail* jumped in on my behalf. John was from a mining community in Bonnyrigg and wasn't having it. He said: 'Hey Wallace... if the laddie goes, we all go!' Mercer backed down."

Super Joe's timely double gave Hibs the momentum they needed for their must-win game at Dumbarton, which was my first experience of Boghead, and one I attended because the club had generously laid on free buses to ensure that we had a healthy and vocal travelling support. Even though I'd seen and played on a few brutal council football pitches like Inverleith Park and Sighthill, I had never seen anything quite as shitey as the surface at Boghead! Still, the must-win game was won, and we were staying up! "Most of these memories have left me but I know it was tight," says Blackley, now 73. "I always remember going down to Dumbarton and how tense it was. But we got the win and stayed up and that was the main thing. By that time, I had asked Tommy Craig to be my assistant, and he was brilliant for me and the club – he was a really good coach and knew so much about football in general. He also played for us a few times when he first arrived, but he was a first-class coach."

John Collins also remembers just how influential a figure Craig was to have around. "I was very lucky to have guys like Pat Stanton, John Blackley and Tommy Craig to guide me – all real football men," says Collins. "All of them took time to appreciate the creative side of the game as well as the physical, and to put the emphasis on skill. For them, it wasn't all about having big strong players, they were all for giving young players a chance. Tommy Craig came to Hibs as player-coach from Carlisle, and within a few weeks he had seen something in me on the training pitch that he really liked and he became something of a mentor for me. He knew I was going to take his place, even though he was still a great talent himself, but he did all he could to push and encourage me. He was a huge influence. He pushed all the young boys actually and would regularly take us out in the afternoons for extra sessions, working on our pinging and passing and shooting. He was always encouraging, but he was a very demanding coach and did not accept sloppy sessions and was always striving for quality."

The final game of the season against Rangers would have been a largely forgettable affair, even though we won 1-0, had it not been for the awful events happening in Bradford that day. I have clear memories of the numbing shock amongst fans at the end of the game, as word got out that a fire had engulfed the old wooden stand at Valley Parade – a disaster which claimed the lives of 56 people and injured more than 250 fans, who like us, had simply gone to support their team and watch a game of football.

Our season was over, and so was Brian Rice's Hibs career. Unbeknown to the elegant midfielder at the time, he had caught the eye of Brian Clough, legendary manager of double European Cup winners Nottingham Forest, and when they made an enquiry about Rice, the wheels were quickly set in motion for a move south. This turn of events took everybody by surprise at the time, especially Hibs – who had offered Rice a new contract they expected him to sign.

"The move to Forest was a strange one," admits Rice. "My contract was coming up and the money I was getting wasn't great – my sister was earning more than me working for an insurance company. I was playing every week and I thought I deserved a wee bit more. I got wind that a couple of teams might want me, but I was still training away at Hibs and working hard. I went home after training one night, a Tuesday, and went down to the park to play fitba with my pals – as we did in those days – and my Dad came down and said there had been a phone call for me and I better get back because they'd be phoning me back in 10 minutes. It turned out to be the assistant manager at Nottingham Forest, Ronnie Fenton. He asked if I would be interested in coming down if they could do a deal with Hibs. I couldn't believe it because they were a top team and managed of course by Brian Clough – I had only ever seen him on the telly and that was enough to leave me scared enough of him! Ronnie told me to go into Easter Road the next day and to knock back the deal they had offered me, but not to tell them the club I was going to.

"I went to Easter Road the next day to seek out John Blackley and Tommy Craig. I went upstairs with them and said to John: 'Gaffer, I'm not signing.' He was surprised and reminded me that Hibs had made what they thought to be a good offer. I said: 'Look, I've had a good offer from an English club and I'm flying down there tonight.' He asked who it was, and I said they had asked me not to say. As much as I wanted to tell them, I couldn't, I didn't want to jeopardise the move. So, sadly, the conversation and my time at Hibs didn't finish well – I just got told in no uncertain terms to get out, get my gear and don't come back. I went downstairs, gathered up my stuff into a black bag and walked out and got the bus home. I didn't get the chance to say goodbye to anyone. Even when I went to Nottingham Forest the clubs could not agree terms and I couldn't play until they set a tribunal date, which was a few weeks into the season. I remember coming up to the tribunal with the club secretary, and John (Blackley) was there with Cecil Graham for Hibs. We were all in the meeting and they eventually decided the fee. John came up to me and asked 'are you going back to Nottingham now?' I said I was going to see my Mum and Dad first and he said: 'C'mon I'll drop you off. It's the least we can do – we've just made close to 200 grand out of you so that will keep us going for a while!' In the end, I think it was great for all parties."

Rice has told the story of his first face-to-face meeting with Clough before, but it's worth telling again. "That was incredible," he laughs. "I was in a wee hotel and Archie Gemmill came along in the morning to pick me up and take me to the City Ground. I had a good head of red hair then and after we chapped the gaffer's door and walked in, he looked up from his desk, looked me up and down, and said quick as you like: 'Bloody hell, it's Steve Davis!' And that was his first ever words to me."

The relationship went from strength to strength, and Rice loved his time at Forest under Clough. "I signed the same day as Stuart Pearce and me and him became the best of friends, and still are. We were room-mates and he's been up to Whitburn a few times with me. I was playing in a team full of internationals, it was just a different level. I made my debut at Anfield, we lost 2-0, and the following week I'm playing against Tottenham, against Hoddle and Clemence. In hindsight, another year at Hibs wouldn't have killed me – it would have made me stronger and better, but sometimes the opportunities come and you have to grab them. Every transfer is a gamble. The gaffer (Clough) took a big shine to me down there and I had a brilliant six-and-a-half years. I made mountains of pals and still have a great rapport with them. Clough was an amazing manager, but he kept it simple – nothing was complicated. We all knew our job and there were no big-time Charlies. If there were, then he would soon cut them down to size. It didn't matter who it was, we all got treated the same and he was fair with everybody. He really looked after me. There are certain lessons I learned, especially around man-management – he was special."

While Rice was beginning a new chapter of his career in England's top flight, Hibs were busy bringing in new faces and a key signing was centre-forward Steve Cowan – one of the fringe players at Fergie's all-conquering Aberdeen, where being on the periphery was understandable given the brilliance of that squad. "I had been there six years, which was quite a long time to be at the one club," says Cowan. "Alex Ferguson had asked me to sign another two-year deal to stay at Aberdeen. I asked him for a bit more money and he wasn't very forthcoming in agreeing to that, so I was left in limbo a bit. It was getting near the end of pre-season, and I had just finished training one Friday when I got a call from Alex saying Hibs had made an offer which had been accepted. He told me to go down to meet John Blackley and Tommy Craig in Brechin, as Hibs were playing a pre-season friendly there. It was all a bit of a shock, the speed at which it happened, but it was the best thing that could have happened to me. Obviously, I had had a great time at Aberdeen, but I needed to get out there and establish myself as a player. So, I thought to myself, I have nothing to lose here – Hibs are a big team, a big name in Scottish football, so I went to listen to them.

"When I met John and Tommy, I instantly took to them, and knew that I could work with them and play for Hibs no problem. I had always considered myself a bit of a student of the game and I knew the history of Hibs, their involvement in cup finals and Europe, and the achievements of the Famous Five, so it was a really attractive move for me. The two of them were a big selling point – Sloop, a Scottish internationalist, and Tommy, another excellent player who had played at Aberdeen himself in his formative years. I just bonded with them immediately and I knew what they were looking for from me as a player – they knew what I could give. I almost agreed terms right away. I went back up the road, spoke to my wife, and that was more difficult – as she was a local girl from Aberdeen, so I had to sell her on the move to Edinburgh. We had just had our first girl who was a few months old. But it all worked out, and within days the deal was done and I was heading down to Edinburgh.

"I was only 22 when I joined Hibs, but I was deemed a very experienced player because I had been in and around Aberdeen for so long. I was still relatively young in terms of football years. But people knew I had played alongside guys like Miller, McLeish, Strachan and understood that I would know what I was doing. I came down with a very simple philosophy – to do what I had been signed to do and score goals."

Cowan did not take long to start finding the net. He was a good old-fashioned No 9, prepared to hold up the ball and bring others into play, and blessed with a natural poacher's instinct for goals in and around the six-yard box. His attributes clicked neatly into place with the dynamic Durie, who had speed to burn and who would terrorise defences with his energy and ability to exploit space.

"I was quite lucky to be in a partnership with Jukebox, who was brilliant to play with," Cowan is quick to acknowledge. "He was an unknown quantity at the time, and defenders often struggled to handle him. He was bursting with enthusiasm and the ability and pace he had was fantastic. He would listen to what I was saying to him, he was eager to learn. I was lucky, as I had some good knowledge to pass on – I had been taught at Aberdeen by guys like Joe

Harper, Steve Archibald and Mark McGhee – you couldn't get any better than that. I was lucky to come to Hibs at that time, because you had Mickey Weir wide on one side, Joe McBride on the other, and other good, dependable experienced players around like Benny Brazil. Loads of quality to create chances. You are only as good as the players round about you, especially when you are a striker. The training was brilliant under Sloop and Tommy, it was all geared towards attacking, creating opportunities, getting the ball into the box, getting it up into spaces for Jukebox to run into, get it into the front post for me to attack. I thought it was great, and it made me feel settled and happy that I had made the right move. It was like a glove fitting perfectly."

Cowan's first goals in a Hibs shirt arrived in style – a hat-trick against Cowdenbeath in a 6-0 Skol Cup cakewalk. It was the first step in a memorable run to Hampden, lit up by the Cowan-Durie partnership. A week after thrashing the Blue Brazil, Hibs hammered another six past Motherwell at Easter Road, five of them coming from the burgeoning strike pairing – hat-trick honours this time for Durie. Not since the days of the Tornadoes had fans seen back-to-back goal-fests like this. This quickfire, exciting cup format was much more attractive than the old League Cup sections of the past, and the midweek ties came thick and fast. Hibs had motored into the quarter-finals in the space of a fortnight and were rewarded with a home tie against Celtic under the lights. The drama that unfolded that September evening was incredible – an epic match which must make any short-list of best-ever cup ties seen at Easter Road. Yes, it was that good! "Breathtaking, a much-abused word, was entirely apposite last night with goals and countless incidents to lift a crowd watching two sides playing at their peak," Hugh Keevins wrote in his *Scotsman* match report the following day.

A fast-paced first half ended 2-2 (Cowan and Durie) and the teams traded goals in the second half to take it into extra-time. Celtic again got their noses in front in the first half of extra-time through Roy Aitken, only for Danny McGrain to deflect in a Durie response to tie the match at 4-4 and send it into penalties, where more twists and turns were to follow. I remember wise old fox Alan Rough stopping the bull-like charge run-up of Roy Aitken to pick up an imaginary piece of litter near the six-yard line. Aitken was forced to retreat and try again, his cool completely gone, and we gleefully watched as Rough's cunning plan paid off and the Celtic midfielder duffed his spot-kick. Peter Grant also missed, as did big Gordon Rae for Hibs. The shootout swung our way and Benny had a chance to win the tie – but he also missed! "What a game of football that was," says Benny now. "If I had scored that was us through. I put it in exactly the same spot as the time I had done before, in the 6-3 game, but he read it and saved it."

The teams were level at 3-3 as the shootout went into sudden death. Stevie

Cowan sent the crowd wild by putting Hibs ahead and then up stepped Pierce O'Leary, most famous for being the brother of David O'Leary, but soon a famous name in Hibs folklore as he ballooned his penalty over the bar and high into The Cowshed. We'd done it, we were into the semi-finals.

"That was an unbelievable night," says Cowan. "You know Celtic are going to come at you, and be expected to pump you, but we set up to have a go right back at them and I was lucky enough to score one goal that night, and I scored what proved to be the winning penalty because Pierce O'Leary ended up blazing his penalty for Celtic over the bar. It was a great night, and the atmosphere was brilliant – both sets of fans created some noise. We had that type of character in the side that we never knew when we were beat, and we always knew we could score goals."

Our cup campaign had a magical feel about it, but this did not extend to the Premier League. To ruthlessly illustrate this, Celtic returned to Easter Road less than 72 hours later after their cup exit and annihilated Hibs 5-0. Same teams, very different result! Alan Rough may have had nine goals put past him in a matter of days, but he stepped up to become a national hero on a bittersweet night for Scotland in Cardiff the following midweek. With Scotland needing a draw to close in on World Cup qualification, a tense first half saw them fall 1-0 behind to group rivals Wales. Jim Leighton had been noticeably shaky in goals, and when he failed to re-emerge for the second-half (a lost contact lens was given as the reason for his substitution) big Roughie was suddenly called upon. The Hibs No 1 shone in the second half and kept a clean sheet, while at the other end Davie Cooper scored a dramatic equaliser from the penalty spot to help send Scotland to Mexico. The match was, of course, overshadowed by the tragic loss of manager Jock Stein, who suffered a heart attack and collapsed in the closing minutes, and died soon afterwards. A nation mourned the loss of a great man, and legendary football manager, who of course had a memorable spell in charge of Hibs before working his European Cup-winning magic with Celtic.

Another great man would be lost before the end of the year, in devastating circumstances. Erich Schaedler, who had been playing for Dumbarton after leaving Hibs at the end of the 84-85 season (434 appearances in two spells at Easter Road), was reported missing by his family and friends in the run-up to Christmas, before he was found dead in a car at Cardrona Forest, near his hometown of Peebles. He was only 36. I covered his life, career and death in my previous book *Shades*, and this much-loved character is still mourned and remembered to this day.

Returning to Hibs' Skol Cup run, after three successive exhilarating midweek cup wins, yielding 16 Hibs goals – 20 if you count the penalties – there was a three-week gap to catch our breath before the semi-finals began, with

Hibs drawn against Rangers and Dundee United paired with Aberdeen, both ties to be settled over two legs, home and away.

That gave Hibs time to make another key signing, and ironically it was the man who had settled the English League Cup final at Wembley earlier that same year, Gordon Chisholm, who had the misfortune of scoring an own goal while at Sunderland to gift the trophy to Norwich City. But big Chis wasted no time in putting that mishap behind him by scoring on his debut against Rangers, as a well-drilled Hibs won the first leg 2-0, the other goal coming from Durie. Before the goals arrived, Alan Rough had shown himself to be the man for the big occasion with a crucial penalty save from Ally McCoist. The atmosphere at Easter Road – undergoing redevelopment at the time as the terracing was transformed into a covered enclosure – was absolutely crackling that night.

"The thought of coming up to Hibs really appealed to me," says Chisholm, who to my surprise reveals that Hibs were actually his boyhood team. "The truth is, as a kid, I was probably the only boy in the school with a Hibs strip. I stood out from the crowd running about in a Hibs strip, because at that time it just wasn't seen in Glasgow. The reason for that was that my old man brought me through to a game at Easter Road and I just fell for the club there and then. At the time that I signed I never mentioned it and never really made anything of it, because I thought it might sound a bit naff and unbelievable if I said Hibs were my favourites as a boy, especially coming from Glasgow. I have never ever really talked about this! I wouldn't say I was a hardcore supporter or anything like that but when I grew up Pat Stanton, Alex Cropley and all that team were my heroes. If I ever watched a game on the telly it would be Hibs, because I thought they were a right good football team.

"So, I was really happy to get the chance to sign for them. I had played against John Blackley when he was at Newcastle, him and Tommy Craig, when I was only a kid. It was good playing under Sloop, and there were a lot of good young boys like Gordon Hunter, John Collins, Mickey Weir and Paul Kane who were just coming through at that time and developing. That was the sign I was looking for when I signed – that the club was going places. There looked like a good development path in place, and guys like big Gordon Rae and Roughie to provide some experience. We had a great set of boys and I really enjoyed my time at Hibs. When I first came up and signed, we were struggling in the league, but were in a semi-final and that's when I made my debut against Rangers. Then we had Hearts on the Saturday. We beat Rangers and we drew with Hearts, so it was a great start for me.

"I had actually been meant to make my debut on the Saturday before, against Clydebank, but the game was postponed, so my first game was against Rangers instead. I remember running out from the tunnel, and what an atmosphere there was at Easter Road – it was buzzing. I had all my family there and my wife's family all there to see my debut, and the place was bouncing. And then to play Hearts on the Saturday straight after that, it was some introduction – I couldn't get enough of it. Having been playing down south, I was blown away by the atmosphere in Scottish football. I had been used to playing at Roker Park, and don't get me wrong – that was a full-house that also could generate some atmosphere, but then I came up here and was so impressed. It was the perfect start to playing up here. It told me I had made the right choice. I scored the first goal with a header and that will live long in the memory. One of my best mates is Nicky Walker, who was the Rangers goalkeeper that night, and to this day I am still able to wind him up about that goal – I tell him I got so high above him that I could see the highlights in his hair!"

Excitement among the Hibs fans was at fever pitch for the return leg at Ibrox a fortnight later. The club had laid on buses for the 8,000-strong travelling support, but the fleet soon got swamped in rush-hour traffic and roadworks on the M8, and the semi-final procession became a crawl. Our heroic driver must have himself been a Hibbie because he burst through some traffic cones and proceeded up a cordoned-off section of the motorway to beat the queue. Proving how sharp and witty football fans can be, this act of derring-do was accompanied by a few loud choruses of the *A-Team* theme tune from those grateful fans on board. We hadn't long taken our seats – and thousands of less fortunate Hibbies hadn't done at that stage – when Davie Cooper scored a scintillating free-kick to reduce the aggregate score to 2-1 and leave the tie balanced on a knife edge. "I can still hear the sound of the ball hitting the net," remembers Stevie Cowan. "It was pouring with rain and you could just hear the sprinkle of water as the ball hit the net."

As the game progressed and nerves began to go through the shredder, the delayed Hibs support started to arrive in numbers and filled up the Broomloan Stand to roar the team on. Somehow, despite intense pressure and countless goalmouth scrambles, we managed to hold on and claim a famous victory, which set up a Hampden cup final against Aberdeen. "After Davie Cooper scored with the free-kick it was an absolute onslaught, one-way traffic, but somehow we managed to hold on for the result. What a fantastic feeling it was after that game," says Ally Brazil.

The only blot on an otherwise glorious night was the booking Gordon Rae picked up, which ruled him out of the final. "Beating Celtic and Rangers in the League Cup took some doing. They were amazing games," says Rae. "I got booked in the second semi-final. It was McCoist I think, but I played the ball. I appealed to the referee Brian McGinlay. I was so annoyed because I had won the ball and I couldn't believe the ref hadn't seen it that way. It was tough but it's all part of football, all about shaping your character and your ability to deal with setbacks when they come along."

"That cup run was brilliant," says a proud Blackley. "The guys really produced their best in that competition. We had Stevie Cowan, who was a great buy for Hibs – honestly, he was an excellent character and player. His general demeanour was first class – he was never down and always up and bubbly, great to have around the place. And having Gordon Durie to play alongside him, it was a great move. They struck up a great partnership, which just took off, especially in the Skol Cup. I have to say Alan Rough was extremely important to us too – he was probably my saviour and Hibs' saviour that particular season. He was just a really nice character, but always a top goalie. And let's not forget Benny Brazil... what a great servant and stalwart, he would give everything for the team. We had lost our way in the league but produced our best in the cup. I remember coming back on the bus from Ibrox and what a high we were all on – there was something really special about getting the club to the final and giving the supporters something to get really excited about and to hang on to. The motorway was great, all the cars and buses coming back and flashing their lights and giving us the thumbs up, it was a special night for the club. A great night and a nice memory that one!"

Team-mates and fans certainly felt sympathy for Rae, but Steve Cowan insists the harsh ban handed out to the big man did not cloud preparations ahead of the final. "Gordon being suspended... I have to admit I didn't give it a second thought. I know that might sound a bit harsh but that's the nature of the beast. We all miss finals and big games, that's just the way it goes, and if someone misses these games then it gives another player an opportunity. He was a great lad though, I liked how he was winner. As soon as I saw him play and train I thought 'you'll do for me'. I needed guys like that around me because I had come from that background at Aberdeen. He was a very good captain."

Captain for the day was Iain Munro, and a huge Hibs support travelled through more in hope than expectation against Ferguson's formidable Aberdeen. Two goals in the opening 12 minutes, first from Eric Black and then Billy Stark, effectively ended the final before it had really started, and it finished 3-0. "Sadly the final didn't work out," sighs Blackley, who was nevertheless honoured to have led Hibs out for a cup final at Hampden. "I always call it the 12-minute final, because they were 2-0 up and out of sight within 12 minutes. We knew to have any chance we would need to keep a clean sheet for as long as possible, but they were a really strong side and everything we had fought for was gone after 12 minutes. But credit to the players who had got us there and it was sad on the day that we failed. It was nice for the fans to get the opportunity to go to Hampden, but we let them down. It would have been so nice to have done it for the fans."

Like the rest of his team-mates, Cowan looked crestfallen at the end, particularly as he was playing against the club he had left just a couple of months earlier, but he insists: "I didn't feel any extra pressure that it was Aberdeen in the final. I've always been a great believer that you play the game not the occasion. It's just 11 guys, but I knew we would need to be right at our best and for them to have an off-day for us to beat them. That's not being pessimistic, that was being realistic. You just had to look at that team and see the quality that you were up against. 2-0 in 12 minutes and it was an uphill struggle. A lot of teams could have put the heads down completely, collapsed, and lost 6-0, but we didn't. We hung in there. It was still a bit of a beating, but we could be proud of the run we had gone on to reach the final. Sometimes everything goes against you, and it did that day for us."

Team-mate Paul Kane reflects: "You look back in time and you realise just what a great Aberdeen team that was. That era was full of great Scottish teams, Aberdeen and Dundee United particularly. They had top players at the peak of their powers. We would have needed something exceptional that day for us to win and for Aberdeen to somehow take their foot off the pedal, and they didn't. They were ruthless and they blew us away. They annihilated us that day."

Alan Sneddon agrees: "It was a thrilling run in the Skol Cup. They were great games and we had players like Gordon Durie and Stevie Cowan who made us an entertaining team. That run was incredible and we genuinely felt we could do something, but that Aberdeen team was unfortunately too good for us, and we didn't do ourselves justice in the final at all. I think we lost goals at bad times and we never got settled or caused them a problem. They had that experience to handle the occasion better."

"We just never got started and found ourselves a couple of goals down inside the first 12 minutes," says Gordon Chisholm, who was completing a rare Wembley-Hampden League Cup final double in the same calendar year. "It was a massive disappointment, especially after the build-up and the amazing run we had been on to reach the final. We let ourselves down to be honest, we got off to a terrible start and never recovered. Against a team like that, they are not going to let you recover. It was a disappointment for the players and the supporters."

It was a double-whammy for Kevin McKee – a player reluctantly rendered a spectator that day. The young full-back was left out of the cup final squad, and reveals that he rather cruelly had to make his own way to the match. "I played in the quarter-final against Celtic and the first leg of the semi-final against Rangers, but I had to pay for a ticket to get into the final, that's the gospel truth!" says McKee. "Those of us not in the matchday squad weren't even on the bus – well I certainly wasn't! I went to the game with my friend. That was towards the end of my time at Easter Road – it is what it is. It was devastating to me as a young kid not to be involved in the final, having played in the quarter-finals and the semis, but that's football and you sometimes just have to roll with the punches.

"When Sloop took over, I don't know if he just didn't fancy me, but my confidence was pretty low at that point. It's very difficult in the 80s, being a young kid with no agents – you had to deal with it yourself, which was difficult. You didn't have people to give you advice and guide you. I probably made a few bad decisions at the time, and I just think it was too early for me in my career. If I'd been older it might have panned out differently for me at Easter Road."

While McKee was moved on, Blackley had shrewdly brought in another young player who would have a big impact in his maiden season at Easter Road, and who developed a happy knack of scoring important goals in big games. Eddie May was a product of the Dundee United youth system, but he was a Hibbie through and through, and he soon settled at the club – after he managed to escape the notoriously iron grip of Jim McLean at Tannadice, where contracts were usually long and binding.

"I had signed a two-year contract with a two-year option, so I was able to leave if I wanted to," explains May. "I played a lot of reserve games, but United were a fantastic team at the time and I had to be really honest with myself: could I really see myself breaking into that team to the extent that I would be playing every week? I had a conversation with Jim McLean: I actually knocked on his door and put it to him. The first time I asked him about potentially leaving he wasn't very nice or pleasant, but that was just the way Jim was. He must have seen a value in me. But the second time and especially the third time I think I succeeded in letting him know that I was serious. I was actually thinking about packing it in altogether and either going back into education or getting a job away from football. He reluctantly said yes and by chance I got the opportunity to go to Hibs until the end of the season, and then after that I got the offer of a longer-term contract.

"The one person I must thank for giving me that opportunity is John Blackley – he was absolutely great for me, but money was tight at Hibs and we probably didn't get the chance to see the best of him as a manager at that time. I don't think he got the full backing that he needed at that moment in time because of the restrictions at the club. I really enjoyed my time at the club, especially as I was a Hibs supporter. It meant a lot to me. I grew up in two places: West Pilton and Southhouse, the posh areas! What I did learn in these places was to become streetwise and that helped me a lot in my football career. It stood me in good stead. I remember the first time I played – I got my game ahead of Ralph Callachan and what a fantastic professional he was. He pulled me aside before the game and gave me a talk and gave me all the encouragement I needed, not only for that game but for the rest of the season."

After making his debut in September, midfielder May scored for Hibs in the Scottish Cup against Dunfermline, again in the next round against Ayr United, and then saved the biggest intervention for a titanic quarter-final against Celtic. On a March afternoon, somehow the intense excitement we had experienced between the sides in the Skol Cup quarter-final six months earlier was reprised in an utterly bonkers second half. This cup tie has to be seen to be believed, and in an era when television coverage was sketchy at best, the only footage in existence is a grainy home-made video effort, sans commentary, which has been uploaded on to YouTube.

Celtic had led 1-0 at half-time, before Stevie Cowan equalised early in the second half. Davie Hay's side then retook the lead through Mark McGhee, and the score stayed at 2-1 until there were just 14 manic minutes left. First, cup specialist Gordon Chisholm scored for Hibs, then Cowan put us ahead for the first time with an 84th-minute penalty – a lead that lasted a mere two minutes as Celtic quickly replied with a penalty of their own, to make it 3-3. A replay at Parkhead loomed before Eddie – on as a substitute for John Collins – nodded the ball home from close range to claim a famous 4-3 win for Hibs and dump Celtic out of the cup for the second time at Easter Road that season. Who says lightning can't strike twice?! "That's another game I won't ever forget," says goalscorer Cowan. "A Saturday afternoon, the Scottish Cup, a muddy Easter Road, a big crowd – it was special! We went toe to toe with them again and I scored two. I remember I was only a few inches away from Eddie May when he got the flying header to get us the winner right at the death. It was against a very good Celtic team with guys like Mo Johnston, Roy Aitken and Murdo Macleod in their team and they won the league that year. There were pitch invasions at the end of both of those Celtic games in the cup, so the fans were obviously delighted with the outcome!"

Bobby Sinnet, the author of a number of Hibs books, says: "It's the only time we've beaten Celtic in the Scottish Cup since 1902 despite beating Rangers frequently, and Celtic regularly in the League Cup. The game itself was a thriller that turned and twisted, and the advantage surged back and forward. Just when it seemed a draw was likely, Colin Harris crossed for Eddie May to score the winner with seconds remaining. It was really windy that day as I recall and the only footage from the game was from a low-quality VHS that Hibs produced as there was no telly deal that season. I converted the VHS to DVD, and the lack of commentary and the low quality just adds to the nostalgia!"

Match-winner May, who you can just about make out from the faded footage, says: "I was fortunate to be in the right place at the right time. I had been sent on as a substitute to make an impression. As a young guy you just run about, without any fear of the occasion, and it was great to get my head on the end of that one. I got brought down for the penalty too. We could be a great attacking team on our day – the problem was that we often left it too open at the back."

The prospect of another semi-final generated plenty excitement among the Hibs support, although that was tempered by the fact it was the daunting Dons who would be the opposition at neutral Dens Park, and that there was a major fitness doubt lingering over our star striker Durie, who was – coincidence or not – being linked with a string of big clubs interested in signing him.

Durie made it on to the pitch, but looked miles off his brilliant best, and in a repeat of the Skol Cup final, Hibs were 2-0 down at half-time before eventually meekly losing 3-0. Aberdeen would face league leaders Hearts in the final and some tough words were said in the Hibs dressing room in the heat of the moment. "I remember Sloop giving Gordon Durie a torrid time," says Alan Sneddon. "Jukebox had been injured before it and there was a doubt over whether he would play, and even though he went out and played, Sloop laid into him afterwards, saying: 'I wouldn't like to be in the trenches with you' and that kind of thing. It was harsh. It was frustrating for us all, and especially the fans, because we all knew if Jukebox had been fully fit, we would have got a totally different game out of him. But Aberdeen had a team full of experience, and Alex McLeish and Willie Miller were up against him that day. They were a hard team to play against."

Blackley tells me he would prefer to keep his own counsel about the exchange he had with his off-colour striker that day but, on the record, he says: "It was a huge disappointment – we needed a good Gordon Durie to have any chance." As it turned out, Durie did not have to dwell long on Blackley's blast – it was his final game in a Hibs shirt and within days he was sold to Chelsea for £400,000. His strike partner Cowan, at least, stuck around, and could reflect on a very successful season. "I was lucky enough to finish on 28 goals, which I think since 1986, only Leigh Griffiths has matched at Hibs," he says. "I am very proud to hold that record. I think I am also the last player to score three hat-tricks in one season as well." So, he must surely still have the match-balls somewhere? "No," he laughs. "I think the club only had two match balls so there was no chance of them giving them away. There was nothing like that, no fuss, it was just right on to focusing on the next game, not the one that had just passed."

With four leagues game to go, the season may have been petering out for Hibs, but across the city, the Hearts supporters were working themselves into a frenzy as they galloped towards a league and cup double. But, as anyone who has seen the clip from the 1956 Grand National knows, you can be miles clear with the finishing post in sight, and still 'do a Devon Loch'. Hibs fans were literally heading for the hills as Hearts went on their logic-defying unbeaten run in the league and cup, taking them to within 90 minutes of the title. Their fate would be determined at Dens Park, while 60 miles away eighth-placed Hibs would host Dundee United.

As TV commentator Archie Macpherson put it as he called the action from Dundee: 'Who, way back in August blessed with the second sight of the seventh son of a seventh son could have foreseen that Hearts, on the very last day of the season would be playing for the Championship requiring only one point?' Not even in our worst nightmares did we think this could ever be possible. But here they were – releasing their cringey 'Chunky Chicken Champions' single and making plans to hoist the flag over Tynecastle. However, let's just say the best laid schemes o' mice an' Jambos gang aft a-gley. To re-imagine Archie's famous line: 'Who, on the final day in May, blessed with the second sight of the seventh son of a seventh son could have foreseen that Hearts, in the very last seven minutes of the season would fuck it up quite so badly?'

Suspecting that Easter Road might be the only safe haven to be found away from the screams of jubilant Jambos that day, I had sombrely joined the paltry crowd of 3,500 scattered around the ground ready to draw a line under our own limp league season. Incredibly, come 4.45pm, we would be leaving the stadium with the weight of the world lifted off our shoulders, dancing down St Clair Street in unbridled rapture at Hearts' incredible capitulation.

I never really took a radio to games, as some supporters did in those days (this was pre-smartphone kids!), but that day I thought I might as well hear the bad news confirmed. I was fully resigned to the Jambos winning the league, had made my peace with the world and was grudgingly willing to admit that they had deserved it. Although probably not to the smug bastards who would be rubbing my face in it down the park that night or at school on Monday. Celtic, after all, needed a six-goal swing to prise the title from Gorgie's grubby grasp. I half-listened as the goals started raining down at Love Street, with Celtic taking care of their side of the equation against St Mirren, managed by a certain Alex Miller... of which, more later, much more!

The clock ticked towards the horror of a Hearts title, before from the wee handheld wireless, David Francey's voice became animated and uttered the immortal words: "It's a goal! A goal by Albert Kidd. The unthinkable has happened, with seven minutes left to play it's Dundee 1, Heart of Midlothian 0. What a terrible disappointment this will be for Hearts. Not so much at the last hurdle, but in fact at the winning post, it looks like they might be toppling."

The problem for me was, as soon as I heard this and screamed 'GOAAAAAAL!', I momentarily panicked and wondered whether I had made a terrible mistake, brought on by a bout of blind optimism. If I had got it wrong, then I faced being ripped apart limb by limb by the growing mob of Hibbies who had converged on me and my wee radio, daring to dream that there had somehow been an act of divine intervention at Dens. But my ears had not deceived me, I had made no such mistake, and as I looked beyond my own huddle, I became aware of other fans around me going absolutely barmy in unison as they saluted Albert's amazing slaying of the Jambos. When the Moustachioed Musketeer scored the second, the roof of the recently re-constructed East Terrace nearly came off Easter Road – which would not have been a major surprise given how cheap and nasty it looked.

Hibs, meanwhile, were slumping to a 2-1 defeat right before our eyes. We didn't care, not many of the players seemed to care too much either, but Cowan reveals that the management did not adopt the same attitude. "Obviously, like you guys in the stands, we were hoping Hearts would get beat," he says. "I don't apologise for that – you don't want your city rivals winning the league and lording it over you. I was up against Paul Hegarty, and the roar went round the stadium, and he turned to me and asked: 'Do you think Dundee have scored?' I looked at everyone dancing on the Hibs terracing, and I said: 'Probably!' And then there was another roar a few minutes later, and we thought to ourselves – Hearts must definitely be getting beat. As you know, we lost 2-1, and I had scored a penalty at the end. We came into the dressing room and heard the result from Dens confirmed. We were all in the bath jumping about singing and gloating and Tommy Craig came in and absolutely destroyed us. I won't repeat his language, but he told us in no uncertain terms that we were an effin disgrace, what are you effin celebrating, you are down near the bottom of the league, shut up, get your bath and go home. I look back on that and admit that was brilliant by Tommy – he was spot on. What did we have to celebrate? He was doing it to send a message for the following season. He needed to put us in our place and remind us that we were professionals. We had under-achieved. We had been rotten all season, so he was telling us to get home, get ourselves sorted for next season and improve."

Joe Tortolano, who came on as a sub that day, is not quite so diplomatic. "It was the best feeling in the world," he chuckles. "Albert Kidd is a God among Hibs supporters that is for sure, and it was a shame seeing that wee Jambo sitting on the steps of Dens greeting – brilliant! But it was a weird game to play in at Easter Road. Tommy Craig absolutely lost it afterwards – when he lost it, you dived for cover. It's the ginger hair you see! He could just turn into the Tasmanian devil if you got on the wrong side of him. A brilliant coach, but he had the capacity to be an absolute nutter when he wasn't happy with you. He was right to make that point after that game. Never mind what was going on elsewhere, we had let ourselves down. I think, in that moment, he just took his entire frustration out on us at the way we had under-performed all season."

Supporters also treasure fond memories of the day Albert Kidd was knighted! "Despite losing the game against Dundee United, Hibs fans had a party on the terracing, doing a big conga when the news came through from Dens Park of the ultimate supersub Albert Kidd spoiling Hearts title celebrations," says Andy Blance, while former *Mass Hibsteria* co-editor Sean Allan recalls: "Everybody seemed to be in huddles around somebody with a wireless. Word came through 'Kidd' had scored at Dens. Easter Road fell silent. If Walter Kidd had scored, they fuckers had won the league. Just after Dundee United scored, word came through that it was actually Albert Kidd, a Dundee player nobody outside Dens Park had heard of, that had scored. Hearts were losing... the league! We went wild. Gordon Rae ran from the bench towards the East Terrace waving two fingers in the air. After the game, me and my pal Mark Lally raced to Easter Road for the bus. We got the No1 to Gorgie, where we were both raised as youngsters, and went on a barry pub crawl along Gorgie Road, bringing smiles and cheery dispositions to an otherwise bleak and forlorn place."

Like the 7-0 game for the generation before us, this day, and later the 6-2 game, was our ultimate weapon of choice to batter the Jambos with at every opportunity. And let's face it, it's the gift that keeps giving. However, as we know only too well as we get older and a little wiser, what goes around comes around, and it's safe to say that we have been on the end of our share of savagings from the Hearts fans too. It's what football's all about, rivalry. Can't live with the Jambos, can't live without them, and there's still nothing that gets the juices flowing like a derby. Some of my best mates are on the dark side, but there is mutual respect for our fanaticism, traditions and allegiance. An amusing footnote of the 'Albert Kidd Day' was that my first girlfriend chose that night to cheat on me – with a weasily Jambo. To be fair, he needed a shoulder to cry on more than me!

CHAPTER 8

The **BATTLE** of **EASTER ROAD**

*"It was disgraceful what he did. Souness has even
been glorified for it by some people. It was cowardly
because I had my back to him." – George McCluskey*

Disgraceful. Stupid. Cowardly. The adjectives George 'Beastie' McCluskey
uses to describe the brutal off-the-ball assault on him by Rangers
player-manager Graeme Souness in a frenzied opening fixture of the
1986-87 season, leaving him needing helped off the pitch in agony and requiring
10 stitches in a gaping wound at the side of his knee.

The game would be labelled 'The Battle of Easter Road' in recognition of
the 21-man brawl that broke out in the centre circle after Souness's studs had
ripped into an unsuspecting McCluskey. Glorious sunshine, a 27,000 crowd on
the very first day of the season, a debut red card for the new moustachioed
face of Rangers, an SFA investigation and blanket bans for all involved and –
above all – a famous Hibs victory. Is it any wonder that many Hibbies rate this
as our most memorable game of the 80s? Me included.

I watched on as a spellbound 14-year-old, scarf knotted round my neck
despite the temperature, and proudly wearing the new Umbro Hibs top,
bought from Thompson's Sports in Great Junction Street, with a blank white
band across the chest where the sponsor should be, but which the club had
thus far been unable to secure. Perhaps this summer blockbuster was the
ultimate show-reel needed to persuade would-be backers to form an orderly
queue – as before long, the name P & D Windows would follow Insave as the
sponsor emblazoned across the strip.

If you look at the TV footage, "as I do now and then", you can see me and my
pals in the throng towards the front of a packed East Stand, swept up in the
scenes of wild abandon, as first we celebrate Souness getting his marching

orders, and then Steve Cowan's winning goal. As an added bonus, you can see me clapping approvingly as Alan Sneddon scythes down Rangers winger Ted 'Tin Man' McMinn right on the touchline. Legendary presenter Arthur Montford brought us the must-see highlights the next day, not from the *Scotsport* studio, but from some windswept golf course – as the quirky show tended to do from time to time, swapping fairways and greens for obscure curling rinks in the winter months! In the months that followed, I just about wore out the video tape watching the 'Souness game', which would have been a problem, as I was about the only poor sucker who had a Betamax recorder while my mates all had the more 'normal' VHS. Cheers Dad!

You could not have written the script: European Cup-winning Liverpool legend and Scotland midfield general Graeme Souness, playing his first ever competitive game in Scottish football, in his home city, is sent off just 37 minutes into his debut as player-manager of Rangers. As soon as his shock appointment was announced, Souness wasted no time in shaking Scottish football to its core by bringing some of the biggest stars in the UK to Ibrox. England's teams were banned from European competition at the time as punishment in wake of the Heysel tragedy, so Terry Butcher and Chris Woods became the first of a procession of big-name internationals to head north. Like Souness, Butcher had just returned from the 1986 World Cup in Mexico, and the England captain had last been sighted on a football pitch facing Argentina in the quarter-final, watched by more than 100,000 fans, as Maradona danced his way past him to score the goal voted 'Goal of the Century'.

Alan Rough, who had been an unused substitute in Alex Ferguson's World Cup squad, remembers chatting to the new Rangers manager in Mexico about his grand plans. "We all had a room each and Souness was in the room two along from me. We were sitting outside one day having a beer, because we weren't allowed to leave the complex, and I asked him: 'What are you planning on doing when you go back to Rangers?' He told me he was going to sign Butcher and Woods and a few others and I started laughing. I said: 'You're going to sign WHO?' But then he started signing other guys like Gary Stevens, Ray Wilkins and Trevor Francis – it was absolutely incredible. It affected the whole of Scottish football, financially – because when all these players came up, the wages went up and that had a ripple effect at other clubs. I know that the average wage at Celtic at that time was around £400-500, but when Souness brought all these players up it wasn't long before the wage was £1,200. He made a big difference on the financial side of the game."

His top earner and marquee signing Butcher would find Easter Road just as hostile a cauldron as Estadio Azteca when he arrived in Leith on 9 August 1986. Within minutes of kick-off, Scotland's new record signing looked like a rabbit in the headlights as he struggled to adapt to the vitriol pouring down on him from the home stands, and beside him his manager was fast approaching boiling point. "It was an incredible atmosphere," says Mickey Weir. "I don't think I've experienced an atmosphere quite like that. Even the games I played in at Hampden didn't touch that game, it was just a frenzy of noise – it was electric.

"It was such a big game, you could feel the pressure, especially on them. We all fed off it. It was the type of game that reminds you why you play football. It was a beautiful summer's day, playing against Rangers with Souness just in the door and vowing to win the league and building a team with a core of players who had just played at the World Cup in Mexico a few weeks earlier. The fact that his first game was against Hibs at Easter Road was great and it was such a big game for the club. It was a great day and the atmosphere both sets of supporters generated that day was just unbelievable, there just seemed to be Rangers supporters coming from everywhere. Easter Road was bouncing. I think they came to Easter Road that day just expecting it to all click into place – that it was going to be a stroll in the park for them, but then they very quickly realised it was not going to be like that and that in the Scottish Premier League, you have to earn the right to win games."

Joe Tortolano, playing left-back and sporting a deep summer tan and a tache to rival Souness's that day, says: "The atmosphere was red-hot, you could feel it building up that day, especially when Souness came running out to do his warm-up. You did look over at him swaggering about and think to yourself: 'Fuckin hell, Graeme Souness on the same pitch as us, what is going on? This is unbelievable.' But it was just a case of being professional, psyching yourself up, and making sure you could compete with them, do your own job and hopefully put a good performance in."

Meaty tackles were quickly exchanged between the teams, and both sides signalled their intent to attack. Even early on, this had all the hallmarks of a classic. When Hibs took the lead, the roof nearly came off the East Stand. Stevie Cowan won a tussle with Butcher on the edge of the 18-yard box and slid a pass to the back post, where Stuart Beedie was waiting to pick his spot past a bewildered Woods. You can see McCluskey, following in, in case the effort was saved, running into the back of the net and celebrating in front of the Rangers masses in the Dunbar End. "It was so all hyped up," remembers Alan Sneddon. "It was a huge start to the season for us anyway, playing Rangers at Easter Road, and they had brought in all the English guys because England were banned from Europe at that time. You could see the way Souness was strutting about, he thought he would just dictate things, but we were so fired up for that game and we managed to get our noses in front."

That euphoria was short-lived, and Rangers equalised when Ally McCoist took an outrageous dive, patted himself on the back, and then tucked his ill-gotten penalty past an incensed Alan Rough, who had been booked for his protests. Minutes later Souness joined Roughie in the book, for a hefty, lunging tackle which put Billy Kirkwood on the deck. It looked malicious and pre-meditated rather than mis-timed and it was obvious the Rangers No 4 thought he had a target on his back that day and was willing to get his retaliation in first.

Things went nuclear in the 37th minute. Souness collected a pass in midfield, skipped a tackle from Billy Kirkwood and strode towards the halfway line looking to pick a pass. Hibs' goalscorer Beedie then came flying in at pace on his blind side and robbed him of possession, getting man and ball, hard but fair, and dumping Souness ungraciously to the ground. This was all too much for the disoriented Souness, who first shoved Kirkwood with both hands to the ground, and then as other players appeared on the scene, lifted his studs and aimed a violent slashing kick with force at McCluskey. "Souness just lost it completely. It all happened in a flash," recalls Sneddon. "Stuart Beedie had tackled him and he didn't like it one bit. He got up in a rage and then made a beeline for George McCluskey for some reason and drew his studs down his leg. There was a fair old gash to George's knee and shin that he left, it was a right mess. Souness got carried away with the whole occasion. Managing Rangers, making his debut in his home town, it was just all too much for him to deal with."

Whether McCluskey was the intended target, or this was a case of mistaken identity and Souness had actually meant to put the boot into Beedie, we will never know. "Souness got the wrong player," is Alan Rough's theory, "he had been meaning to try and get Beedie. Graeme told me later that when he was in the Rangers dressing room before the game, someone told him that there was a Hibs player who was going to deliberately target him and when he asked who it was, Beedie's name came up. It was a case of mistaken identity that he got George instead! But you should have seen the state of poor George's leg – there was five holes in the wound."

Joe Tortolano also believes Souness had been fed a story before the game that Hibs were out to get him. "The rumours were that Souness had heard there was going to be a couple of players who were going to try and do him during the game – Kirky and Stuart Beedie," says Joe. "He had obviously come prepared for it."

The touchpaper had been lit, and Woods, Butcher and others hurtled from all corners of the pitch into the melee, as the Hibs players did likewise. While Souness tried to buy himself some time by adjusting his boot and tying his shoelace, the others went at it. A combination of Ally McCoist and Colin West put Mark Fulton on the deck, and Kirkwood, Sneddon and Co stood their ground with giants like Butcher and Dave MacPherson. Even wee Mickey

Weir was in there somewhere! "I was just to the side, and I just let the big boys get on with it," laughs Weir. "I was still just a young guy at the time, just getting used to playing in the first team. But it was a mad game, just crazy! It was everything that was good about football in these days – players absolutely going at it and getting stuck into each other. It makes me laugh comparing matches like that to the modern game where you see boys rolling about feigning injury. In those days, it wasn't just about football, it was a battle and you had to be a man. You had to roll your sleeves up and scrap."

One man was not in the thick of it, Alan Rough, who chose to watch the Wild West-style dust-up from the safety of the six-yard box in front of The Cowshed. Rough insists that his earlier yellow card – rather than being 'chicken' – prevented him from joining the melee. "Peter Martin still winds me up about that, saying I was the only chicken – the only one that never got involved in the barney. But he never realised WHY I didn't get involved," says Rough. "The truth is that having been booked, if I had got involved in the free-for-all then I would have been off the park, especially the way the referee was handling it. Not that I would have got involved anyway – it would have been too far for me to go running away up there to the centre circle!"

Tortolano says: "Everyone got involved, 21 players in there, apart from big Alan Rough – who was leaning on the goalpost watching. I remember at half-time, Tommy Craig saying how great it was that we had all stuck together and fought our battle as a team, and if we stuck together in the second half we would definitely go on and win the game, and big Roughie piped up: 'I think you're all very immature.' One or the two of the lads were saying to Roughie: 'Where the fuck were you?' and calm as you like he said: 'There's nothing to be upset about.' He was so laid back it was frightening, not a care in the world."

Gordon Chisholm, who was not so hesitant about joining the fray, says: "I knew quite a few of the boys in the Rangers team that day from my time playing down south, but that was an absolute cauldron that day – the crowd at Easter Road and the adrenaline was something special. The whole thing with Souness was incredible. It was handbags... there was no-one actually properly fighting, the only person that didn't get booked for that afterwards – and it won't surprise you – was big Roughie, who stayed in his goals and let us all get on with it. He was just standing there laughing. I think there were more people in there trying to break it up rather than start anything. It had got very explosive and most of us were trying to pull everyone apart. For me, there was no malice in it, just two teams going at it and trying to look after their team-mates."

Meanwhile, Hibs physio Tam McNiven had wasted no time in racing on to the pitch to attend to the stricken McCluskey. McNiven, wearing his usual flat cap, took one look at the blood dripping down from a wound next to George's knee on to his white sock, helped him unsteadily to his feet, then wrapped an arm round his waist and another round his shoulder to help walk him over to the tunnel. Meanwhile, Mike Delaney wasted no time in showing Souness the inevitable red card and his walk of shame began, uncomfortably almost side by side with his victim and Tam McNiven, who were heading for the treatment room. A dazed Souness shook his head in a mix of embarrassment and disbelief, and was stalked by Kirkwood, who left a few choice words ringing in his ears as he trudged off. "It was disgraceful what he did," McCluskey tells me, 35 years on. "He has even been glorified for it by some people. It was cowardly because I was talking to the ref at the time and had my back to him. I didn't feel any pain but could see the blood. It felt more like he'd sliced it open and I've always thought that maybe his studs had been sharpened. I remember big Billy walking with me as I went off, giving him a hard time. He tried to come into the dressing room to apologise but the wee groundsman wouldn't let him and sent him away with a flea in his ear. I was taken to ERI for stitches."

It also looked like Colin West – a big dumpling of a striker and one of the least successful Ibrox recruits – was about to be sent off along with Souness, but he escaped with a yellow. The TV replays suggested that it was McCoist rather than West who had decked Fulton with a sneaky punch. With their player-manager gone, Rangers were reeling and Ian Durrant was also lucky not to be sent off for putting Weir up in the air with a crunching tackle in front of the dug-outs. Mickey laughs at the memory of that challenge now: "That was just part of the game – it was ferocious and you had to be prepared to take a few hefty tackles along the way. It was brilliant though. I couldn't imagine those tackles being accepted now, half the players would be sin die for life! You just wouldn't get away with it now, but for me that was real football and the supporters used to love it. I'm pretty sure the older supporters who watched football in the 80s would say the same, and they enjoyed that physical contest. It wasn't so much tactical, it was just blood and thunder and getting wired in.

"That's not to say it was all about who was the strongest physically, there was loads of skill around in the Scottish league then. I played with a lot of unbelievably good and talented players during my time at Hibs. We used to be playing against teams like Aberdeen and Dundee United, who were getting to European finals, then you had the Old Firm and other teams like Hearts, St Mirren and Dundee who were all good at that time. But Souness coming in changed the dynamic. Rangers started chucking money around."

Weir got up and got on with it, as players did back then, and Hibs scented more than the blood running down Beastie's leg. The winning goal arrived shortly before half-time when Kirkwood fed substitute Willie Irvine (mark 2) on the left, and the former Stirling man sent a daisy-cutting diagonal ball across goal, for poacher Stevie Cowan to prod it home before galloping off on a gleeful goal celebration, arms thrust aloft, all the way to the halfway line in front of a jubilant East Enclosure.

"I do some after-dinner speaking and I still talk about the game, the Battle of Easter Road," says Cowan. "For me, before we even came out that day, the noise coming from the fans was unbelievable. Running out of the tunnel was quite a sight. You saw three sides of the ground totally green and white, then the red, white and blue at the Rangers end. The sky was piercing blue, the grass was lush green – it was just a real peak of all the senses. It was a vision. As for the game itself, it goes without saying it soon turned into a battle. John Blackley gave us the easiest team talk ever. Referring to all their new signings he said, well this lot think they have come up the road to hammer you 6 or 7 nothing, what are you going to do about it? And that's all he really needed to say. We just looked at each other and said: 'C'mon then, we are going to go toe-to-toe with you. We're not scared of Butcher and Souness and whoever else you bring in.' It just shows you what can be done when you're fired up in the right way. It was a fantastic occasion and a great memory. To imagine a game of that physicality being allowed to be played for 90 minutes today... it just wouldn't happen. The challenges, the kicking, the elbowing, there was all sorts going on. It was a fantastic game and I'm just glad we won it."

Gordon Chisholm agrees: "It was a good physical contest. The truth was that the Rangers team that day was bursting with top-quality players and it was our job to compete with them – and if it upset them then too bad, that was it. That was the gameplan – to get out there and work as hard as we possibly could, get in round about them and if it upset them, as it obviously did, then no problem. And we got a great result by doing that."

Eddie May says: "I think Rangers thought they could just turn up with their players costing multi-millions, and win. They were good players, make no mistake, some of them had just come straight to this game from the World Cup, but for Hibs to give them a game and beat them was incredible. I think most of the supporters in the ground that day will say the same – it was absolutely phenomenal. We had just done pre-season and I got pulled aside the day before the game and was told that I'd be playing and that my role was to try to go and stop Graeme Souness having an influence on the game. It was an enjoyable game to play in, and very high-tempo – it was always great play-ing against those type of players. We proved again that day we could rise to any occasion and be competitive."

Blackley fondly remembers the victory, but not the tackle which left him without McCluskey for weeks. "They had spent huge money on the best of players in England and Hibs' performance was out of this world against them," says Sloop. "We showed the desire. The lads battled and played some really good football to win that day. But when you see an incident like that, the studs over the top on to McCluskey's leg, it doesn't endear you to football."

Certainly, the tabloids went to town on this 'shame game' in the days, weeks and even months that followed. They were positively frothing when the SFA slapped retrospective yellow cards on all involved and warned both clubs about their behaviour. Appeals were lodged, and while most were rejected, the SFA later relented and removed the cautions from Alan Rough, Mark Fulton and the unfortunate victim McCluskey. Big George, who lived through in the west, became a target for mindless threats and abuse from Rangers 'fans', who somehow held him responsible for the self-combustion of their new Fuhrer. "Graeme Souness had come back to his own country with the reputation of being the man who had seen it all and done it all in England and Italy, but I was surprised he allowed himself to get carried away by a game against Hibs," said George in a 2002 interview with the *Daily Record*. "I couldn't believe the incident because I didn't even have the ball at the time. But Souness must have had something sharp on his boot because he sliced my leg open.

"I needed 10 stitches inserted in my wound and I wasn't prepared for the explosion of publicity that followed the game. The pressure on me was so great I had to move out of my home and temporarily leave my wife and family to seek refuge with a friend. My privacy was being disrupted by people calling to ask if I had any intention of suing Souness over the tackle. But the outcry was so great the callers who drove me from my home forgot to ask one thing – how my leg was. I was put out of the game for a month and he got a one-match ban from the SFA for what I still consider to be an act of stupidity on his part."

In the same *Daily Record* article, Alan Rough claims, "I had a drink with Souey afterwards in the players' lounge and he was totally unconcerned by the collision with George", but Souness has since given a number of interviews where he lays his shame and regret bare. In one, he said: "I've never felt so alone. I'd let my Dad down, humiliated him in his own street. That was my lowest moment in football." And in another, with *FourFourTwo*, he said: "My experience from Liverpool and also being a foreigner playing in Italy was that other teams treated it as their cup final when they played against you, so I was prepared for what lay in store. However, it was far more intense in Scotland. I was regarded as some big-head coming back to Scotland to show people how it was done, but that was never my intention. Of course that first day is something I would like to change. Getting sent off wasn't the best of starts – especially as my Dad was watching."

Whether you believe Souness's contrition or not, as the song says... we don't care what the animals say, what the hell do we care? For we only know that there's gonnae be a show, and the Edinburgh Hibees will be there!

Those that were there still marvel at what they saw themselves. Hibbie Alan

Woodhouse recalls: "The 2-1 victory over Rangers on the opening day of the 1986/87 season was mainly memorable for the sending-off of Souness on his debut, but I can clearly recall 35 years on just how febrile the atmosphere was in the sun-drenched stadium that day. I was with my pal in the old East Terrace and it was absolutely jam-packed, with a feeling within that things could tip over into something wild and uncontrollable at any second. When I left the ground that day, I realised someone had poured Bovril over my jacket, much to the amusement of my mate. I stank all the way home, but it was worth it. And looking back now, it seems like a nice metaphor – it was meaty and hot!"

Graham Ewing, the *Mass Hibsteria* editor, says: "The game of the decade has to be the Rangers game at Easter Road in August 1986 when Souness made his debut. The hype during the week leading up to the game was off the scale, with the media fully expecting an easy Rangers victory – nothing changes, eh? The game was mental, tackles flying in at all heights, with a dose or two of actual bodily assault added in for good measure. Justice was served courtesy of Stuart Beedie and Steve Cowan with a McCoist dive worthy of Greg Louganis giving Rangers an undeserved penalty. We headed back to the Beau Brummel in Hanover Street, where I worked at the time, after the game and celebrated in fine style!"

Mike Burns, the 'Raving Reporter' for *Hibs Monthly* and *Mass Hibsteria*, also highlights this game as the most memorable of the decade. "Even as I walked to the game with my mate, there was an atmosphere that you could feel in the air which got more intense the closer we got to Easter Road," says MB. "Any 'normal' Hibs v Rangers game is not for the faint hearted, but this was extra special, extra intense, this was the debut of Graeme Souness for that lot. For me personally, it was a combination of two things coming together that I, to put it mildly, had the greatest of dislikes for, Rangers and Souness – a man to this day that I still can't even stand the sight of.

"On approach to the ground, there seemed to be more than the usual expected amount of visiting fans, and after we took our usual season-ticket seats in the old North Stand there were sounds of a commotion downstairs (in the Enclosure). Next thing we knew, there was a smallish invasion of unwelcome 'guests' clad in non-green colours. They were quite amazingly ushered up to the back of the stand by the old volunteer steward, before they were eventually escorted out of the stand and away to safety by the police.

"The game had started but gone largely unnoticed by most of us in the North stand, but as we settled down, things on the park were kicking off, and that man Souness was at the heart of it. A quite despicable and brutal attack on George McCluskey resulted in Souness rightly being sent off. One who got off lightly in my eyes was the so-called cheeky chappy Ally McCoist, who sneaked round the battling pack to lay a punch on Mark Fulton, then ran for cover behind his team-mates. In a decade of disappointment, this was right up there as one of the highlights. I remember many years later Terry Butcher was asked for his recollection of that game. He replied along the lines of: 'I have played in some of the biggest games and biggest stadiums in the world for England and in England but never have I ever experienced an atmosphere like I did that day.'"

Looking back, Hibs may have dealt so comfortably with facing the so-called stars in Rangers' side that day as a result of a shrewd strategy developed by John Blackley – to play the occasional glamour friendly against high-profile opponents. Blackley did this in the hope that it wouldn't be long before he was able to lead the team back into Europe, and it would give them some valuable experience of facing top-class players. In early 1985, Hibs beat Moscow Dynamo (as they used to be known) 2-0 at Easter Road, and then followed that up in December with a 4-2 win against a Feyenoord side that included Johnny Rep – best known to Scotland fans for thundering a long-range strike past Alan Rough in the World Cup match made famous for Archie Gemmill's wonder-goal. A few days before facing Souness and Co, Hibs first faced Seville, managed by Jock Wallace, losing 2-1, then produced a tremendous performance in a 4-1 win over Chelsea at Easter Road, in which the new Willie Irvine scored a hat-trick to overshadow the returning Gordon Durie and his new side.

Durie may have been put in the shade that day, but his loss was soon felt by the team and his old partner in the forward line, Steve Cowan. "It was a bit of a change for us when Jukebox was away," he admits. "We all knew it was coming and I think the club got 400 grand, which was great money in those days. You couldn't turn that kind of money down, so he was always going to go sooner rather than later. It was disappointing but to be honest I didn't give it much thought other than wishing Jukebox well. I got on really well with Gordon, still do, and he was away to carve his career out."

As sweet as the opening-day success of beating Rangers was, it was starting to look like a flash in the pan, and before long Hibs' frailties were exposed. A new 'Famous Five' – crudely coined by the tabloids – turned out to be anything but! Only George McCluskey could be considered a success of a quintet of new recruits who were paraded at the start of the season. The other four: Billy Kirkwood, Willie Irvine, Stuart Beedie, and the frankly fat and useless Mark Caughey, failed to make any meaningful contributions. As Blackley chopped and changed his side in an effort to find the right formula, it would be a full two months after the Rangers win before they recorded their next league victory. Hibs started to sink down the league and the pressure started to grow on the manager.

"A few new players came in, and there was a bit of a transition, but they didn't gel in the way it was hoped, and it just didn't happen at all that season,"

Hibs chairman Tom Hart pulled off a stunning coup when he lured George Best to Easter Road in 1979. The maroon tie was soon forgiven!

Best, the legendary former Manchester United man, put thousands on the gate, and got on brilliantly with his new team-mates, but he failed to stop Hibs being relegated and would be on his travels again in 1980.

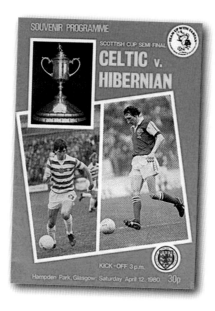

Eddie Turnbull took Hibs to the 1979 Scottish Cup final, but his attempts to do the same in 1980 ended in a crushing 5-0 defeat to Celtic - his final game in charge.

With the club heading down to the
First Division, they were thrashed 5-0
at Easter Road by Aberdeen as Alex
Ferguson clinched his first league title.

After Turnbull came his Famous Five team-mate
Willie Ormond, who had not long been sacked by
Hearts. Ill-health would limit Ormond's tenure and in
came an altogether different style of manager –
Bertie Auld, the third Hibs manager in six months.

Bertie Auld unveils his backroom team of John Lambie, Pat Quinn and Tom McNiven, with Hibs secretary Cecil Graham overseeing the paperwork.

Bertie meets his new squad – already a lack of smiles and enthusiasm appears evident!

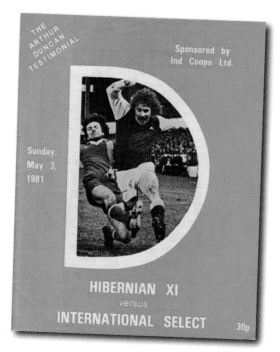

Hibs' second highest appearance holder (behind only Gordon Smith) Arthur Duncan is rewarded with a testimonial, and Jim McArthur would get the same honour soon after – although no programme was produced for his game.

IMAGINE . . .
PELE IN A HIBS' JERSEY

Edinburgh businessman Kenny McLean, chairman of the Testimonial Committee, wanted a superstar to appear today and, after consultation with Hibs' chairman Tom Hart, an approach was made to the legendary Brazilian, Pele, through George Best.

A five-figure cheque was dangled as bait for a one-match stand in Hibs' colours but Pele, as famous for his white suits as his immense skill, couldn't be hired due to previous engagements on a world tour.

Just like Mohammed Ali, the great Brazilian is always in demand for personal appearances despite having retired from serious competition.

He quit after a spell with New York Cosmos though it was in his years with Santos and Brazil that Pele won everything in sight.

Only the American fixture list prevented George Best from flying over today. Last night the Irishman was needed to play against San Diego abd that match wrecked his intention to fulfil a promise to Arthur.

However, there are plenty other big-name players on call to make it a memorable afternoon for all concerned.

Not content with his George Best signing, Tom Hart also tried - and failed - to get Pele in a Hibs shirt.

Out of the First Division at the first attempt under Auld, Hibs line up for their first season back in the big time and get up to some hi-jinks during their media day.

Fans catch up with George Best when Hibs headed to California to face San Jose Earthquakes on their 1981 end-of-season tour.

The Hibs group pose by the poolside before heading to Haiti to face their national team in a game which had to be abandoned after a free-for-all.

Pictures: Alan Hart

Craig Paterson, perhaps wondering 'what's it like to be a Hun', was vilified by Hibs fans for moving to Ibrox, but there were mitigating factors.

Ricky Hill made the trip from the Caribbean to Edinburgh in 1981 hoping to win a deal and become Hibs' first black player, but the coldest winter in 100 years thwarted his chances. I tracked Ricky down to his home in Bermuda where he was delighted to re-establish his Hibs connection.

In the absence of European football and following the installation of undersoil heating, glamour friendlies became the norm at Easter Road.

Hibs entertain Ron Atkinson's Manchester United on Boxing Day 1981.

George Best is reunited with Ally MacLeod and co as NASL team San Jose Earthquakes pay a visit.

The old Easter Road terracing, including 'no man's land', provides the backdrop as Craig Paterson, Jim McArthur and Alan Sneddon try to keep Celtic at bay.

The sudden death of Tom Hart hit the club and a memorial trophy was staged in his memory, with Snoddy collecting the trophy from Jock Stein after a 1-0 win against Hearts.

Kenny Waugh would be the
man to take over as chairman.

S.O.S. - aka Stanton, O'Rourke
and Stewart - brought the feelgood
factor back to Easter Road.

As Pat got familiar behind his desk, young fans flocked to Easter Road for an Open Day.

Hibs line up for the 82-83 season, with Fishers Garage as their new sponsor.

BACK ROW (left to right): Ally Brazil, Gordon Rae, Peter Welsh, Jim McArthur, Bobby Thomson, Ralph Callachan, Gary Murray. FRONT ROW: Derek Rodier, Arthur Duncan, Erich Schaedler, Jackie McNamara, Alan Sneddon, Jim Turnbull, Bobby Flavell, Billy Jamieson.

Erich Schaedler – a huge inspiration and example to young team-mates. News of his devastating death followed three years later.

Jackie McNamara shows typical
fighting spirit against his old club
Celtic as future Hibs captain Murdo
MacLeod says his piece.

The arrival of Alan Rough in November 1982 proved to be a great signing.

The fanzine Hibs Monthly was born in 1987, and evolved into Mass Hibsteria, still making the occasional cameo for special occasions.

By the 1983-84 season, prolific
striker Willie Irvine could not stop
scoring, but other shortcomings in
the team were starting to surface.

A conveyor belt of talent was coming through the ranks at Easter Road, and it wasn't long before this crop of youngsters burst on to the scene in the first team, including John Collins, Paul Kane, and Mickey Weir.

Kano would get his first goal in a game against Dundee, re-arranged when fog cut short the original fixture.

Callum Milne, pictured as a youth, came through the ranks at Hibs, but would be frustrated by injuries... and managers!

Gordon 'Geebsy' Hunter also broke through and would become a popular mainstay of the Hibs team.

The 1983-84 season saw the renewal of top-flight Edinburgh
derby fixtures. A 3-2 win for Hearts at Tynecastle in the first
clash sadly set the tone for much of the decade.

JACKIE McNAMARA TESTIMONIAL

SUNDAY, AUGUST 5, 1984

50p

HIBERNIAN v. NEWCASTLE UTD.

Kick-off 3 p.m.

Sponsored by the TOMMY YOUNGER BAR

A well-earned testimonial for Jackie Mac, which included a glamour game against a Newcastle team featuring Chris Waddle and Peter Beardsley.

Picture: David Cartledge

John Blackley would hang up his boots and fill the vacancy left by Pat Stanton, when the Hibs legend quit with the club in relegation trouble.

John Blackley gets
his man – as Gordon
'Jukebox' Durie signs.

Alan Rough, a study
of concentration and
professionalism.

Another true pro, Ally 'Benny'
Brazil, celebrated his day in the
sun – a hat-trick against Celtic
in a thumping 6-3 win when
the clubs got together to play
a snap friendly at Easter Road
when the undersoil
heating beat the frost.

Steve Cowan is welcomed to Hibs from Aberdeen
by John Blackley and Tommy Craig and went on
to form a deadly strike duo with Gordon Durie.

1985 new kit promo: Ally Brazil, Gordon
Chisholm, Joe McBride, Gordon Durie,
Steven Cowan and Colin Harris.

John Colquhoun is the meat in the sandwich as Geebsy and Alan Sneddon get wired in.

Three Gordons – Hunter, Rae and Chisholm – gang up on Ally McCoist as the Rangers forward strikes a familiar diver's pose in the electrifying 1985 Skol Cup semi-final.

Some of the games on the cup run were played while Easter Road underwent a transformation, with the East Terrace becoming a covered enclosure and Justice Popplewell paying a visit as part of his UK-wide safety review.

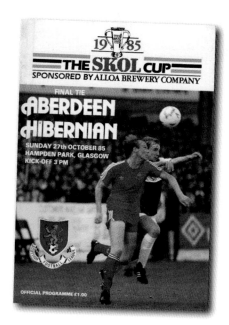

All good things come to an end: Aberdeen were just too strong for John Blackley's Hibs in the 1985 Skol League Cup final at Hampden, ending an amazing cup run.

Hibs defeated Dutch side Feyenoord
in a December 1985 friendly.

John Blackley was fond of arranging friendlies against top-class opponents,
and arranged two games against Sevilla, then managed by Jock Wallace.

In 1986 Hibs edged one of the greatest Scottish Cup ties ever seen at Easter Road – a surreal 4-3 victory over Celtic, who they had also knocked out of the Skol Cup that same season. Eddie May came off the bench to grab a dramatic last-gasp winner.

The not-so Famous Five. Only George McCluskey could be considered a success among this batch of summer signings in 1986. Mark Caughey, Wille Irvine mark 2, Stuart Beedie and Billy Kirkwood did not stay long.

McCluskey would go on to become a cult hero, with the 'Beastie Branch' supporters' bus named after him.

Kirkwood at least left his
mark on a derby or two.

Terry Butcher went from trying to catch Maradona in the Hand of God game in Mexico, to the white-hot atmosphere of Easter Road when Rangers came calling with their new manager Graeme Souness for the explosive opening game of the 1986-87 season.

Picture: Mark Leech/Offside Sports Photography

It's all too much for Souness on his debut as player-manager, in his home city. First, he picks up a booking for clogging Billy Kirkwood...

... then minutes later Souness loses his mind and
attacks George McCluskey, resulting in a red card, a
free-for-all and stitches in a gashed leg for his victim.

Hibs' sponsorship deals were in a state of flux in the mid-80s. Fisher's, then Insave, then P & D Windows – a deal celebrated in typically sexist style!

From the dazzling smiles of models, a more sombre tone was struck with the arrival of Alex Miller as manager in December 1986. He had plenty to be serious about as he took charge of his first game – a 0-0 draw at home against Rangers.

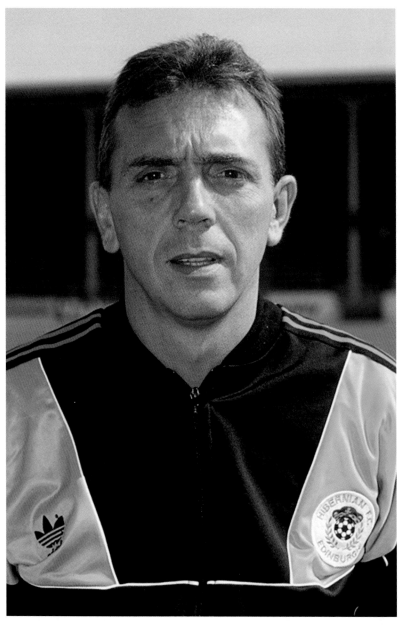

Miller would spend a decade in charge, win the 1991
League Cup for Hibs, and divide opinion along the way.

Miller soon set about bringing in reinforcements, Dougie Bell and Graham Mitchell becoming his first signings.

The cool and dependable midfielder Neil Orr arrived from West Ham.

Gary Mackay and JC tussle in the Edinburgh derby. We were still waiting for our first league win over them in years, but that was about to change.

1987 was a year of change and transformation at Hibs. In came new chairman David Duff and managing director Jim Gray.

Duff and Gray soon laid down a marker by
splashing out £300,000 to bring Andy Goram
in from Oldham to take over from Alan Rough.

The 1987-88 season began in glorious
sunshine and a 3-3 draw at Dunfermline...

...but our brightest day would be on 17 October when we finally beat Hearts thanks to goals from Paul Kane and Eddie May. At last, at last, at last! Champagne flowed in the Hibs dressing room after that one, provided by chairman Duff.

The notorious Hibs v Celtic match in
November 1987, which resulted in 45
people being taken to hospital when a CS
Cannister was chucked from the Celtic end
into the Hibs terracing. Incredibly, no-one
was seriously hurt. Equally incredibly, the
game was not abandoned and Celtic were
allowed to close out a hollow 1-0 win.

Fans packed into Easter Road in 1988 to pay tribute to Gordon Rae, a tremendous servant to Hibs. His testimonial against Manchester United took on an unexpected twist when Joe T (pictured in his infamous Electric Beach ad) went bananas and got himself sent off for halving Gordon Strachan early in what was meant to be a friendly – incurring the full force of the Alex Ferguson hairdryer!

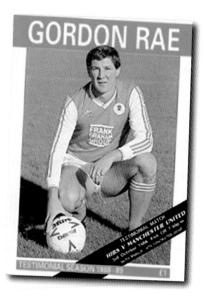

Hibs looking the part in 1988 and still
good value at £40 for a season ticket.
I'm now nearer to OAP than a junior!

The headline signing Duff and Gray craved was delivered in style – in the shape of Barcelona star Steve Archibald.

A complex, controversial character but a hell of a player, Archibald is fondly remembered by Hibs fans for his displays in a green and white shirt – none more so than his match-winning performance against Hearts in November 1988.

Hibs lost the Scottish Cup
semi-final against Celtic on
16 April 1989 – 24 hours after
the disaster at Hillsborough
had numbed the country.

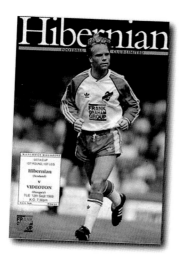

Hibs qualified for the 1989 UEFA Cup, ending an 11-year wait for European football to return to Easter Road, and emphatically beat Videoton home and away.

Houchy with the flag he was thrown by supporters at the end of the famous 3-0 win in Hungary.

Houchy missed a penalty in a goalless
first leg against RFC Liege.

The second leg ended in extra-time heartache in Belgium,
but thousands of Hibs fans had the time of their lives.

There may be trouble ahead: Jim Gray and David Duff prepare to float the club on the Stock Exchange – a move that led to Wallace Mercer's nonsensical merger bid in 1990.

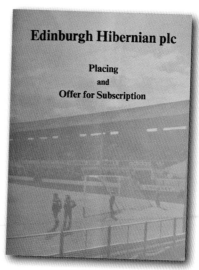

Edinburgh Hibernian plc

Placing
and
Offer for Subscription

Copies of this prospectus, together with the documents specified herein, have been delivered to the Registrar of Companies for registration.

This prospectus includes particulars given in compliance with the Regulations of the Council of The Stock Exchange for the purpose of giving information relating to Edinburgh Hibernian plc and its subsidiary. The directors of Edinburgh Hibernian plc have taken all reasonable care to ensure that the facts stated herein are true and accurate in all material respects and that there are no other material facts the omission of which would make misleading any statement herein whether of fact or of opinion. All the directors accept responsibility accordingly.

Application has been made to the Council of The Stock Exchange for the ordinary share capital, issued and now being issued, of Edinburgh Hibernian plc to be traded on the Third Market. It is emphasised that no application has been made for these securities to be admitted to listing or to be dealt in on the Unlisted Securities Market.

Transactions in the ordinary shares of Edinburgh Hibernian plc will be effected in accordance with the Rules and Regulations governing the Third Market. This investment may carry a high degree of risk.

Edinburgh Hibernian plc
(Incorporated in Scotland under the Companies Act 1985 No. 112772)

Placing and Offer for Subscription

by

CGS Securities Limited

and

Stirling Hendry & Co.

of 3,650,000 ordinary shares at 55p per share
payable in full on application

The Application List for the ordinary shares now being offered for subscription will open at 8pm on 14 October 1988 and may be closed at any time thereafter. The procedure for application and the application form are set out at the end of this prospectus.

Share Capital

Authorised			Issued following the Offer	
£	No.		£	No.
240,000	12,000,000	Ordinary shares of 2p each	146,000	7,300,000

The ordinary shares now being placed and offered for subscription will rank pari passu with the existing ordinary shares.

Indebtedness

At the close of business on 16 September 1988 the Group had outstanding secured bank overdrafts of £912,000, secured loans of £917,000 (of which £500,000 will be repaid immediately following the Offer), hire purchase commitments of £30,000 and outstanding mortgages of £24,000.

Save as disclosed above and apart from intra-group indebtedness and borrowings at that date the Group did not have any loan capital (including term loans) outstanding or credited but unissued, or any other borrowings or indebtedness in the nature of borrowings, including bank overdrafts, liabilities under acceptances (other than normal trade bills) or acceptance credits, mortgages, charges, hire purchase commitments, guarantees or material contingent liabilities other than that disclosed in paragraph 6 of Part 7.

Hibs had some classy strips throughout the 80s and into the 90s. Paul McGrath gets his hands on Gareth Evans' away shirt during a friendly at Aston Villa in 89.

The 'Planet Saturn' crest sits behind JC, Torto and our devoted celebrity fans The Proclaimers.

Hibernian Sign The Proclaimers!

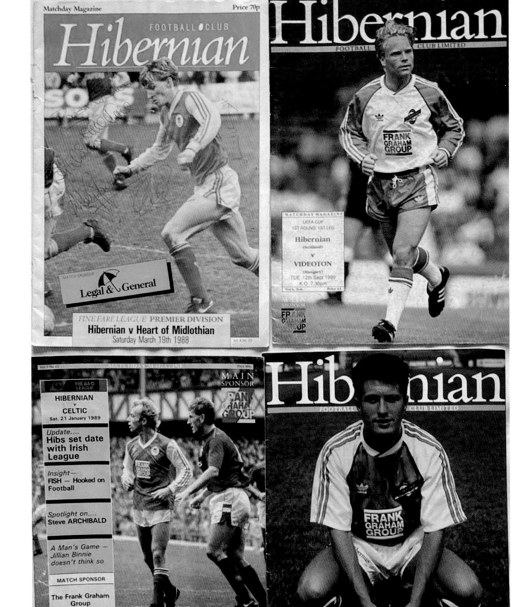

The arrival of Duff and Gray saw a transformation in the club programme,
going from the traditional format to snazzy 'matchday magazines'

says Cowan. "I think 12 games in, I had to get another knee operation, so I missed three or four months of the season. That was my fourth operation, because I had already had three during my time at Aberdeen. I still don't know how I passed the physical examination at Hibs and then later at Motherwell because I was told to stop playing. It took me three or four months to overcome that. Soon we started to struggle, for whatever reason. There was a sense that things had gone wrong and the season hadn't happened for us the way we had hoped. With Jukebox away and me out for three or four months, then there's a whole chunk of goals that is missing. The transition was difficult, particularly for the new players."

After a run of just one win in seven, Blackley quit. Tommy Craig stepped into a caretaker role, and when he failed to win any of the four matches he was in charge, he too was gone. One of the senior pros in the squad, Alan Sneddon says: "Coaching-wise they had good ideas, but the man-management side was a bit more tricky at times. I think that was because they had not long stopped playing themselves, it was maybe a little bit harder to man-manage a group of players. Sloop could be quite a hothead and probably looking back on it he would admit that there were certain situations that he might have handled differently – but that's all about experience and learning, he was a young manager at the time."

A philosophical Blackley adamantly refuses to blame anyone for the poor run of form which cost him his job. "I just wish I could have done better than I did," he says candidly. "I know we did well in a lot of cup ties and enjoyed some special nights, but I would love to have won us a trophy – for the fans. You do need a bit of help along the way, and when you start selling your better players, you are losing your impact – that's maybe me putting an excuse up, and I don't want to be making excuses, but the loss of Durie hurt us. I did the right thing for me, and I did the right thing for Hibs by leaving. It was painful but I had to go. I was honoured to get the chance though.

"It was a tough season. Although I wasn't getting as much help from the board as I would have liked, I was bringing more pressure on myself than the board were. My relationship with the board wasn't bad at all. I would say, if anything, they maybe could have delved into their pockets a little more to help us along the way, but Kenny Waugh was a really nice man and he had his heart in the right place towards the club. But at the end of the day, he was a bookie, and bookies are never too far away from the odds. It was my job to do better. I didn't make a great job of it, and I don't blame Kenny Waugh or anyone else. It was a hard time for Hibs.

"I had always been a Hibs man and I wanted the best for my club, and when it came to the crunch I just felt I was not delivering the best for the support. I didn't think I was doing as well as I should. It's a lot of pressure going back to the club that you love, as the manager – it's a different feeling. You feel under pressure to do that wee bit more. I just felt it was time for me to step aside and let someone else come in."

CHAPTER 9

HERE COMES the MILLER MAN

"After my first game, I took all the underpants home. We had no-one to wash them. My wife said to me 'I hope this is not going to be a regular Saturday night tradition!'" – Alex Miller

Has a manager ever divided the Hibs support and players as much as Alex Miller? At the time of writing, he is one of only two men alive who has led Hibernian to glory in a cup final and his decade in charge at Easter Road should surely be interpreted as a success... shouldn't it? Two cup finals, two European adventures, and some inspired signings can certainly be put in the plus column. But the feeling lingers that he stayed too long, and never fully embraced the romance and traditions of a club built on attacking football and entertainment. Mediocre, dour and over-serious are widely held perceptions of a man who undoubtedly ate, slept and breathed football 24/7. As editor and contributor to the fanzine *Hibs Monthly/Mass Hibsteria*, I was personally responsible for hurling some brickbats in his direction back in the day. Some of it was justified, some of it not. Time has softened my attitude to the man we dubbed Lexo, but what about the man himself – has he mellowed down the years and, looking back, was he just misunderstood?

I'm about to find out after he agrees to be interviewed for the book, face-to-face after the lockdown restrictions have finally been relaxed. I should never have doubted him really, as even in the fanzine days he would front up and agree to meet us in person to 'discuss' our views and, occasionally, scathing criticism of his performance – as did the chairman who proved to be his No 1 fan, Dougie Cromb. Old Dougie would wait for us in his office, fanzine open on desk, with any offending paragraphs marked out in yellow highlighter pen to be dissected and debated during our showdowns.

I meet Alex in the clubhouse of his local golf course, where he spends a fair chunk of his spare time, once family commitments and his self-confessed fixation with football are factored in. What follows is a fascinating – even thrilling – 90 minutes, with not a single question ducked or fudged. And while I still think there were times between 1986 and 1996 that he deserved to be held accountable, I at least come away full of respect and admiration for the man, having heard another side to the Alex Miller story, straight from the horse's mouth. Jeez, he even LOLd a few times! A Chuckle Brother he is not, though, and when it comes to me shaking his hand and thanking him for his time and insight, my earlier bold thoughts of asking him to pose with me for a selfie wither, and I bottle it in fear that he might just rip my head off!

After John Blackley had departed the Hibs post in 1986, and caretaker Tommy Craig had attempted and failed to steady the ship, chairman Kenny Waugh decided to turn to one of the brightest managers in Scotland, the former Rangers full-back Miller, who had been working minor miracles at St Mirren. Ambitious from the word go, Miller wanted to climb the ladder, and saw Hibs as the challenge he was ready for. From day one, he was curious to understand why such a big club in Scotland was mired in such difficulties.

"I saw potential. It was a big club with great traditions," says Miller. "They always had good players and a good team when I played against them. But as an outsider looking in, when you see a club go down and down like Hibs had in the 80s, you ask 'what's happening?' You wonder whether there are divisions within the dressing room. When I got there, I found it was all a bit disjointed. I got appointed on the Friday, a couple of weeks before Christmas, and they played Rangers in my first game on the Saturday, a 0-0 draw. It was actually wee Jim Rodger, the journalist, who first phoned me whilst I was at St Mirren and asked me: 'Would you be interested in the Hibs job?' I said: 'Yes, I would consider it.' So a meeting was arranged for me to go through and meet Kenny Waugh. I met him, and the deal was done."

Miller was given a rousing reception from the fans when he stood on the pitch before that draw with Rangers, scarf aloft, and while he was happy to have made the move, he soon realised how disorganised and under-resourced the club was. "It was quite funny because immediately after the Rangers game, we had to go and play Sevilla in a friendly that had been arranged for the Monday night. Jock Wallace was their manager and when he arrived at the airport to greet the Hibs party and saw me, he said: 'What are YOU doing here?' I went: 'I'm the manager of Hibs.' He hadn't heard, such had been the speed of the move from St Mirren. We had to leave on the Sunday to go and play against Sevilla and I said to wee Danny Lennon, who was on the groundstaff, 'where is all the equipment kept?' He took me to this cage and there was nothing, apart from some blue and yellow socks – all the goods had been snaffled! Excuse my French but I said to Danny 'what the fuck is going on here, are you at it?' But he went: 'No boss.' So after the game on the Saturday, I took all the underpants home – centres we called them. We had no-one to take them and wash them, so I had to take them home to get cleaned. My wife said to me, 'I hope this is not going to be a regular Saturday night tradition!' I also found there was no physio – Tom McNiven had just retired and there was nobody, which gave me an indication of how disorganised it was.

"That was in December 86 and by March 87 I had moved through to Edinburgh. I am really hands-on and I didn't take days off. I worked morning, noon and night. I wanted to be around all the training sessions with the young kids, to work with them and help them develop. So, I was leaving home at first at 6.45 from Bearsden, to be at my desk for about 8.15 and do all my paperwork before the players came in. Leaving home at that time every morning was a strain and if we had a night game, it would be after midnight before I would get back home, it was killing me, and I said we need to move."

Waugh had at least promised to back Miller in the transfer market, and by New Year, there were three new faces – Graham Mitchell from Hamilton, Dougie Bell from Rangers and future Skol League Cup hero Tommy McIntyre from Aberdeen. Later in the year, when the club was under new ownership, Neil Orr would be recruited from West Ham. "It was a hectic time for us, because in the New Year I remember playing Falkirk at Brockville and if they had beaten us, we would have been in a real serious position down near the bottom of the league. But we beat them 3-0 at Brockville and Dougie Bell scored. Graham Mitchell, who could play centre-back and left-back, was a great signing for us and we got Dougie, who didn't cost us any money other than his wages. Graham Mitchell was, pound for pound, one of my best ever signings. I actually met Mitch two years ago at a Barbara Streisand concert in London! I was heading into the toilet just as he was coming out of there, and I said: 'My God, fancy seeing you here.' The thing about Mitch was that he was a typical Glasgow boy, he had a bit of steel about him. The bigger the game the more he gave you."

Insisting their encounter at the Barbara Streisand concert has not influenced his judgment, Mitchell reciprocates the admiration and is keen to emphasise how much he rated Miller. "I always thought he was a brilliant coach," says Mitchell, who like his old gaffer, stayed for 10 years. "He maybe wasn't a great man-manager, but as a coach he was the best I played under. Before I came to Hibs, I had played under John Lambie – he didn't worry so much about the coaching side, but he was a brilliant man-manager. If you could have combined the two you would have had the perfect manager."

Miller adds: "Neil Orr was another really good signing – the calm presence and influence we needed. I remember once we went to play Rangers and I played Neily Orr as a sweeper and someone leaked my team to Rangers. Walter Smith and Souness told me that they had known my team beforehand, but they didn't believe that we would play with a sweeper and thought it was nonsense. We won 1-0 and Neily was magnificent. He had the cleverness to drop off when he needed to."

As new faces arrived, old faces left to make way. "Every manager has their own ideas, and when Alex came in, obviously he was going to come in and make changes," says Gordon Chisholm, who played for a while under Miller before moving on to Dundee. "I don't have a bad word to say about Alex Miller, it was just circumstances at that time. I was out of contract, and I was looking for a new contract that equalled what I was currently on, and they were saying they couldn't do it. There were prolonged negotiations about it, but I had to look after my future. I had a phone call from Jocky Scott at Dundee and, after speaking to him about a potential move, he gave me 24 hours to make a decision. It all ended up a bit bizarre, I will never forget it. I went up to Dundee and I hadn't signed anything... then they said, 'let's get the photos done'. So, I'm sitting there, with an unsigned contract, still a Hibs player in name, and they've taken a photograph. Then, if that wasn't bad enough, the door swings open and who's standing there – Peter Cormack, who was assistant manager at Hibs at the time. I was gobsmacked. He had been sent up at the last minute to see if Hibs could change my mind. Peter just looked at me, and said: 'Too fuckin late then eh?' And, the truth was he wasn't. But before we knew it he was back out the door and I was left there to complete the paperwork and sign for Dundee. It was just funny the way it worked out.

"I didn't even have time to pick up my boots from Easter Road, that's how quick it all happened, and I had to send wee Joe McBride down to pick them up for me the next day. There is always a tinge of regret that I left Hibs when I did, because I enjoyed it so much, but it worked out well for me at Dundee and I had eight years up there and had a great time."

Steve Cowan was another player soon on his way. "I was still recovering from an injury when Alex came in and wasn't fit to play," he says. "I remember his first game against Rangers, and I chapped the dressing room door, because you always wanted to pop in to wish the guys well and then take your seat in the stand. But Alex said, 'No Steve, come and sit on the bench' which was great. So, we started our relationship reasonably well, but it didn't last very long. I think my knee injury took more of a toll on me than I thought. But also, Alex wanted his strikers to do different things. My game had always been based around playing in the penalty box, playing between the posts, and being in positions to get goals. Alex was thinking differently in terms of working across the line, working back. When it was me and Jukebox, I would take the ball to feet most of the time, while Jukebox would do the running into space behind the play. Alex wasn't looking for that same set-up with his strikers and I think that's where we disagreed. I respected that he was the manager, he was in charge, and that's the way he wanted his strikers to play – and if you don't want to do it, then you're on your way.

"I hadn't long signed a new two-year deal, but I wasn't in the team, wasn't getting a game, and I wanted to be playing. I think Alex knew that he needed to get me out the door and I got it – it was a totally professional decision. I get on great with Alex to this day and I don't have a problem with that at all. I would have done the same, and I have done the same in my time as a manager. Sometimes you have to get players out of the door, so they don't disrupt the dressing room. To be fair to Alex, he didn't force me out. Motherwell had come in for me and he said: 'Steve, nobody is forcing you out. You've just signed a new deal. But if you wanted to go and speak to them you do that and decide what you want to do.' I thought that was very fair.

"I was disappointed to be leaving Hibs, a big city club, but being a professional I thought to myself 'the manager doesn't fancy me here.' I got that, didn't have any problem with that, so I thought it's time for me to move on. By the time I left I was edging close to 100 appearances for Hibs. If I hadn't been out injured for four months then I would have got that 100 and another few goals, which would have been satisfying, but I am just so grateful to have played for Hibs – the club still means a lot to me."

Miller was starting to put his stamp on the squad and bringing in other seasoned players he felt he could depend on to get the club moving up the league. Additionally, he knew that a vibrant youth team could provide solid foundations for the future, but he was alarmed at what he found. "By the end of the first year we lost Gordon Chisholm on freedom of contract to Dundee, and we sold Billy Kirkwood back to Dundee United and Stuart Beedie too. No disrespect to Billy, who was a good player, but he was more in tune with Dundee United's way of playing," he says. "My first night at the youth training, I turned up at Riccarton at the Walled Garden and there were only three players there, one who wanted released and went to Rangers. I said: 'How do you want released when you've never seen me work?' I found that strange. But I started trying to build up our youth system and improve the scouting network. Over the years we tried to improve the playing staff and I think we did that. I know a player when I see one.

"I think we did well with what was available. We got Pat McGinlay for nothing when he was freed from Blackpool. It was big Martin (Ferguson) who got alerted to him. I took him on trial for a month initially but after a week I could see what a good prospect he was and decided immediately that I wanted to sign him. I saw a lot in him that I could work with, and he proved to be a great player for Hibs. Wee Gareth Evans was another who was brilliant for us, and we got him for something like 60 grand. He would put himself all about the place and disrupt defences and always be on their tails. He was a good player. I would drive anywhere to watch a player – I could be driving to Birmingham for a reserve game then driving back up the road that same night. I would do anything to get us good players."

The chequebook was about to come out of its moth-infested hidey-hole when Kenny Waugh ceded power and sold up to new chairman David Duff, and his brother-in-law Jim Gray, with the latter working closest to Miller on a day-to-day basis in his role as the club's managing director. "Kenny Waugh was good to me, but he was only there for a short time, and then it was Duff and Gray," says Miller. "When I went in, I think the first team's wages were £170 and then I tried to step it up. In my latter stages they were maybe getting paid £500 with £400 bonus if they won. We just wanted to make the place much more professional."

Miller also implored the club's new custodians to address a paucity in training facilities. "We were at Wardie mainly, which was all lumps and bumps with a wee slope. What they have now (at East Mains) by comparison is fantastic."

Even Paul Kane, a player who clashed with Miller in their time together at Hibs, admits: "For years, we would train anywhere – next to Craigentinny golf course, Gypsy Brae, you name it – if it was available, we would have it. There were no purpose-built training pitches. You would just jump in the minibus and try and find a pitch. Forgetting all that I dislike about Alex Miller as a guy, to be fair to him, he got the club professionalised. In the early days, you had to make sure you were in early to get the decent kit. It wasn't until Alex Miller came in that things changed and we started getting nice Adidas gear and training kit."

Miller adds: "As I prepared for my first full season, and the players were due back after the summer, the stadium was looking dilapidated, with seats flaking and crumbling. So I went to one of the fans, who had a painting and decorating business, and asked him how many season tickets he bought each year. When he said six, I said 'right, I want to paint the stand and all the benches in time for the players coming back. You give me the paint, then six groundstaff boys and myself will paint the stand and the benches and I'll speak to the board and get you your six season tickets'. He agreed, we painted the seats, the kids and me, and the boys came back and loved it. It gave them a lift. I wanted them to feel that we were big-time again."

Standards were important to Miller and that applied to the players' fitness, diet and professionalism. "I gave players a personalised training programme to stick to over the summer, so they would return ready for pre-season," he explains. "In the first year, Graham Mitchell and a couple of others didn't do the training programme they had been given, so I fined them a week's wages because I had gone to a lot of trouble with the sports scientist to tailor their plans. I knew they hadn't done it, no matter how much they argued – you couldn't beat the system. But, after that, I never had a problem. They would go away and do the programme, some of them getting up to peak fitness quicker than others. There was a lot of thought that went into it, and I used to tell players not to tell anyone else what we were doing, because other teams might start to copy you and you lose any potential advantage you might have had over them.

"The boys that were with me for years, will say 'boss, what they are doing now, we were doing 20 years ago'. We really worked them, in innovative ways. In 1989 we were one of the first clubs to get heart-rate monitors. The club didn't have the money to buy them, but out of the players' fines I bought three heart-rate monitors – one for a striker, one for a midfielder and one for a defender. I wanted to see how my training was impacting on work levels. We had ice baths, massage, and a psychologist who came in, all ahead of our time. I would pick up new ideas by studying and reading up on what was happening elsewhere in the world.

"To give you an example, I noticed that for pre-season training everyone was running uphill. During sessions in Holyrood Park, I started to run downhills as fast as they could go, because the Russian Olympic sprinters were running downhill to improve leg speed. I changed other methods after looking into an Italian study about aerobic and anaerobic fitness and our fitness index improved markedly. When you went off in the summer, they would be off for 6-8 weeks, so a player would be allowed two weeks of doing nothing – play with the kids, play golf, swim, just take it easy and rest because your body needs to recover from the hard season you've had. Then, after that, three times a week you had a four-mile run. The pace was something like an 8-minute mile, which you could do standing on your head being a footballer. Then the next two weeks was a bit more intensity – 300-yard runs, 500-yard runs, bit of rest, bit more pace. Then the last two weeks, we would change the ratio between work and rest. By the time they came back, we knew where they were at. As for me, I always took a month's holiday at the end of the season because I was really drained, and then we were good to go again.

"The only reason they usually got fined was on-field discipline. I would fine them for stupid bookings or orderings off, because we didn't have the squad size to cope with suspensions. They wouldn't just be letting me down, they would be letting down their team-mates and the supporters just for opening their mouths. We started to have a Christmas party for the players' families and kids and buy them presents, so they got their money back."

Further down the line, the arrival of Andy Goram led to another high-profile departure, when the evergreen Alan Rough was eased out, first via a spell in the United States and then at Celtic. Roughie admits the manner of his exit could and should have been handled better. "Alex had his own ideas and I think his idea was that he wanted more young players coming in and the older ones moved on – meaning me, Iain Munro and a few others," he says. "He just wasn't my kind of manager. The first three-year contract I signed it was fine. The next three-year contract I signed, Kenny Waugh, John Blackley and Tommy Craig said they didn't have a lot of money but 'would you be prepared to wait until near the end of your three years and we'll give you a testimonial game?' I said yes, fine, I'm happy with that. When Alex came in, he knew I would be due a testimonial in a year's time. He called me into the office with those two nutcases Duff and Gray. They were all sitting there, and they said: 'We've just noticed that you've got a testimonial next year.' I said: 'Yeah that's right,' and they said: 'Just to let you know that won't be happening.' By telling me that, they knew I wasn't going to stay. We had the testimonial committee all sorted and organised, but his gambit was – and he was probably quite right as well – 'Gordon Rae should get a testimonial before you.' I didn't debate that for a second. Gordon had been there for a long, long time and absolutely he should get one. I said: 'I was promised one too and that's the agreement the club gave me when I signed my contract. I'm sorry, but maybe Gordon could wait another year?' He knew I wouldn't wait and play a year in the reserves, so I decided it was time to move. These things happen in football, but it had happened to me in my career once before, so it perhaps felt more sour than it should have been. I was gutted the way it happened (leaving Hibs) but I went to America for a year and then while I was over there I got a call to come back and play for Celtic. As fate would have it, one of my first games back was against Hibs. I think it was 3-1 and Stevie Archibald scored."

Mickey Weir has the unusual distinction of leaving not long after Miller became manager, and then returning. After he decided to sign for Luton Town, with the transfer fee decided by a tribunal, he was quick to realise he had made an awful mistake and pined for Hibs. "The transfer to Luton came about mainly because I was at loggerheads with the manager at that time, but there were other factors," explains Mickey. "Away from the pitch I was getting abuse and things were happening – my car was getting targeted and it was all getting on top of me, I was getting fed up with it to be honest. I became impetuous and when the chance came to go somewhere else, I took it. I made a snap decision that I wanted to get out of here and try a wee change some-where else. Luton were in the top league in England at that time, the old First Division, so that tempted me. Never ever did I want to leave, but at that time even wee things were annoying me and niggling away at me. I was headstrong, and if I wanted to do something then I would do it, so that's exactly what I did and left.

"When I went down there, I realised very quickly that it was not the right move for me, both in terms of the football on the plastic pitch and my home life. I started to miss Hibs and Edinburgh pretty quickly. I had been used to training with Hibs every day, alongside good friends, and I had loved playing for Hibs, so when that was no longer there for me, I struggled.

"I got word back to Hibs that I would be keen on coming back. I got on the phone to Paul Kane and said 'Look, I should never have come here. I'm looking to come back up the road, would you be willing to speak to people to see if there's any chance of them taking me back?' And he did. I think he went to Peter Cormack and asked if they would be interested in bringing me back. It all happened very quickly. Believe it or not, when I was heading back, I got a number of calls from a few teams in England who wanted to keep me down there. Graham Taylor at Aston Villa called me and asked if I would go there and asked me to think about it. I mulled over it for about 24 hours, and told him I had made my decision – that I was coming home, where I was happiest... at Easter Road. And the Hibs supporters were fantastic with me – they always have been. I wasn't overawed or nervous about facing them, but they made it easy and welcomed me back with open arms, which I really appreciated.

"I was at that age where you think the grass is greener on the other side – I was lacking a bit of life experience. I was just delighted to be back. It did take me a little bit of time to get settled back into the club, because I wasn't fully fit and I wasn't right, and my back was giving me problems. So I had a big fight on my hands to get back to form and fitness and it was difficult at times, but I knew I would get myself right eventually and it was just a case of plodding on and persevering until that happened."

One thing that did bug Weir was inaccurate rumours that he was a compulsive gambler, due to his passion for training greyhounds, and that he had engineered the transfer to Luton for purely financial reasons. "Because I used to keep dogs it used to infuriate me that people assumed that I would be a gambler – I was anything but. I paid enough to get in and I very rarely even had a bet. I was just into the dogs, and then training them. The rumours that I was a gambler and all that nonsense used to do my head in. I never drank either, but I would also get accused of being a drinker – but that's just the way it is and the rumour mill in Edinburgh could be outrageous."

Miller offers a far more straight-forward take on Weir's extended 'holiday' at Luton. "Mickey is a home bird and there was no way he was going to survive down there at that stage of his life," he laughs. "You need to have your wits about you and be able to cook a dinner! Mickey's car was an absolute shambles, the bin lorry was cleaner than Mickey's car! I was delighted to take him back."

Despite all the changes in personnel, and the reshaping of the team, Miller maintained a fairly united dressing room, and team spirit was improving. It didn't mean everyone liked his style or manner though, and there were a handful of players he clashed with on a continual basis. "I didn't see eye to eye with Alex Miller at all," says George McCluskey, who scored Celtic's winner against Rangers, with Miller in their side, in the 1980 Scottish Cup final. "He would tell me to play up front and stretch the game but, as soon as the match started, he would be shouting at me to track back.

"I loved that the fans took to me, and I was pleased to have such a good relationship with them, and maybe Alex was a bit envious of that. I think they saw that I was a trier and that I was willing to put myself about and take some punishment. I remember one of the boys from the Beastie Bus ran down to the front of the terracing and gave me a T-shirt to wear, so I stuck it on and wore it during the warm-up. Alex Miller gave me a row when I came off, saying it wasn't official club training gear, so I told him: 'You go and tell the boy that I cannae wear his top then!' We didn't get on very well."

Hibs fanatic Kane also got off on the wrong foot with his new manager, and the relationship never really recovered. "I remember sitting at Easter Road and seeing a red, white and blue jacket, and I knew it was his. I asked whose it was, and when he said it belonged to him, I said: 'How would you like it if I walked into Ibrox with a fuckin' Hibs jaiket on? It wouldn't happen, would it, and it shouldn't be happening here!' So it was all downhill with him after that really! I was a Hibs man through and through and I felt I had to say something. If I look back now, I probably got too much involved in the politics at that time. To be fair to him, he rated me quite highly at first, but he was more defensive than he was attacking, his teams would often be set up more for a point than three points.

"We fell out again after I had played in the Tennent's Sixes and been top scorer. After seeing that I had my eye in for scoring goals, he asked me if I would play up front, against Motherwell or whoever, and I said I would. He started me there, but put me to right-back in the second half and after the game he said: 'See you, yer nothing but a lazy bastard, you didn't try!' I asked to see him after, away from the rest of the boys, and told him: 'You can slag me for whatever you want, but not for not trying. I am not a non-trier. I will always try my best for Hibs, I might be the worst man on the park, say that to me and I can take it, but never accuse me of not trying.' He later accused me of wanting him fired. Our relationship was way beyond repair. Looking back, there's some things I said that I shouldn't have done, but I couldn't keep my mouth shut back then and it came because I wanted the best for Hibs."

Of the crop of apprentices who had blossomed under Pat Stanton and then John Blackley, Callum Milne was another player who did not click with the new man in charge. The fact that they had history did not help. "I couldn't get a run of games under Alex Miller and I just didn't like him," says Milne. "He broke my ankle before he came to the club. I played against Hearts on the

Saturday in a derby, then on the Sunday there was a five-a-side competition through in Falkirk at Coasters Arena. I went for a tackle with Alex Miller and I think it was just the way I went in, but I knew I was in trouble as soon as I did it. I tried to stand on my ankle, I went 'Oh no, this is bad news' and I fell to the ground. But Alex Miller came up to me and said, right to my face: 'Next time, it will be even fuckin harder.' So I never forgot about that!"

With that painful experience still raw, how did Milne feel when Alex Miller walked through the door as the new Hibs manager? "It was an absolute nightmare," he says, "but I was so much of a Hibbie I just wanted to be there. If I only got a handful of games I would keep my head up, and by the time we were back for pre-season I'd be telling myself: 'This will be your season Callum.' It never happened – I was in and out, in and out. Nowadays, if that happened to a player, you would go in and speak to the manager and try and sort things out, but I was a shy laddie and I felt I had no-one to fight my corner. I couldn't bring myself to knock on the manager's door, but in hindsight I wish I had done that.

"Nowadays you have man-managers, who know when to put an arm round you and build your confidence back up when you're struggling a bit, but Miller was nothing like that. He was just a horrible person... to me anyway! I remember one day we were up in the Highlands for pre-season, and after a game I'd played really well in, I was in the changing room and he said to me: 'You know what Callum, Scotland are looking for a right-back.' To say something so positive like that and then go back to blanking you is odd. I just couldn't stand the guy and couldn't take to him. Don't get me wrong, he was good tactically, and did everything down to the last detail, including scrutinising the opposition. He was very professional, but he was soor-faced. He never smiled and looked like he was never happy."

Gordon Rae, the club captain at the time, says: "Alex was a good coach and a great football man, but for me he was lacking a bit on the man-management side. He looked after some of the guys like Johnny Collins and Andy Goram, but he was happy just to let the rest of us get on with it. His man-management style was a bit dour. If you were an employer in football, he would be your dream employee, because you could be guaranteed he would put absolutely everything into the job. He was totally obsessed with football, and I'll always be grateful to him for organising my testimonial."

Alan Sneddon, another one of the older heads in the dressing room, would also go on to receive a testimonial in 1991 with Miller's support, for which he is thankful. His assessment of the manager is: "Alex Miller was a really good coach, but he was very much about stopping the opposition. It wasn't always so much about what WE were going to do and using our strengths, the game-plan was instead focused on what the other team could do and how we could stop them hurting us. It was a very negative approach I felt. I always thought we could get more out of our attacking side of the game."

John Collins, whose game went from strength to strength under Miller, before he moved on to further his career at clubs such as Monaco, Fulham and Everton, says: "Alex was more organised, more defensive-minded than a couple of the other managers, but he knew everything about the opposition. He picked me every week and we got on well. He showed faith in me and trusted me. He probably made the defensive side of my game stronger, but he had been a defender himself so that was his forte. He was always making sure we were well disciplined and frustrating the opposition when we didn't have the ball, which is part of football as well, but he was a workaholic – never away from the ground and was very thorough and dedicated."

Collins, towards the end of his time at Hibs, would form a close friendship with team-mates Neil Orr, Keith Houchen and Gareth Evans, and they too have strong opinions on Miller. "Me and Gareth used to call him 'The Bad Man' behind his back," says Houchen. "I was always messing about and that used to rankle with him. I just felt he needed to crack a smile every now and again. I didn't do myself many favours mind you, especially when he caught me hiding his white board. He had his board for the complicated tactics, and I would say something like: 'I'm a footballer, I don't have A-levels.' When he caught me hiding it, I would either get a scowl or the death stare.

"I just wanted him to be more on my side, to see things from my point of view a bit more instead of opposing me all the time, which is how it felt to me. It was just making me worse, more rebellious. The lads could see it and they were brilliant with me, but he seemed to have that personality that he wanted to butt heads with people. He could have been better with his man-management I think, and to recognise when it was the right time to put his arm round someone and explain things more kindly. He was hard work. We all mellow with time though. He was football through and through, completely, and you have got to be able to do both. What I had been used to at Coventry was the complete opposite – it was all about fun, camaraderie and being able to have a laugh between yourselves. Alex Miller was so rigid with his training and how we had to play, that it took the fun out of it.

"After Duff and Gray, Dougie Cromb became the chairman and I got on really well with him. Alex made a big thing about me calling him Dougie, insisting that I should always call him 'Mr Chairman'. When I called him Dougie, it must have felt to Alex Miller that I was always trying to undermine him, but I wasn't. We had a massive barney in his office because I was saying to him 'don't say to me who I can and can't talk to or call people'."

Evans laughs: "I got on well with Alex Miller, it was just Houchy that never! I have nothing but 100 per cent respect for Alex Miller. He was nothing but good for me and he had a loyal bunch of boys at that time. He looked after us and we kind of looked after him as well. He treated us with respect and we treated him with that same respect back, it was mutual. If you look at the achievements he had during that period, especially the early 90s, it was somewhat remarkable given the situation the club was in at that time and the turmoil it was going through. I think people will look back at the history and say 'Jeez, how did he manage to do that?'"

Miller knew it was part and parcel of football and he responds: "I hate the statement: 'He doesn't like me.' What a load of nonsense. I didn't care what type of person a player was, if they performed on a Saturday, I could handle them. By the way, I accept criticism. I am not above or beyond criticism. I am not the type to say I did everything right, but as far as training the team and as far as tactics, my players will tell you I was up there with the best and even above the best tactically at times."

Mike Aitken of *The Scotsman* believes Miller did exceptionally well in difficult circumstances at Hibs: "If you buy into the ethos that Hibs play fancy, free-flowing football, then did Alex really fit that bill? Probably not, but Alex was wonderfully knowledgeable about football – one of the most knowledgeable about football I have met. I have never listened to a manager after a match give a more honest or succinct appraisal than Alex. Unlike most football managers, where you would go into the press conference and be waiting 30 or 40 minutes for them to appear, Alex was usually waiting on you, ready for you. Immediately, you would get a completely fair analysis of what had just happened. He didn't gild the lily, but he never tried to pretend that black was white. If you wanted someone to give an honest opinion, it was him. And if you were critical, but had a point, then Alex would not have a problem with that, whereas there were plenty of other managers who just did not like the truth. Maybe his teams were not always the most exciting to watch, but I did not accept the claims that Alex wanted to field nine centre-halves and one forward. I thought that was unfair. If you look back now at what Alex accomplished it was pretty good."

Simon Pia covered the Miller years for a number of national newspapers, until the bitter end in 1996. "I get people casting up to me that I cost Alex Miller his job, but I was actually really fair to Miller until the last six months of his final season when I started to put the boot in," insists Pia. "Miller used to say to me: 'I know who you run with! You hang out with that lot in the Hibs Club – they've never liked me, they've always had it in for me.' So, I think he always had that paranoia that he hadn't been fully accepted. But what sort of guy would turn up to take the Hibs team for training in a Rangers tracksuit? Kano went and told George Stewart and all the guys in the Hibs Club about that. Miller was quite a miserable guy, but he was a steady manager and he definitely brought some professionalism to the club. The players spoke very highly of his training too. Under Pat and under Blackley, there wasn't the structure or stability that Miller brought to Hibs. But he was fortunate to get that length of time."

Looking back, Miller – who post-80s would lead Hibs to Skol League Cup glory in 1991 – is satisfied and proud of the work he did at Hibs, before a globe-trotting career that took him to Champions League glory as Rafa Benitez's first-team coach at Liverpool, plus spells in management in Aberdeen, Sweden, Japan and Siberia! "To be fair, I must have been doing something right when I survived three boardroom changes at Hibs," reflects Miller. "No doubt they all did their homework by asking people about me – and the most important people at the club were the players. I always knew that if I could get money I could really do well. I told Sir Tom Farmer that if he allowed me to spend a real good bit of money, I could split Rangers and Celtic at that stage."

My 90 minutes, plus some added time, are up and I thank Alex for his time and honesty. He has been open and expansive, and I ask him if he regrets not being a bit more outgoing and friendly in the public eye during his time as a Hibs manager. "Aye maybe," he says, "as a young player, I got advice when I was at Rangers to watch what I was doing with my press, and maybe that influenced me and stayed in my head. I took it too literally and stepped back from it too much. I am a private person and I am unassuming. I am a normal guy, and I have had a great life. When I left Hibs I went to Liverpool and had some fascinating jobs – you're no a daftie if you can survive all these places!"

CHAPTER 10

A **CASUAL INTERLUDE**

*"The 80s was a like a car crash, but for us it was like heaven.
I've been slashed, attacked, hit with a brick and had some right
kickings. Would I do it all again? ... Aye!"* – Andy Blance

There were a few pivotal years for Hibs in the Eighties, but the one that the winds of change registered on the Richter Scale was 1987. It was the year the new manager Alex Miller started to build his own team. The year that Hibs signed Andy Goram. The year we finally beat Hearts. And the year the fanzine movement exploded into the public domain. Above all, the sale of the club from Kenny Waugh to David Duff, backed by David 'Spotty' Rowland (a right banker if ever there was one) would mark 1987 as a milestone in the history of Hibernian Football Club.

The takeover was welcomed at the time, and some promised razzamatazz duly followed, but there's no getting away from the hard fact that Duff's involvement left us wide open to the pudgy, predatory claws of Wallace Mercer. Duff, a 33-year-old solicitor, concluded the near £1 million deal to take over Hibs in early 1987 and promptly made the club's MD his brother-in-law Jim Gray, formerly a director with a construction company. To try to ensure a smooth transition, outgoing Kenny Waugh initially stayed on the board along-side Gregor Cowan.

"We came in not long after Alex Miller had arrived as manager," says Duff, who grew up a Hibs supporter before moving down south. "Kenny didn't really want to sell the club and he didn't really want to keep it – he had such an emotional tie to the club, but at the same time I think he accepted that he had taken it as far as he could. Kenny Waugh wasn't a bad man and nor was he a bad chairman – he was maybe just there at the wrong time. The club needed a regeneration. Although people hadn't heard of me, I had a Hibs background. My uncle was a Hibs supporter and my mum's side of the family got me into watching Hibs. I first went when I was 8 and I sat on the wall of the old terracing, with the scoreboard in the corner, and I was smitten by the sounds and smells. From the age of 12-16 I lived in Bromley, Kent, and then we moved back and I went to Trinity. We would play rugby in the morning and go to the Hibs game in the afternoon. At that point I joined the Carlton branch of the Hibs Supporters' Club – I was a real Hibernian soldier!

"So, when the opportunity came to buy the club, I jumped at it. I had been sitting in the stand, watching one of these games when Kenny Waugh was the chairman, and thinking things could be so much better – the service, the general atmosphere, the team. They weren't terrible and probably weren't going to get relegated, but they just seemed like another St Mirren or Hamilton – and you look at Hibs' history and they shouldn't be like that. Hibs are the great pathfinders in Scottish football, were the first club in Europe, had the Famous Five and all that rich history, it had to be better than this. I was with Jim [Gray] and just said casually – 'can this be bought?' It was just a throw-away comment and then the guy who was with us, he knew one of the directors and set up a meeting over a pint. Then he talked to Kenny and that was the start of it.

"I had talked to the Spurs chairman at the time (Irving Scholar), so I had a clear vision for Hibs. He had taken Spurs in a brave new direction, doing some great stuff with sponsorship and television rights and so on. I was doing a lot of conveyancing for Irving at the time. I got to know David Rowland through Sheila, who proved to be a Hibs hero in the future, and who is his ex-wife now. I liked him because he was an expert at the Stock Exchange and all that could bring. The other thing was, and it's been proved now, that football needs to have diversity of income because if you have a bad season, or you get relegated, then you can't depend on gate money alone. I felt Rowland could offer that expertise."

"The price for the club was £800,000 and we needed £900,000 to do everything. I put £100,000 of my own money in, he put in 200k, and we borrowed the rest from his company. For him to get his money back, it was an interest free loan on the never-never until we floated (on the Stock Exchange) and so off we went and concluded the deal."

The new chairman arrived in a blaze of publicity and promises, and he wasted no time in assuring manager Alex Miller that they would back him in the transfer market. "Alex had a wish-list when we came in and the first player he wanted was Neil Orr from West Ham, so we bought him on the day that I took over at the club," says Duff. "We knew a week before that I would be coming in, even though we hadn't yet announced it, and I worked with him that week to help with the Neil Orr deal. Neil was a bargain, coming from the top division in England. He wasn't a flair player, he was an 'Alex player' let's be honest, but he was a good defensive midfielder. So, I came in, and although the players thought it was very odd this young guy coming in, I was down to the dressing room from day one and they seemed to accept me."

Orr, back in Scotland after a spell living in Australia, remembers: "Yes, I was Duff and Gray's first signing. I had been at West Ham for five-and-a-half years, and the club had offered me another year. But six months earlier they had just brought Liam Brady and Stewart Robson in. I was playing in midfield at the time and my first thought was that my first-team games would be limited. I actually played the first game of the season, at home against QPR, and that's when Hibs came in. I had said to our manager John Lyall to let me know if there was any interest, and that's when he let me know about Hibs. My wife and I went over to Heathrow to meet Alex Miller and Jim Gray.

"Jim Gray was with Alex Miller, and when Jim went to the bathroom, Alex was honest with me and said: 'Look, I don't know these guys from Adam, they've just bought the club.' So, he didn't know what to expect."

Around that time, I had not long launched the fanzine *Hibs Monthly* while still at school with my lifelong Hibbie pal, Stevie Burns. Early copies were a crude mish-mash of typewritten articles thrown together under Letraset or magic marker headlines, on photocopied A4 sheets and held together with staples. I even had to borrow a few quid off a Jambo pal to pay for the first photocopying costs – if only he'd known what he was unleashing!

Issue No 1 appeared in March and splashed on Alan Rough's heroic performance in a 1-1 draw at Ibrox, and featured match reports, star ratings and snippets of news, including the arrival of Duff and the departure of Waugh as chairman. It was the start of something new in more ways than one. We were initially oblivious to the growing cohort of football fanzines in the UK, and we entertained no grand plans to make it a long-standing venture. By the time we got the number of issues into double-figures, the sub-culture of the fanzine had become an unstoppable force, and it just so happened Edinburgh had its own champion for the fanzine movement in Alan Cunningham (a Partick Thistle fan if my memory is correct) who stocked a smorgasbord of titles in his Football Crazy shop in Spittal Street.

These early fanzines were a huge inspiration to wide-eyed young guys like us, who were just starting out and experimenting in the printed word. We feasted on the ideas and creativity to be found around the country, from the wonderfully-titled Gillingham effort *Brian Moore's Head Looks Uncannily Like London Planetarium* to the razor-sharp *AWOL*, produced by Meadowbank Thistle's Brake Club.

Leading the way for Hibs in 1987 was the *Hibees Glasgow Gossip*, which – in the hands of older and more experienced editors – eschewed the rather bland, serious content we were producing at that stage and gave readers a winning mix of humour and attitude. Copies were sold outside grounds and provided an alternative to the staid and stale approach of match programmes. As soon as I leafed through it, I knew that's the direction *Hibs Monthly* had to go.

With the encouragement of Alan at Football Crazy, it was time for a revamp and to take it beyond our own bubble. An appeal went out for writers to contribute, and those who boldly stepped forward – talented guys like the Hibbie Hippie and Octopus (a certain Mr Irvine Welsh, you may have heard of him?) would soon transform the title into a full-blown fanzine with an agenda fuelled by mischief and mayhem. There was still room for more thoughtful pieces from Hibs historians like Brian Mark and Robert McCutcheon, but by and large it was a riot of jokes, pot-shots at Hearts, cartoons and chaos.

Although football hooliganism was a constant throughout the decade, as it had been in the 70s, 1987 took a particularly sinister twist when a CS gas cannister hurled by a Celtic fan towards Hibs fans packed into the by-now covered East Terracing at Easter Road, caused mass panic and a stampede that spilled on to the pitch. It left 45 people requiring hospital treatment and thousands more thanking their lucky stars that this despicable act had not resulted in deaths and disaster.

I had always held aspirations to embark on a career in journalism, and I adopted the tone of a war correspondent when giving my on-the-spot account of the tear gas incident in Issue 7, writing: "Hibs supporters spilled on to the pitch to escape the choking fumes after a gas grenade was thrown into the packed covered enclosure. After the grenade was thrown, a loud bang followed and then gas started to emerge. People immediately panicked and made their way towards the fence. The police were at first unaware of what was happening, and it was a while before they realised and opened the crowd safety gates. Hundreds poured on to the pitch, some collapsing, vomiting and choking, their eyes streaming. It was an unbelievable scene of chaos. Chairman David Duff said: 'What happened today was a major criminal act. This sort of thing has nothing to do with football. Throwing a cannister of gas into a crowd of innocent people is the work of a very sick mind.'"

As worthy as the CS Gas incident was of reporting, we would soon steer clear of such high-brow, hard-hitting news pieces and give the readers what they told us they wanted – an independent voice. Meanwhile, the cretinous Celtic fan who hurled the cannister was later jailed for four years in an era when football-related convictions were commonplace, largely due to the rise of casuals.

There will doubtless be people reading this book who would prefer not to see space given to the casuals and football hooliganism, but I believe it is hard to write a book about Hibs in the 1980s without acknowledging their presence and prominence. I don't seek to defend or glorify the violence, at grounds and city centres, and nor do I want to go into their exploits in detail as there are other books, written by Hibs boys, who have comprehensively covered this.

I would, however, like to scotch the frankly ridiculous myth that these guys cannot be regarded as 'true Hibs fans'. Sure, there were many voyeurs on the periphery who were drawn to the heady mix of mob mentality, fashion, music and drugs. A lot of the hangers-on came and went, especially when the police finally got their act together and curtailed their numbers and activities. They were never really into it for the football or for supporting Hibs anyway. But you still see many of the old Hibs boys, following the club home and away, some of them grandads now, and there is absolutely no doubt in my eyes that they are Hibs through and through.

A prime example is Andy Blance, arguably the most notorious member of the CCS (Capital City Service), given his high profile in the media and the fact he put his head above the parapet when writing his casual memoirs, *Hibs Boy: The Life and Violent Times of Scotland's Most Notorious Football Hooligan*. Andy is one of these familiar faces I have seen throughout my entire Hibs-supporting life, and even during the lockdown months I had spotted him on TV watching the cup tie from outside a mesh fence at Stranraer and sitting on top of someone's garage overlooking Queen of the South's ground – dedication and a handy set of portable ladders demonstrated his commitment to the cause! Despite my big brother's delinquent years as a casual (I was the angelic one!), I had never properly met Andy before I wrote this book. When I caught up with him for a chat in South Queensferry, across the water from his native Fife, he was still bearing the marks of a scrap in London during Scotland's Euro 2020 clash with England at Wembley. Old habits and old enemies die hard it seemed.

Blance became hooked on Hibs from an early age. A family friend would take him and his brother to Easter Road one week and Tynecastle the next, but it wouldn't be long before he decided there was only one club for him, and by the age of 11 he was heading through to Hibs games on his own from Rosyth. "By the time I moved to Leith I was a skinhead," says Blance. "You would occasionally get in bother at games, but we were getting in bother whatever we were doing, not just at the football. The casual scene kind of came along, bang at the right time for me. I was getting mega-hassle from the police for being a skinhead, but when the casuals came along you could go to places like Glasgow, up to Dundee, and nobody knew you. And once the police arrive and the fighting stopped, you just walked away and blended in with the crowd.

"Me and my mate Girvan stayed at the bottom of Leith Walk and we were already going to the games. The casuals had just started and when we saw a whole load of boys fighting, without any colours on, we recognised them as Hibs fans and steamed in and helped them. The next week we were going through to Glasgow and a young guy called Alan Robb said: 'Are you coming with us?' I had a skinhead jacket on, we were young and daft, and thought 'why not?' Virtually by the next week we had Pringles and stonewash jeans on, and we were growing our hair a wee bit longer. My primary concern was Hibs and the football – if there was a fight before, during and after, then obviously I was a willing participant.

"Predominantly at the beginning it was all just a case of Hibs fans coming together, ready-made guys who were going to the games anyway. We were going robbing and fighting folk before the casuals came along, and naturally we gravitated towards the scene. You would have Hibs buses all over town with some handy boys on each of them, and the natural thing to do was to join together."

Hibs certainly had some crazy, chaotic buses back in those days. Supporter Rod Macleod says: "I remember coming back from an away game and stopping off for a pint in Whitburn. We are all sitting enjoying a beer when the polis burst into the pub and tell us to get out and get back on our bus and get back to fucking Edinburgh. Reason being, the young team who could not get served in the pub started a rammy with the local neds in Whitburn, and we all know what flavour they would be. I used to travel on the Gardiner's bus with Uncle Dougie Sneddon as the convenor – it was such an eclectic mix on the bus, Gilmerton and the Inch, Niddrie, Muirhouse, Pilton and Drylaw. We had a lot of great times and I still see a few of the lads at games."

Not that every supporters' bus was a rabble on the road. For example, passengers on the Hawkhill bus were usually on their very best behaviour, or they would risk the wrath of legendary convener Maude MacFarlane, who sadly passed away in 2010 at the age of 93. I remember travelling through to Ibrox in the 80s on the Hawkhill, and Maude would make everyone take their scarves off and hide their colours in case the bus windows got tanned. By the time the casuals had arrived on the scene, hiding colours – even green and white ones – just made you even more of a target, as some Rangers fans would assume it was a bus-load of Hibs hooligans. But you didn't argue with Maude, as John Campbell – the 'Hibstorian' – can testify: "Some of the best days out I had back then were travelling to away games in the early 80s on the Hawkhill bus. Maude MacFarlane was a character to say the least and when we stopped on the way back from a game, God help you if you weren't back in your seat at the time stipulated. I recall one occasion where she gave me a dressing down for being drunk and late to return, when in fact I was stone cold sober and newly back from the chippy with my pie supper!"

By and large Hibs fans were a united bunch, while the Old Firm followings often got bogged down in factions and rivalries within their support, and that extended to their hooligan elements. "You would think Rangers and Celtic would come together but I think there was always a bit of friction and in-fighting," says Blance. "In the grand scheme of things, for Hibs to be acknowledged as being the best firm in Scotland, I think it always rankled with Rangers, and to a lesser extent Celtic. They were the big fish as football clubs and with their supporter bases, yet we were the ones with the reputation. Whenever you go down south, people still regard Hibs as the main firm. It was kind of amazing how it did turn round, because there's no doubt about it the Gorgie Aggro were a fearsome bunch.

"People don't see it, but I felt you were fighting for your club, because you love your club. I know people disagree with that, and think casuals can't be true supporters, but that's not the case. I know that (fighting) is not right, but it's just something that's part of human nature. If you think back to the 70s, you could come out of Easter Road – never mind Tynecastle or one of the Glasgow grounds – and your scarf would have to go inside your jacket or pocket because you were in danger of getting a kicking.

"The Gorgie Aggro, or even going up to the old Muirton Park in Perth, or either of the Dundee grounds – they used to be dangerous places for a Hibs supporter. It was time to start fighting back. I can mind going to Ayr United way back, before casuals, and we got booted to fuck and chased back to our buses. And going to Ibrox was just like being in a suicide squad back then. We changed things. I know Brad Welsh's 'Bridge of Doom' comment (referring to the footbridge connecting Bothwell Street and Albion Road) was tongue-in-cheek, but it was the truth! Away casuals still look back and admit: 'you wouldn't go through to Hibs in the 80s, you were taking your life in your hands.'

"I think a lot of the older fans, although they disapproved and didn't like it, on some level they were proud of the fact that we stood up for our club and Hibs fans could go to these places and watch the game knowing that the casuals were there to make it a bit safer. We might not have been there to protect them, but we were there to deflect from them. The hooligans at Rangers and Aberdeen wouldn't be interested in the ordinary scarf-wearing fans, they would be looking for us. That element of safety can go out the window a bit at derbies, but most of the time no-one would ever touch innocents."

There will, of course, be 'innocents' who would dispute that statement, including myself. I got a kicking in Dundee city centre when I was 14 for rather naively strolling around near the Overgate with a Hibs scarf round my neck. True story: when I later explained the grazes on my bruised face to my inquisitive mum, I told her I had been struck flush in the puss by a wayward shot from Benny Brazil that had cleared the Dens Park perimeter wall. And she bought it!

Hibs fan Alan Woodhouse also takes a less romanticised view of the casuals and the trouble that was constant in and around stadiums and city centres. "The worst thing about the 80s was the constant, malevolent threat of hooliganism," he says. "I was chased, punched, spat on by opposing fans, and we were treated like shit by the authorities. It was an awful time to be a football fan."

The roots of CCS can be traced back to around 1984, and within a couple of years, there were a couple of offshoots like Blackley's Baby Crew (later Hibs Baby Crew when Sloop got the heave-ho) for the younger hoolie, and – you have to applaud the equality and diversity here – the LST (Lassie Soccer Trendies). "Some of them would probably do more damage than some of the guys," jokes Blance.

An early clash at Easter Road with the other emerging mob in the country, the Aberdeen Soccer Casuals, left one Hibs boy in a coma for a week, and battle lines were drawn. It also brought casuals to the attention of the media for the first time. Journalist and author Simon Pia says: "When the casuals came along, I remember Stewart Brown of the *Evening News* sending me off to find out if a guy had been killed when Hibs were playing Aberdeen. He hadn't been, but there had been a lot of rumours sweeping the stadium. They decided in the press box that I was the only one the casuals might speak to!

"The whole casual thing was interesting at the time, and it grabbed the attention of the media. I was also working the day of the Celtic game with the CS gas cannister. You could smell the gas – it was pretty scary. There was lots of battling and fighting during the Eighties. I did a couple of articles with the casuals and got to know them a bit. Derek Dykes (author of the 2007 book, *These Colours Don't Run: Inside the Hibs Capital City Service*) and a few others, including Bradley Welsh. They could be a very entrepreneurial bunch! Most of them were good guys, and they were mainly just busy kicking lumps out of each other."

With news desks now paying attention, it brought widespread publicity for the casuals in the tabloids, but it was often unwanted and inaccurate. "We were under the radar to begin with, but reporters could cause you problems," admits Blance. "They got the majority of what they wrote wrong, and just made up what they thought would sell papers. The CCS has a Wikipedia page now, which is an accurate account of what really went on."

By the end of the decade, Hibs had gained recognition as the most notorious 'firm' in Scotland, and they were starting to have a big influence on nightlife in Edinburgh too, running doors of pubs and clubs and often wreaking mayhem away from the football. Road trips like Wembley for the 1988 England v Scotland fixture, and Millwall two years later, would generate more headlines and kudos within the casual network, but a return to European football was manna from heaven for the Hibs boys.

"I wasn't allowed to get a visa for (the Videoton game in) Hungary, but Liege was something else," says Blance. "We went into Brussels on the way and ended up fighting with everyone – there was gangs of bikers, Anderlecht boys, and Moroccans. Fifty-odd of us got lifted, and it was splashed all over the papers and telly back home. They let us out the next morning. I had paid for a hotel in Liege but never got to stay in it because the next night I got lifted again. In Liege, we were at the top off this hill and the police were trying to stop us. One of them said to me, in broken English, 'you don't want to go down there, it's all Liege hooligans'. But that was exactly what we wanted to hear, so we all went off charging down this hill and started fighting with them. And of course, I got lifted again and spent the night in the cells. I got a burst nose for my troubles too."

Blance's list of football-related convictions neatly matches his age, in the 50s, and the first of them came in a derby. "My first arrest as a casual was before a game at Tynie," he recalls. "We were in Luckies at Gorgie Road, whatever it was called back then. Someone was sitting with their foot up on a seat. The landlord at the time came in and told him aggressively to put his foot down. Someone said: 'Who the fuck are you talking to?', picked up a pint glass, threw it, missed, hit a light on the wall and the next thing the whole place was plunged into darkness. Everyone started raiding the bar, the cellar, we took the fucking lot – bottles of beer, boxes of crisps and peanuts, stuff we didn't even need or want. It was just daftness.

"Then we were out on the streets, swaggering about as you did, and a car came along full of Jambos, so we put that on its roof. Then a supporters' bus came along full of Jambos so we tried to do the same again. We were rocking it back and forward, but it wouldn't topple. The polis arrived and we scarpered. I had this polisman chasing me along Gorgie Road on a motorbike – even though there were mums with their prams and old women with their shopping, he was up on the pavement, so I ended up turning round and pulling him off it. He radioed for help and I got lifted further along the road. I got done with all sorts, but back then the police and courts didn't have computers like they do now, and I only had convictions in Fife, so I got treated like I was a first offender and let off lightly."

The courts didn't stay lenient with Blance for long, and he would go on to miss cup finals, games in Europe and other notable matches, because he was behind bars. So, any regrets? "For the outsider the 80s was a like a car crash, but for us it was like heaven," he says emphatically. "I've been slashed, attacked, hit with a brick in Motherwell and had some right kickings. Folk often say to you, 'would you do it again?' Aye! Even if you had to take all the bad with the good, you would still do it. You've got pals that you've made for life, and I'm not just talking about the fighting. Even now, when you're going to a Hibs game it's not just about going to the game – it's the whole day out, it's meeting up with your mates, having a day out, having something to eat, everything that goes with it. The whole camaraderie of it all was special. Nowadays, even if I'm up in Aberdeen I can catch up with some of their main boys from back then. There's lots of boys at Hibs who will have different mates at different clubs."

When journalist Simon Pia wasn't being despatched to shed light on the inner sanctum of the casuals, he was busy writing Hibs books of his own in the 80s. The arrival in 1987 of goalkeeper extraordinaire Andy Goram soon gave Pia the idea to collaborate on an autobiography entitled *Scotland's For Me* – a nod to the future Scotland No 1's Lancashire birthplace.

The son of 1940s Hibs goalkeeper Lewis Goram, who did not feature in the first team before moves to Third Lanark then Bury, Andy was a big presence as soon as he set foot inside Easter Road. He had actually played against his new side that summer in a pre-season tournament. In the *Scotland's For Me* book ghost-written by Pia, Goram said: "The only time Hibs had seen me was the Isle of Man the year before when they beat Oldham 3-0. That day I had a stinker. Gordon Rae scored his first goal in three years, Johnny Collins nutmegged me and to top it all Mickey Weir scored with a header."

Goram's arrival also accelerated the departure of Alan Rough. After all, the £325,000 splashed out to sign him from Oldham Athletic, was not going to be wasted on an understudy. It proved to be money very well spent, but ironically Goram had not even been the first-choice target for Alex Miller, and the move only happened when preferred option, Leicester City's Ian Andrews, chose Celtic rather than Hibs. He played five forgettable times for Celtic on the way to obscurity, so it was a very lucky escape.

Chairman of the time Duff remembers how the focus shifted from Andrews to Goram. "The first time we went to Tynecastle that season we lost 1-0 and Roughie was in goals. He had gone wandering around his penalty area and had conceded the goal, and Alex Miller never forgave him for that because he came into my office the next day and said: 'Chairman, we need a fuckin goalie or we will get relegated.' So, I said all right, who have you got in mind? His first choice was Ian Andrews, or Eamonn Andrews as we called him. He went to Celtic and had a terrible time, so we were lucky not to get him.

"How Andy came to us was that we had Martin Ferguson with us (brother of Sir Alex) and he was a great source to us with his contacts. We used to say ring your brother and see who is available. It was through Joe Royle that we got Andy. Joe said: 'I know you're looking for goalkeepers, and we have got a great one here for you if you're interested. He's brilliant, I love him, but he's a handful.'

"Joe even brought him up and helped negotiate his contract, because that's the kind of guy he was. Andy came up with Joe Royle and we took one look at him and thought: 'Are you kidding? Big fat 5ft 10ins goalkeeper' – but what a keeper he proved to be! Perhaps he wouldn't be able to come out and catch crosses all the time because of his height, but he was a fantastic stopper and without doubt he had the best hand-to-eye co-ordination of anyone I had seen – he saw a ball coming before it was kicked, literally. That was his strength, as well as his confidence. We thought we would take a chance on him, and it was the best move we ever made."

Goram made an instant impact. His debut came in a 4-0 cakewalk against Dunfermline, a game that remains an emotional but happy Hibbie memory for future *Mass Hibsteria* editor Graham Ewing. "My Dad joined me for that game. It was the last Saturday game he attended before he started suffering from a progressive neurological illness which he suffered for a good 20 years until his death in 2011. After the game we drove back to Bonnyrigg and had a few beers in the Calderwood after picking up a *Pink News*. It was nothing short of a perfect father/son day."

Goram's debut was the perfect tonic ahead of his second match – the visit of Hearts, who we still hadn't beaten in the league for 10 years. "I couldn't believe no-one was giving Hibs a chance and was unaware of recent derby history," said Goram in his book. "I was interviewed on TV the night before and said I couldn't believe all the talk was about Hearts. They were just another team and we would go out and beat them."

Hibs did exactly as Goram predicted, his injection of confidence and self-belief helping to get a grossly overdue job done. Poor Roughie had never played in a derby victory in five years of trying, and here was his replacement nailing it at the first attempt. Goram and Rough were pals for club (briefly) and country, and there were never any hard feelings or animosity between the pair. "I felt a bit awkward as I had got on well with Roughie in the Scotland squad, and here I was pushing him out of the team," Goram recalled. "Although it's part of your job as a professional, it is still not a nice feeling. But full credit to Alan Rough as he never showed his disappointment and bore no grudge."

Rough agrees: "Andy actually stayed with me for the first fortnight that he came to the club and we got on really well with each other. I've always got a good word to say about Andy and I could see then that he was going to become a great goalkeeper. You could see it in training. He may have been a bit short in height in goalkeeping terms, but he was just different class in everything else he did."

Goram's short stay with Rough was followed by a stay in the Hilton Hotel, and then a move – at his own request – to something a bit more relaxed and friendly, which led him to the Lady Nairne Hotel in Willowbrae Road. He occasionally took the relaxing part a bit far.

Ahead of his first ever Tynecastle derby, on 2 January, Goram arrived at our rivals' ground bleary eyed and hungover – yet still produced a superhuman performance that fans of both clubs remember well. "I used to ask the hotel to stick a bottle of wine aside for me whenever I missed a meal as I had full board," said Goram. "Come the New Year I had built up quite a stock and there was big party at the hotel. I went over the score and had a few too many. The next day I played in one of the best 0-0 draws I've seen. Hearts dominated in the first half and we took over in the second. It was my best game so far for Hibs and I ended up with the man of the match award."

Joe Tortolano already knew his 'big mucker' Goram from their time together as youngsters. He explains: "I knew Andy from way back because he was at West Brom when I was there, before he left to go to Oldham. We recognised each other and hit it off right away. I had a close relationship with the big man, he was aff his heid, but what a brilliant keeper! One of the best you will ever see. We were blessed with good goalkeepers during my time at Hibs: big Roughie, Goram, Budgie (John Burridge), Jim Leighton – all top class. We had Scotland's best goalkeeper for the best part of a decade

"That New Year derby was classic Andy – he had been bevvying all through the night and then had the game of his life. Lots of times he was doing things he shouldn't have been doing but he got away with it because he still believed in himself and knew he was going to make great saves. You would never have known that he had been out the night before because he was that good. He was brave, a hardy boy. If that ball came into his box, if you were in his way, he would just splatter you all over the place."

Goram's fast and loose style also became evident to Pia in his regular meetings with the gregarious goalie, usually on licensed premises, as they started to build a relationship and work together on the book. "A lot of the Hibs players used to come into the Dean Hotel and that's how I first met him, and got to know him pretty well," says Pia. "He was quite a character. I remember going back to the flat he was staying in and he would get you to throw fruit at him, so he could save it – same as Budgie used to do. He used to say in that accent of his: 'I never eat the fookin stoof', but he had fantastic reflexes.

"When we did the book together, about 1989, I spent a lot of time with him. He was always out on the piss, always tapping people for money, forever skint. I would go and meet him at Easter Road on a Friday, and then we would go for a curry and a chat. One day we left the ground, went to the bookies, then had a curry for lunch, then a few bevvies. He used to start off on the white wine spritzers. Then after that, about 2 or 3pm, we would go up to the snooker hall at McDonald Road and play snooker and drink pints. One night we were drinking there till about 7, then went across to the Windsor and had a few more pints. It would be getting on for 9 or 9.30 by then, and we split and went our different ways. The next day, we were playing St Johnstone, and he had a brilliant game. I was working and saw him after the game and I said: 'You were in surprisingly good nick today, Andy.' And he said: 'Yeah, felt great. We had a brilliant lock-in back at Bonnyrigg after I left you.' It turned out he had gone into this local in Bonnyrigg and stayed there until after 2 in the morning!"

Perhaps Goram's greatest claim to fame at Hibs came in the final game of his first season at the club, against Morton, when his huge wind-assisted kick down the old slope bounced and beat his opposite number, David Wylie, who admittedly shat it when he saw George McCluskey marauding towards him. Recalling his goal, Goram said: "There was a superb response from the crowd and every time I got the ball they were shouting for me to shoot. I think it helped build my relationship with the Hibs fans."

That game also marked a cringeworthy publicity stunt from the new chairman David Duff and his managing director Jim Gray, which did not sit so well with Goram. "David Duff and Jim Gray carried out a public relations stunt beforehand, going round the ground waving at fans, and went in to watch the game from the terracing. A few of us were a bit cynical about it even then. Their efforts to be men of the people, at one with the fans, just didn't ring true. When Morton went 1-0 up, Duff and Gray must have been thinking, 'we've made a mistake here, we could get lynched'."

That was also the view of a bemused Alex Miller. "I was sitting in the dug-out watching this unfold," he chuckles (yes, he does chuckle from time to time!). "When they first went into the terracing, it was all smiles and clapping and joking and saying 'hallelujah' boys, and then when we lost a goal they were out of there sharpish. I remember nudging Peter Cormack and saying 'look at the fuckin pair of them coming back round the track getting pelters'. I couldn't stop laughing at that. We won 3-1 in the end and Andy Goram scored, so the smiles were back by the end of the game."

Tortolano, who joined the name Goram on the scoresheet that day, says: "I scored the third one that day, not that anyone will remember that. I work doing the Opta stats for Sky – me and Graham Mitchell – and that's three times I've seen a goalkeeper score. Goram's goal, Mark Oxley's goal against Livingston and one in a Brechin v Stirling game. That's my hat-trick and claim to fame! It was great to see Andy score and it put him on a pedestal with the fans, who loved him. Goram was brilliant to have around the place. He was great at golf, snooker and cricket (he played for Penicuik during the summer months and was capped for Scotland) and a brilliant centre-forward in the five-a-sides – putting himself about and smashing bodies all over the place. You would make sure big Goram was in your team.

"Goram would always have fun and a joke at my expense. If I was playing left-back, the first chance he got he would fling it to me with all this spin on it. It would bobble over my foot and the Hibs supporters would be screaming at me from behind the barriers, wanting to kill me: 'Get a grip Tortolano, you're fucking shite' and I would turn to Goram, pissing himself laughing, with me pleading: 'Will you stop it?'"

It's sad that Goram's legacy has been tainted in the eyes of Hibs supporters by his association with Rangers, as he was a joy to watch in the four years he graced our No 1 shirt. Hibs fan Alan Woodhouse sums him up well: "He was astonishing. He looked too small and chubby to be a keeper, but he ended up being on another planet when it came to doing what was necessary between the sticks. That he went on to have such a great career is no surprise."

CHAPTER 11

D is for **DISASTER...** and **DERBIES**

*"We had a terrible record against Hearts, and wee
Robbo just could not stop scoring against us."*
– John Collins

You could say that popping champagne corks in the home dressing room was a bit OTT after Hibs had beaten Hearts 2-1 in a bog-standard league game in October 1987. But this self-indulgent, over-extravagant show of back-patting went beyond the fact that our new chairman David Duff was a flash git and fond of the Bollinger. These celebrations stemmed from the unbridled relief that a bleak, barren run against the Jambos, stretching to 17 games and eight years, had finally been halted. The Gorgie monkey was off our backs... for now. Only Hibs could somehow contrive to go an even worse run of 22 winless games against their arch-rivals in the early 90s!

So, as painful and gut-wrenching as this is, a chapter has been dedicated to the Edinburgh derbies of the 80s, and more to the point, how the fuck did we not win a few more than we did!?

It should be pointed out at the outset that there were no league derbies between the sides from the start of the decade until 1983, when both sides were finally reacquainted with each other in the Premier League, having had respective spells in the First Division. Perhaps signaling that luck was not often going to favour Hibs in derbies for some time, they twice led in that eagerly-awaited renewal of old rivalries at Tynecastle, before losing the match 3-2. The name 'Robertson' on the scoresheet would become almost as predictable in this fixture as Hibs' inability to win.

Whether we were cursed, overawed by the occasion, or at times simply up against a stronger Hearts team inspired by the goal machine Robbo, the derby record of the 1980s (and the early 90s) was a source of deep embarrassment, and it probably led to the arrogance and sense of entitlement that has seeped into an element of their support to this day. Prior to the 1983 game, Hearts hadn't beaten Hibs in five years, and managed only two league derby victories in the entire 1970s.

Player by player, manager by manager, I cross-examined each of them on their memories of the derby games of the 80s and sought some insight and an explanation – if indeed there was one – as to what had gone so horribly wrong.

Gordon Rae, who scored in the first Edinburgh derby I ever saw (a Hibs win in 1979), was never one for ducking a tackle and nor does he duck the question. "My memories of those games are not that good actually," he sighs. "Those derby matches were so intense, and they meant so much, that you couldn't always just go and play your natural game, the way you would want to play it. I had played in these matches towards the end of the Seventies, when it was Hibs that dominated and won a lot of them, and then when Hearts came back up to the Premier League in the 80s they took over that mantle, and we found it hard to beat them – for whatever reason."

Pat Stanton was Hibs manager for the opening salvos in the 1983-84 campaign, and he looked very much the man for the occasion given his magical association with the fixture, especially at Tynecastle where he was in beguiling form in the 7-0 game of 1973 and then two years later nodded in the famous '5 o'clock equaliser' at the McLeod Street end. Horses for courses? No, much like the horse racing, the form book often counts for diddly squat and even the ultimate Hibernian thoroughbred Stanton was unable to work his magic from the dug-out. "It was a strange experience being in the dug-out," he says. "There's an edge to these games and I did my best to keep the lads calm and focused. I always felt there was already enough tension surrounding these games without adding even more by having a long-winded pre-match chat with them. At the end of the day, it was what they felt and did on the pitch that was going to matter. Even though these games carried the same number of points on offer as any other game, if someone has to point out to you just how important a game a derby is against the rivals you share the city with, then there is something wrong with you. The majority of players knew exactly what was required of them."

Tynecastle was absolutely bouncing for that first game in 83, and while the fixture later developed an unwelcome reputation as a more turgid affair, this was a bona fide thriller – albeit a hard one to take for the Hibbies crammed into the uncovered Gorgie Road end. "That defeat at Tynecastle was followed by three draws in the other league matches against them that season," notes Stanton. "They were always tight affairs. I knew a few of the Hearts lads when I was playing and I liked them actually, but when it came to the derby game you forgot about friendships and did your job."

Just as the boss had done, Ralphy Callachan had experienced a Hibs victory over Hearts – but he had the distinction of featuring on the other side of the divide too, facing the team he supported as a boy six times in his adopted maroon and not registering a single victory... although the late Stanton goal of 75 had much to do with that. "I was lucky enough to be in the winning side against them once for Hibs, and I can also remember playing for Hearts... I had scored for them, and then Pat equalised about ten minutes after opening time in the pubs," he laughs.

"It was important for the city and the rivalry that Hearts came back up, the fans needed the derby game," adds Callachan, referring to the period the clubs yo-yoed past one another during those relegation-plagued years. "Supporters would always be able to give each other stick anyway but you need the actual competitive games in the league, and that was the same for players – we really wanted to be playing in them. Because I played for both sides, I also got stick from both sides, I was on a hiding to nothing! After that 3-2 game, Hearts had the hoodoo over us for a wee while and we couldn't beat them!"

Ally Brazil had played in the previous league meeting between the clubs in 1979, and four years on still found himself in the strange position of getting pelters from supporters of both teams – something that was very harsh on him from our perspective considering he never gave less than 100 per cent when playing for Hibs. "I think one of the biggest problems for me was that I was a Hearts supporter as a boy, and a schoolboy signing for Hearts, and some people latched on to that after I went to Hibs," says Benny. "I never hid the fact I had been a Hearts supporter before, but that didn't stop me giving my all for Hibs. Being at Hibs was absolutely fantastic and I loved every single moment of my time there. You can never change certain people's attitudes or feelings towards you. Lots of people still come up to me when I'm driving the buses and give me praise and tell me what a fantastic servant I was to Hibs."

Like Brazil, Alan Sneddon, spent around a decade at Easter Road, after he joined Hibs from Celtic, and he admits: "Our derby record was horrendous. In my time there, I think we beat them two or three times. I suppose I at least had the distinction of captaining the side against Hearts and beating them 1-0 at Easter Road – even if it was just a friendly, it was the Tom Hart Memorial Trophy. Jackie scored and I received the trophy from Jock Stein.

"There were just too many draws against them, many games which we should have won. I don't know what it was, but they just seemed to have the hoodoo over us during that particular period. No matter what we were doing they seemed to be able to have had that hold over us and grind it out. They had John Robertson for a start – he could not do anything wrong in derby matches. There are players like that in football, who can't stop scoring against certain teams, and sadly for us he used to score for them against us all the time.

"These games were very similar to the Old Firm matches I had played in –

you could cut the atmosphere with a knife. I don't think there was the same real hatred, where the religious factor in the west was inbred. The Edinburgh derby still had the same passion, and the desire to win the bragging rights, but it stopped short of having that same level of hatred, that was the big difference. On match days for the Edinburgh derby, you would be just as nervous and as desperate to beat your opponents, as the Glasgow derby. A lot of the time you can get carried away with the whole experience of it being a derby and that's where players can let themselves down when they play the occasion rather than the game."

That went for players in both dressing rooms. While the Hearts players celebrated their win over Hibs in the 3-2 game, Gary Mackay was less than pleased with his own contribution, a week after turning 19, having been hooked at half-time in favour of player-manager Alex MacDonald, when Hibs still led the game 1-0. "That experience in the 3-2 game probably helped me in the future because I only played for an hour and was taken off. I had the desire as a Hearts supporter to do well, but personally I didn't. I had a really poor game because of all that nervous energy," says the Hearts midfielder, who went on to play in another 56 Edinburgh derbies.

"(Player assistant manager) Sandy Jardine took me aside after the 3-2 game – that was the quality of their management style. He stressed to me that apart from the win bonus, you still got exactly the same number of points from beating Hibs as any other team. He said he knew how much it meant to me but told me how important it was for me to relax. The day before the next derby he sent me home with a pill and told me to take it before I went to bed and I'd sleep well that night. I took it and I did play well the next day. When I saw Sandy on the Monday he said to me: 'There you are... that was a paracetamol I gave you.' He had used psychology to calm me down and it worked."

The 3-2 defeat had been a bitter pill for Hibs to swallow, but the first derby of the following season was even more acrid, especially as it came at Easter Road, with Hearts again coming from behind to snatch the points. With Frankie Goes to Hollywood topping the charts at the time, it was a day that Two Tribes went to war as a handful of Hearts fans invaded the pitch and made a bee-line for the nearest Hibs players after Paul Kane's opening goal. Hibs' young full-back Kevin McKee, who was attacked by a Rangers fan at Ibrox a month later, must have been wondering what the hell was happening that season. "I remember the fans coming on, it all got a bit heated. I think we got taken off the park for a while until it all calmed down. Sadly, it was a sign of the times, the hooligan element in the early to mid 80s was a big problem, and something we had to deal with."

Shades and Jackie Mac were quick to restore order by 'persuading' the interlopers to retreat back to the terraces, but this flashpoint seemed to knock Hibs out of their rhythm for the second half. An equaliser from Craig Levein looked set to give Hearts a point they scarcely merited, before Hibs were completely blindsided by a 90th-minute winner from Derek O'Connor. A right sare yin as they say! "The game they beat us 2-1 at Easter Road in 1984 still sticks in the memory when their fans ran on and challenged Jackie (McNamara)," says Ralph Callachan. "Hooliganism was still a problem and the fans were getting a bit carried away for a while. It could be pretty wild at times, but it wasn't enough to ruin it for us, and I loved playing in front of those big crowds and in that atmosphere. It was brilliant to play in and I loved the build-up. You wouldn't be human not to feel nerves going into these games, but they were just tremendous to be involved in."

Paul Kane also has vivid memories of that sun-baked day of mayhem. "I scored the goal and I remember them pouring on, and one of them going for Jackie McNamara. Erich Schaedler grabbed him by the throat until the police came and got him. Erich was such a dominant figure at Hibs. He was the senior player and would stick up for all the young lads. He would not let anyone take liberties with the young players."

Brian Rice reveals just how volatile the atmosphere could be in those matches. "There was a lot of crowd trouble at the time," he says. "After that 2-1 game at Easter Road I remember going in the next day because I had an injury and Tom McNiven, who was a magnificent man and top physio, was giving me treatment. Before we got started Tom said, 'Come and look at this', and there was a couple of police officers sorting through all the missiles that had been thrown during the game – you should have seen them... there were golf balls with nails in them, half bottles of whisky. I remember playing once at Tynecastle when a knife got thrown at Ralphy from The Shed. In those days it was horrible, it was just a sign of the times."

It was unacceptable, but if there is anyone who can find some humour in the mindless savagery of it all, then it's Alan Rough. "I always remember the wee ball boys at Easter Road fighting to see who could get behind the goal, because if they went behind the goal they would get all the coins that were thrown on the park. There was one wee boy that came away with about five quid – not bad in those days," Roughie chuckles. "The atmosphere in these games was intense, but it could be fantastic too. Obviously, Rangers v Celtic games was and is the biggest in terms of a derby in Scotland, but Hibs-Hearts wasn't far behind – it was just an incredible atmosphere and the rivalry in the city was brilliant.

"My derby record (8 draws, 9 defeats) gets thrown in my face on numerous occasions. Peter Martin, my co-host on our radio show, gets on my case all the time about that. We drew a lot of the games and at that time wee Robbo was the Jonah for us. He could have slipped on a banana skin and still put the ball in the net against us. He was a terrific player and him and big Sandy Clark were a formidable pair of strikers. Robbo was like wee Joe Harper. You knew if anyone made a mistake anywhere from 6-10 yards then he would pounce and it would be in the back of the net. I remember getting the man of the match in a game at Tynecastle, but I actually lost a bad goal that day. I came out to get a through ball at the side of the 18-yard line and, all of a sudden, who was there? Who else? I can still hear wee Robbo laughing as he ran round me to put the ball in the back of the net. I think it was 1-0 and I had to stay behind and get the man of the match award!"

Many of the players on the pitch in derbies had come through the youth ranks together, either in the same team or from facing each other representing rival boys' clubs. Kane and Mackay were both products of highly successful Salvesen sides, and while the Hearts man was a year older, Kano still knew him and his family well, especially as Mackay's dad Peter coached the younger Salve team. "But me and Gary just never got on," explains Kane. "I got on fine with Robbo, Davie Bowman, and a couple of other Hearts lads, but not Gary. It was just one of these things in football, we were probably too close to each other. But as we've got older, respect has grown as we've grown up. I've got more respect for Gary Mackay now than I ever did."

Mackay agrees what's in the past is in the past, and recognises that as he's matured, so have his relationships with people on the green side of the city. But on the day of the 2-1 game, he was as partisan about Hearts as Kane was for Hibs. "I was in the stand that day, injured. Unfortunately for me I was right behind the Hibs enclosure, because I couldn't stop myself from getting up and cheering, and that did not go down too well. But when you went through as much heartache as I had been through watching them in the 70s, it was nice for the shoe to be on the other foot for a change. Derek O'Connor was another guy who had been through the same as a supporter, he was a massive Jambo from Carrick Knowe. There was a lot of crowd trouble that day. There were lots of reasons for things being so volatile in stadia when we played back then."

As it transpired, this game would be Pat Stanton's last shot at beating Hearts as a manager, but his successor John Blackley was also unable to break the mounting run of winless derbies. "That got under my skin, it certainly did," says Sloop, reflecting on his own derby record as boss. "But they had a good side and John Robertson was a thorn in our flesh. Alex MacDonald and Sandy Jardine had them well drilled."

Kane also points to the glaring difference between the sides. "If you look at it over the period of time, they had a prolific goalscorer in John Robertson. Okay, we had guys like Willie Irvine, Steve Cowan, Gordon Durie, Stevie Archibald but we didn't have a goalscorer for a sustained period of time in the way that they did. Over 8-10 years, he would be getting between 20-30 goals each season. He was the difference. Quite often we would be the better team and, out of nothing, wee Robbo would get a sniff and score." Kevin McKee agrees: "I loved the derbies, but was not fortunate enough to be in a winning side against Hearts, who had a certain John Robertson in their side. He was a bit of a nightmare to play against. He was just a pest and had the hoodoo over Hibs."

Neil Orr didn't have to wait too long for a win against Hearts after his 1987 move to Easter Road, but he did not taste many more, and he too blames the influence of Robertson. "When I came up I couldn't believe the poor record we had against Hearts," says Orr. "We had some close games and a lot of draws, and I think even when we did finally manage to start beating them it coincided with Robertson being down at Newcastle! I remember a game at Tynecastle we were drawing the game, and the ball got played up from their left-back position. You could see Alan Sneddon watching it, and then at the last minute he ducked. It sounds like an excuse for him, but there was a low sun and it was shining through the terracing. He misjudged the ball and it hit the back of his head and fell for you-know-who – John Robertson, and all of a sudden we lost that game too."

Gary Mackay acknowledges: "It must have been really difficult for Hibs because he was always such a thorn in their side. From opposing players, there are players who have good spells against teams at particular times, but Robbo just seemed to score against Hibs all the time – it didn't matter how he played, and that was a huge benefit to us during that period."

Brian Rice, like Rough another Hibs player who has the unwanted record of failing to bag an Edinburgh derby league win, sighs: "Every time we were 1-0 up, Robbo would score two. He had the Midas touch. I still look back with great fondness on the derby matches, because I think they were my best games and I loved playing in them. I had grown up playing against Mackay, Bowman and Robertson and all these guys, so I was really comfortable playing against them – they never fazed me in any way. One game I do remember well is the 2-2 game at Tynecastle, because someone had died in my family and it was a sad time for us, but I still had the game to play. My Dad used to come to every single game, home or away, but he never went that night. I remember I had a chance from about three yards out and I should have scored. Thankfully Joe McBride scored two late goals and got us a point, which spurred us on to beat relegation and stay up."

Gordon Chisholm, who arrived soon after Rice's transfer to Nottingham Forest, did not fare much better in his two years at Easter Road. "We got a few draws, but we never really got the better of them. They seemed to find that wee bit more than us. Wee Robbo knew where the net was. That was disappointing, but they did have a good quality team and I don't know why, but they seemed to have the edge on us. It was strange, because we regularly picked up wins against Rangers and Celtic, but Hearts just proved hard to beat during that period. We had it in our locker to do it, but for some reason we just never could deliver and push it over the line against them."

Joe Tortolano, in common with most of the Hibs players I ask about the derbies in the 1980s (and early 90s) recoils at the question and admits: "It was a nightmare to be part of. We drew a lot of these games, but for some reason, if they scored and got their noses in front, we just couldn't get it back. I hated getting pumped by them. Hearts always seemed to be up for it more than us. We could often be the better footballing side, but they just seemed to have extra aggression. Hearts could play a bit as well, don't get me wrong, but they had that edge on aggression and getting in about us. We eventually got the monkey off our backs and started beating them regularly, but those long runs of not winning were not a good feeling!"

Stevie Cowan regards the derby record as "shocking" but he rejects the theory that it was a mental barrier the players faced and insists he treated the fixture against Hearts as just another game. "I scored in a derby but would like to have won one. You might not like the sound of this as a Hibs supporter, but I didn't view that as the biggest game of the season because of where I had come from (Alex Ferguson's Aberdeen). The big games were against Rangers and Celtic. Of course, you really wanted to win the derby, but it was just another win, another two points. It was more Rangers, Celtic, Dundee United and Aberdeen you had to beat if you wanted to be in the finals and to win cups. To be fair to Hearts, they had loads of good players. What I hate is that Henry Smith stays ten doors down from me and I see him a lot and I still take quite a bit of ribbing about those derbies!"

Alex Miller takes a similar view to Cowan and tells me: "I never used to put a lot of pressure on the players in the week of a derby. It may sound strange, but Hearts wasn't the be all and end all to me. My bigger picture was to get the team up towards the top of the league challenging, to improve the squad. I know you can look at the record from that time and be disappointed, with good reason, but we were a bit unfortunate in a lot of derbies. I was very friendly with Doddy and Sandy because I had been brought up with them at Rangers, but tactically we sometimes gave them the run-around – we just couldn't finish our chances in the same way they did. Hearts had seven internationalists in their squad, while we were scrambling around trying to build a team. We would start games really well and then lose a stupid goal and the heads would go down. This may sound silly, but some of the boys were just too much Hibs supporters – they would let the emotion creep in and affect their heads. They wanted to win too much. When you are on the pitch you need to have a clear head. And they had John Robertson of course and that's basically what the difference was in some of these games."

From a Hearts perspective, Mackay thinks that the personalities of the respective management teams and their approach had a bearing on results. "You look at changes that occur in football clubs at any point in their history, and in Hearts' case it was when Wallace Mercer brought in Alex MacDonald and Sandy Jardine – two people who had such stature in the Scottish game," he says. "The assurance we had from having somebody like Sandy on the pitch, and someone in the dugout with the passion of Alex MacDonald – you couldn't fail to be motivated for these games. All credit, particularly to the gaffer Alex – he loved beating Hibs. I'm not saying he got as much pleasure as Rangers beating Celtic, but it felt that way for us and it gave us that extra incentive. I'm sure he had a good relationship with Alex Miller from their time together at Rangers, but Alex MacDonald was someone who loved winding people up as a manager as much as he did when he was a player. Whenever we beat Hibs at Easter Road he would open the changing room door, and we would have the Hearts song belting out of the old ghetto blaster as we were in the shower, to rub salt into the wounds. That must have got in their heads because it would make the Hibs players angry. If I was second guessing, and I had been one of the lads in the Hibs dressing room, I would be saying to myself 'fuck that, we'll sort them out next time and show them.' But there's a difference speaking about it and putting it into action, and it didn't always work."

Mickey Weir, like Paul Kane and other boyhood Hibs fans, had the added pressure of facing extra abuse from the Hearts supporters because of his allegiance, but he brushes off that special attention. "We got abused the most because they knew we were Hibs fans through and through, but then the Hibs fans would do the same to the Hearts players in a similar mould, guys like Gary Mackay. That was part and parcel of the occasion, you just accepted they would go after you because you were Hibs people and you just had to get on with it and rise above it. I actually quite enjoyed that – it didn't bother me. I loved the derbies, and I would have played in derby matches every day of the week! It was the games you were brought up watching and wanting to be involved in."

Weir played in 26 derbies, but won only two, and he has no choice but to admit: "We didn't win enough games. We played in a lot of draws too. There were times that we played them off the pitch and absolutely battered them, and then wee Robbo would pick his moment, a chance or a half-chance, and that would be the difference on the day. It was difficult for us, but I still loved playing in these games, because derbies are special, and you knew you had to be playing at your absolute best to have any chance of success. You were always pushed and tested – it was so competitive to play in. They had a good side too – they had some good players, but it was a disappointing sequence of results."

On the other side of the city divide, Mackay says Hearts' dominance during these years was down to self-belief. "There were games where Robbo didn't play or didn't score, but whether you wanted to call it a hoodoo or anything else I think we just had some edge," he says. "Alex Miller was so totally respected in the game as a coach, but Sandy Jardine and Alex MacDonald – and this is no disrespect to Alex Miller – in footballing terms as players were a level above Alex Miller. And I think in a way that gave us a confidence and narrative to take things forward, while that burning desire Hibs had to break the two winless runs actually worked against them because they probably tried as hard as I had done in that first game, the 3-2 game. It backfired for them in a sense.

"From our point of view, the confidence we had from having someone like Robbo, who was so prolific in most games, but particularly the Edinburgh derby, did give you an added confidence going into the games. I had witnessed it the other way round in the 70s, when Hibs had a team who were better than Hearts. There were big results in that decade, including 7-0 for Hibs and 4-1 for Hearts, but Hibs were in general better than Hearts. We turned that round and more, in a way, in the 80s. We had guys who knew what the derby was about, having been supporters themselves, and been part of it, and I like to think that my dislike of Hibernian from a supporter's perspective helped my performances in those games.

"You could feel the tension among the Hibs fans. I used to go out and warm up in front of the Hibs fans on the far side (East Terracing) so that you would feel the venom and the hatred. It also allowed me to realise that during these runs there was a desperation from their supporters' perspective that they wanted so much for their team to put an end to it. Of course, a lot of it came down to luck – there were breaks of the ball that didn't work out for Hibs. There are games you look back on, and we admitted at the time, thinking 'how the hell did we come out of that one with a draw?', or in some cases a victory, because it might have been the case that Hibs had dominated most of the game, but it was just the fact that there was a continued self-belief in our team, and that came from the management, there's no doubt about that.

"I know people continue to debate this, but from a personal point of view I far preferred winning at Easter Road. I know the Hibs fans must have loved that 7-0 game being at Tynecastle, and I had always wanted to see Hearts win and win well at Easter Road. I didn't have good memories as a fan – I remember Hibs getting late winners, or late equalisers, and Drew Busby, who was an idol of mine, being sent off there. So, I had seen all that during the 70s, and to then go to Easter Road in the 80s as a player and really turn things round meant a lot to me.

"My derby record was in the match programme for the derby recently and I think I played 52 derbies and lost 7. It's not the be all and end all, and in hindsight I would probably have gladly swapped places with some of the Hibs guys who were on the end of some of those results, for a medal that they won in the

1991 Skol Cup win. Robbo was fortunate enough to still be there when Hearts won the cup in 98, but it wasn't to be for me."

Journalist Mike Aitken says: "I was the main football writer at *The Scotsman* for most of that decade and I covered most of the derbies. I don't think either Hearts or Hibs were that brilliant then but it's not like Hibs didn't have some really good players – like John Collins and Steve Archibald. Even when Hibs played well in the derbies it seemed like they always found ways to make life difficult for themselves and my recollection is that there just seemed to be an inevitability about Hearts coming out on the right side, even if they didn't particularly deserve to. They didn't necessarily need to have played the better football to get a result. It's just that thing in football that once something starts to slip and you get a mindset that is not positive it becomes very difficult to get out of that, and that was what seemed to happen to Hibs in the derbies in that decade. John Robertson did make the difference. It was always horrendous for Hibs that John made it clear that he could easily have been a Hibs player, but for Tom Hart. John could easily have gone there, which would have rewritten history quite considerably I think!"

If you've not already stopped reading this chapter, or stabbed yourself in the eyeball with something sharp, then let's remind ourselves that there WERE a handful of Hibs victories – and the deep rot finally stopped on 17 October 1987 at Easter Road. With Andy Goram in goals for his first derby, and Hibs heading into the game on the back of a morale-boosting 4-0 demolition of Dunfermline – a third successive home victory – the signs were good. The only issue, as it always was, was that this was Hearts we were playing! The old cliché about the form book going out the window was usually spot-on whenever we faced the Jambos. It had been eight-and-a-half long years and 17 gruelling games since we'd beaten them. This time though, it would mercifully prove to be different.

There was autumn sunshine on Leith and we dared to dream as early as the third minute when Eddie May gave Hibs the lead, only for the master bogey man Robertson to haul Hearts level 11 minutes later. With half-time approaching, the player in our team who ate, slept and breathed Hibs – Paul Kane – was the fitting scorer of what proved to be the winning goal, when he headed in a corner from May. "We had a horrendous derby record, so to score that goal and help give us our first win in nearly 10 years was the best feeling I'd had in a Hibs jersey," says the hero of the hour Kano.

It was a great day to be a Hibbie, whether you were on the pitch or on the terracing. Supporter Richard Payne says: "This match sticks out in my mind for so many reasons – mainly because it fell on my ninth birthday. I can remember the excitement I had to see Hibs' new signing, Andy Goram, having missed his debut a week earlier against Dunfermline. It felt the start of an exciting time to follow Hibs with Duff and Gray splashing the cash, and Goram was the first of the big-money signings. My recollection of the match itself was that violence spilling off the terraces was never far away, with supporters from both sides clashing on the side of the pitch as fans spilt on as they celebrated the goals. The sunshine was beaming down that day and we had to shield our eyes at times sitting on the benches in the old Cowshed. At full-time the place was overcome with emotion as the final whistle was greeted with a bigger celebration than any of the goals that day. It was the first time in 17 games Hibs had beaten their bitterest rivals."

Graham Mitchell, signed at the turn of the year, had only played in three derby games before he took to the field that day, and he had the mindset that the run had to end – for the players' sanity as well as for the supporters. "We hadn't beat them for that bloody long," says Mitch. "Any victory over your rivals is sweet, because it's the victory that matters and giving your fans the bragging rights, but if you play well as well and get the victory it makes it that little bit more sweet. But it was long overdue, it was getting embarrassing that you were coming into these games and the newspapers were full of how many games it had been since we had beaten them. And it likely did play on players' minds – it must have, because I thought we were often the better team.

"Those early games I played against Hearts, I remember only one game that Hearts could say they outplayed us, and that was when it finished 0-0 and Andy Goram had an outstanding game at Tynecastle. Even the Hearts fans were applauding him off the park. But the other games we lost, I would say we deserved at least a draw and actually deserved to win most of them. It felt like there were other forces at work."

After seeing out that 1987 success, the jubilant Hibs players returned to the dressing room to find chairman David Duff and managing director Jim Gray waiting for them with bottles of champagne. "They came into the dressing room and doubled our bonus on the spot. I was tee-total and didn't drink at all back then, but the place was awash with champagne," says Kano.

Duff further explains the gesture: "By that time, Goram was the person who would negotiate the players' bonuses. Players' bonuses aren't as important so much today, but in those days the wages weren't all that great, and the bonuses could be a week's wages and more. They got £1,000 a man to win that game and I gave them it – it was my thank you. We had a bit of champagne in the dressing room after that one. I bought the champagne before the game and I wanted them to see it going in the fridge before they even faced Hearts – I had confidence that, if they saw that, they would go out there and win. Some of them needed help with their confidence."

Even a broken nose could not dampen Eddie May's joy. "One of the ambitions I had, and something I had always wanted to do as a Hibs fan growing up, was to play in a winning team against Hearts! I fulfilled an ambition I had always had since I was a little boy, and it is one of my greatest memories I ever had. It was an amazing feeling getting that goal, but the other memory I still carry to this day is the broken nose that John Robertson gave me – I'll never forget it! But I have a wry smile about that incident, because we won 2-1. He elbowed me at a throw-in, for whatever reason. Maybe I was unfortunate being the same height as John Robertson – he couldn't elbow many people – but he caught me flush on the nose. I had to come off for Dougie Bell, but I would take a broken nose every day of the week to win that game of football and to experience that thrill of scoring. I scored the winner a couple of years later against Hearts too, which was also something I will never forget."

The winning derby goal May is referring to was the only goal of the game in the 1989 New Year Derby at Easter Road, which became a sixth unbeaten derby in a row for Hibs after their breakthrough moment in October 1987. It would also prove to be the last time Hibs beat Hearts in 22 games before Gordon Hunter ended that dismal sequence with his Tynecastle winner in 1994!

As good as the 1987 win at Easter Road was, most Hibs fans' favourite derby success of the decade (from an admittedly select short-list!) will be the November 1988 win at Tynecastle when ten-man Hibs won a rousing contest 2-1 thanks to a goal of brilliance from the nonchalant boot of Steve Archibald. The scenes in the away end that day were unforgettable – and are covered in a later chapter. The Hibs player sent off that day was Gordon Rae, and when I diplomatically put it to the big man that he was perhaps a bit unfortunate to have been shown the red card, he laughs: "Harsh? Nah, it wasn't really when you see that one back – I think I couldn't have too many complaints. It was John Colquhoun that I kicked both times, for the yellow and the red – it was a bit like Joe Tortolano's tackle on Strachan if I'm being completely honest about it!"

Colquhoun, like Robbo, was often a nuisance to Hibs during those derbies, and he was also never flavour of the month in the Hibs dressing room. "I hated playing against John Colquhoun," says Callum Milne. "I always had bad blood with him and got sent off a few times playing against him, when he was at Hearts and when he was at Celtic before that. I remember a reserve game at Parkhead and he was involved in a nasty incident with John Collins, I saw him do it and the next tackle, smash, I was off! I didn't like playing against him, he was very quick over the first 10-15 yards. I was no slouch myself, but he was just hard to play against."

Even without their skipper Rae, Hibs managed to hold on at Tynecastle, even though Hearts pulled a goal back in the 90th minute. Lady lucky finally shone on Hibs when Allan Moore missed an absolute sitter in stoppage time. "The game at Tynecastle when Stevie Archibald scored the winner was a great day – I have happy, happy memories of that one," enthuses John Collins. "We had a terrible record against them and wee Robbo just could not stop scoring against us, so it was a huge relief to break the duck, first at Easter Road and then Tynecastle. They were a strong team in those days, and so were we by the time we beat them. It was a huge lift to see Steve Archibald come in, knowing that he had been at Tottenham and Barcelona, and he wasn't that old, so he was still at the peak of his game. I think he was only 31, he was still fit as a fiddle, lean and muscular, and technically terrific, mentally focused, just such a clever footballer – the ultimate professional. It was great for us young players him coming into the dressing room. A good opportunity to see a guy like that up close and learn from him. He was really good with the young boys, always talking and passing down advice – you would listen, that's for sure. And he showed his class with that finish against Hearts."

I remember drinking with boys from the Whelahan Bus before and after that game in the old Barley Bree pub off Morrison Street, just down the road from the Centre Spot pub run by Gary Mackay's mum and dad. I ask Mackay if that boozer also attracted many Hibs fans on a derby day at Tynecastle: "Aye, we got a few… and also got a few that partook in smashing some of the windaes too after games. There was always an extra glazing bill on the Monday after an Edinburgh derby!

"It's well documented, but my Dad was a Hibs supporter when he was growing up, and my uncles too, so he had plenty friends and guys who would come into the pub that were Hibs supporters. I like to think that on the park – and as I know guys like Kano, Mickey Weir and Gordon Hunter feel the same – what we played for was the badge on the jersey, but off the park I'd like to think that we were human beings who showed a bit of respect and humility towards each other and supporters of the rival team.

"We did a lot of commercial and charity stuff together, there were relationships between the two sets of players. There was respect there, but there was added incentive as local lads to want to come out on top. I remember Gordon Hunter and I once doing a karaoke together in the Dean Hotel. We sang *These Boots Are Made for Walkin'* and Gordon's line, which had parallels in the way he might deal with me in a derby, was 'these boots are gonna walk all over YOU!'"

CHAPTER 12

TORTO goes TONTO

"Sir Alex Ferguson came down into the changing room after the game and he ripped into me big time. He wasn't very happy, let's put it that way!" – Joe Tortolano

The Sir Alex Ferguson hairdryer. We've all heard of it, and many an Aberdeen or Manchester United player or match official has experienced it. But Joe Tortolano may be the only Hibs player to have ever felt its full unfiltered force. And let's face it, he deserved it... and then some!

I'm referring, of course, to the infamous moment Joe T lost his mind in October 1988 when Fergie brought up his star-studded United side to Easter Road for big Gordon Rae's glamour testimonial. In what was essentially a friendly, the Italian blood in Torto reached boiling point minutes after kick-off and he savagely cleaned out Gordon Strachan down in front of the old North Stand, leaving him entangled with the advertising hoardings and requiring treatment for the next two minutes. By the time a dazed Strachan had groggily returned to his senses, Joe – having taken leave of his own – was trudging sheepishly down the tunnel, after a red card was promptly brandished in his direction by referee George Smith. That was the least of his worries, as he still had to incur the wrath of his embarrassed manager Alex Miller, and more worrying – an incandescent Alex Ferguson!

When I apologetically ask Joe now about Gordon Rae's Testimonial, his cherub-like response is: "What happened like?" quickly followed by the quip: "I've still got Gordon Strachan's legs up here on my mantelpiece! At least I have a Guinness world record to my name: for fastest ever sending off in a testimonial match!"

Those who were there that night, and it was a bumper crowd under the flood-lights, still wince or laugh in disbelief at the memory of Joe ploughing into wee Gordon. What made it worse was that Strachan was a lifelong Hibs supporter and had been full of excitement at the prospect of returning to Easter Road as a Manchester United player, especially for such a worthy cause.

Joe, who gets reminded of his moment of madness regularly, recalls: "Because Gordon Rae was such a loyal servant to the club, Alex Miller was really keen to get a big club to play us for his testimonial and because Martin Ferguson was on our coaching staff, he was able to help swing it for his brother Sir Alex to bring Manchester United up. Ferguson was good enough to agree, but he added that it was as long as there are no heavy tackles or anybody going off their heid... Anyone who has played football knows there are moments when the red mist comes down and you panic and regret what you've done or said, and that was one of these moments for me. George Smith the referee came up to Alex Miller and said to him: 'Look, I can't let him play on, he's just halved Gordon Strachan in two!' So, that was that, he had to send me off. Alex Ferguson came down into the changing room after the game and he ripped into me big time. He wasn't very happy, let's put it that way!"

Miller, who watched the embarrassing incident through his fingers, had been instrumental in ensuring that United would come to town and put on a show, a fitting tribute to hugely popular club captain Rae, who had made his Hibs debut in 1977. "Big Gordon had been a great servant and given so many years at the club, and it was going to be the first testimonial at the club during my time as manager, so I wanted to make it special for him," says Miller. "I had never got a testimonial myself and had been really disappointed about that at the time, because I'd been 17 years at Rangers, so I thought I'm going to do my best by big Gordon.

"I knew that if we wanted to build something for the future at the club and encourage players to be loyal and stay, then we needed to recognise that, and testimonials were a good incentive. So I phoned Sir Alex and asked him if he could do us a turn and send up a team to play in his testimonial. He said they would send a team up if we covered the flights, which was great. He said: 'We'll come, but we've got a European tie the next week, so it needs to be a friendly.'

"When he came up to Edinburgh, I thanked him and we were having a cup of tea together before the game, and he made a point of reminding me, 'We've got a European tie coming up so make sure you tell your guys we are here to play, it's for a good cause, but no stupid tackles.' I had already told them this, but just to be on the safe side I went back into the dressing room to reinforce the message. I said: 'Look guys, I have just spoken to Alex and he says try and watch what you are doing with the tackles, nothing stupid okay? I'm not telling you to not tackle, but don't go over the top with anybody. Have you got that?' Lots of nodding heads and 'ayes' and off they went up the tunnel.

"I always remember the tackle. Strachan was out on the touchline, close to the dug-out, and wee Joe ran in and put him over the boundary wall. George Smith just looked at me and said: 'I can't keep him on'. Joe was ordered off and as he was shuffling past me, he said, 'I'm sorry, I had a rush of blood boss.' Fergie was screaming at us: 'I fuckin told youse! You fuckin maniacs!' He was going bananas. He came into the changing room after too for another go at Joe. It didn't feel like it at the time, but looking back on it now, it was so funny."

Rae himself harbours no grudges. "To be fair to Joe, it was just one of these things that happened in a flash," he says. "The whole testimonial game and day was a surreal experience for me – I mean, what a team Fergie brought up! I look at the team-sheet now and their team was scary, there was so much quality in it." For the record, United's starting XI, containing 10 players who were already or became internationals, was: Jim Leighton, Viv Anderson, Lee Sharpe, Steve Bruce, David Wilson, Jesper Olsen, Bryan Robson, Gordon Strachan, Brian McClair, Mark Hughes and Peter Davenport.

Hibs were in sparkling form at the top of the league going into the match and could be fancied to give United a decent contest. "And then, for some unknown reason, Joe went flying into Strachan," groans Rae. "It's not like we didn't know Gordon Strachan, or had something against him – the opposite was the case, he was a friend of the club. Gordon used to sometimes come up the road, stay in Edinburgh, and would come and train with us down at Letham Park. We all knew him and liked him – he was a great guy, and then Joe just went and fuckin smashed him. Joe wasn't like that, he was a bit chicken, and could be scared of his own shadow. He would never go and try and hurt somebody, and he goes and smacks Strachan – what's that all about? It's not so much that it was out of character, it was just unbelievable. If you were going to pick somebody out of our line-up who might blooter somebody, or do something a bit naughty, Joe would have been your last pick because he just wasn't like that. Fergie had brought up a team full of stars, with a bench full of young guys, so it ended up being a really hard shift for us."

Alan Sneddon, in the back four alongside Rae that night, agrees: "It would have been hard enough playing against that Manchester United team with 11 players never mind 10, and I was playing against Jesper Olsen, so I got the runaround something terrible. It gave our confidence a real shock. Playing against that quality of team and getting such a going over absolutely shattered us, mentally and physically. We always felt that we could match or get a result against anyone at Easter Road. But we got a lesson that night. You always wanted to do well against the big English teams when they came up to play us on our own patch, regardless of whether it was a friendly or a testimonial or not, so to lose a man that early in the game was a right downer. It was a shame, because Joe was a smashing lad and not that type of player. I don't know whether the occasion got to him, but he never lived it down – big Gordon used to give him pelters for it."

Despite the drama created by Tortolano, the most important thing the evening represented was Rae getting his big night, and all of the guys who played with him at Easter Road are quick to pay tribute to his character and strength. George McCluskey, by no means a weakling himself, laughs: "We used to have a game where you would be in the press-up position and you had to try and slap the hand away of the guy you were matched against. I was paired with Gordon Rae and thought I'd get an early blow in. I absolutely thumped his arm but he didn't even flinch. So I just stood up before he had a chance to have his shot and said: 'Well done big Gaz, that's you through to the next round!'"

Neil Orr says: "I loved playing alongside big Gordon. I remember there were games, we might be winning 1-0 and trying to hold on a bit, and Gordon would boot it high into the stand and turn round to me and say: 'They'll no score from there big Neily!' He was a great character and the type of guy you could depend on."

Eddie May, another to consider himself fortunate to have played alongside Rae, says: "One of the people I have always had time for – either during my time as a coach with the club or back in the days when I played for Hibs – is Gordon Rae. As a captain, as a man, Gordon Rae was absolutely magnificent."

Rae himself was as proud as punch, but is typically humble, and regrets that it coincided with a slump in Hibs' form. "It was great getting the testimonial, but to be honest it all seemed to pass in a flash," he says. "Before I knew it, it was all over and done with. It was brilliant in the build-up, it was like a script had been written – we were towards the top of the league, winning games, playing well, and we were playing Manchester United in front of a full house, with Easter Road really buzzing. So, it was absolutely brilliant... apart from the result, the red card and the aftermath obviously. Before that game we had just beaten Celtic on the Saturday, 3-1 at Easter Road, and we were flying. We had drawn with Rangers, I had scored a goal at Dundee United to put us top of the league. But things just went downhill from the testimonial onwards. I actually got injured about a week later and struggled my way through the rest of the season."

David Duff, chairman at the time, was delighted to host the testimonial at Easter Road, if a little embarrassed at what transpired: "I'll never forget Gordon Rae's testimonial – I mean Joe ran the length of the field to put Strachan in the stands. We were looking on dumbstruck. What you might not know is the manager said to him before the game: 'Joe, I'm thinking of playing you on Saturday so you get out there and show me what you can do.' So that backfired!

"Another thing I remember is that the first time The Proclaimers ever sang

I'm Gonna Be (500 Miles) was at Gordon Rae's testimonial dinner. Jonjo O'Neill, the jockey, was there, and his wife carried him out over her shoulder to *500 Miles* – it was great stuff. Alex Ferguson was there too. Gordon Rae deserved his occasion – what a great player and a mammoth Hibbie. What a nice big guy he was."

In the end, United won the testimonial match 3-0, and Strachan lived to tell the tale, not that he's let his aggressor ever forget it. "I've seen Gordon Strachan a few times since," explains Tortolano. "He came to Easter Road again in Gordon Hunter's testimonial (in 1996) when he was player-manager at Coventry. Big Geebsy was telling us how when Hibs were selling the idea to him of bringing Coventry up, and how he would perhaps play one half for Coventry and the other for Hibs, apparently the first question Strachan asked Alex Miller was: 'Is that cunt Tortolano still on your books?' And when he was told yes, he said: 'Well I'll play on the same team as him in one half, and I won't play in the other!' But he was absolutely superb with me, given what happened, and he always has been since that night. I ask him how his leg is, and he says: 'It's still not the same ya bee bastard!' But what a player he was, and what a brilliant person he is."

Joe's a great lad himself, and while he finds his name filed under the dubious category of 'Cult Hero' by most Hibs supporters who followed the team in that era, his enduring popularity was underlined at the 30-year reunion of the 1991 Skol Cup-winning squad when he was given a standing ovation in Saint Stephen's Theatre by a crowd singing in unison: 'Joe, Joe, Super Joe, Super Tortolano!'.

It was also amusing watching Joe come face-to-face with his ex-manager Miller when the pair were guests together on Hibs TV during one of the lockdown matches. When I interviewed Joe soon after that, I commended him on managing to not look too terrified! "When they asked me to come on the show I didn't even know it was going to be him (Miller) alongside me, but he was absolutely brand new and I was his best mate by the end of it," laughs Tortolano. "I was thinking to myself 'he's definitely changed his attitude towards me!' There were times when I wasn't playing that I'd be telling him to get tae fuck and get out my face because I hadn't been picked. But I have to admit that he's changed into a proper nice person. He had to do what he had to do back then, for the team's sake and the club's sake. He knew his stuff to be fair – he was obsessed with football."

Joe used to be famed in the Hibs dressing room for his uncannily accurate imitations of Alex Miller's voice, usually done behind his back and out of earshot. The former manager laughs about that now and says: "Off camera, I had a wee word with him about that, saying 'I hear that you used to do a pretty good send-up of me. Did you think I didn't know about that?' I was only winding him up, but I could see poor Joe squirming and getting redder and redder in the face!"

Joe's relationship with Miller was indeed a difficult one at times, but he had lost his way a little bit by the time the new manager came in, having made a bright start under his first Hibs boss John Blackley. Joe reveals that he almost became a Jambo, before he joined the club he grew to love. "I was actually at Hearts when I first came back up to Scotland from West Brom," says Joe, sounding furtive, like he's confessing to a heinous crime. "When players were released by a club down in England, their name would be sent up to the SFA and a list would be circulated to the clubs up here. It was well known that I was available, and I ended up going to bloody Hearts for a couple of weeks.

"Looking back now, I think what the hell was I thinking about and I'm glad it didn't happen! Their training was intense, and I was super super-fit because they just ran up hills and sand dunes and did hard runs carrying tyres. I was thinking to myself we've not seen a ball yet! I was going to be a contender for the 100, 400, 800m Olympic record with tyres wrapped around my back, it was like being in the Army. But there's no doubting they were really fit. Eventually, Alex MacDonald had me into the office and said, more or less, they didn't really think I was what they needed. We don't rate you. That boiled my head big time. That was on the Friday, and they were just about to start their pre-season tour. I was still staying with my Mum and Dad at the time, and my Mum said there's been a 'Blakey' on the phone – like the character from *On The Buses*. I thought that's my fitba career over if someone wants me to be a bus driver! But when he called back, it turned out it was John Blackley, and they were offering me a chance to come into training on Monday. Very quickly I signed a three-year contract. I met all the boys then, it was brilliant. I couldn't wait to play against the Jambos and shove it down wee MacDonald's throat."

Rejection was motivation enough for Joe to want some derby revenge, but his love of Hibs went deeper than that. "This is absolutely gospel, but I always liked Hibs," he explains. "My Dad was a Celtic fan and so were all my brothers, but there was one stage I supported Hibs and I had the big poster on the door of my bedroom. I also got the Hibs Bukta strip for my Christmas one year, green and white with the trim down the sleeves – it was a cracking strip, the one George Best had worn. Little did I know I would be playing for them.

"My debut was as a substitute against Clydebank on a Wednesday night. It turned out to be a happy hunting ground for me and I scored a couple of goals there. It was a miserable place, a tight wee ground, but that didn't bother me – I just wanted to get out there and show people what I could do so I could break into the first team. Joe McBride was playing in front of me, and he was a great player and example to follow. He was an old-fashioned winger and a great crosser of the ball, his free-kicks were tremendous too. We played Clydebank in the cup a couple of weeks later and Joe did his cruciate and he was never the same after that. I played regular after that, but I felt bad I was in the team at Joe's expense. I started off as a left-winger, but I was doing so shite they stuck me at left-back, just to keep me out of the road!"

Tortolano is a twin, and I have a story to check out with him, submitted by Hibbie Paul Clark, who says: "Mickey Weir was on holiday with us one time in Corfu and told us of the time Joe Tortolano sent his identical twin into Easter Road in his place for the first day back after the close season. Alex Miller went mental thinking Joe had put on a couple of stone, then Joe walked in."

Joe, laughing, says: "I cannae mind that one, but it does sound a bit like something I might have done! There was another time, though, where there was a good story involving my brother, when John Blackley was the manager. The gaffer had gone to check on a young amateur player, playing for Milton near Bannockburn. He had no idea that I had a twin – we were identical, same size, same build, so when he heard someone shouting 'Tortolano' the gaffer was thinking to himself: 'That surely cannae be Tortolano – what's he doing playing in this league on this pitch?' He thought I was at it, so at the end of the game he went marching up to Mario and tells him: 'You fuckin come and see me tomorrow morning, you're going to get fined, you're not going to play for four weeks, maybe even longer. How dare you!' My brother said: 'Whoooah, wait a minute, who do you think you're talking to? I'm no Joe, I'm his twin ya daftie.' John Blackley just went: 'No way, yer joking – there cannae be TWO Tortolanos!' There were times that people thought he was me. Mario would sometimes stand and sign autographs outside Easter Road, even when the game had started and I was inside the ground on the pitch warming up!"

Tortolano literally lived up to his reputation as a colourful character when he and John Collins were chosen to front an infamous advertising campaign with one of Hibs' commercial partners, 'The Electric Beach' tanning salon in Lothian Road. "Players always got a kit sponsor at the start of the season and my one was Electric Beach," says Joe. "I think they had sponsored me and Johnny Collins, so they wanted us to go up to their salon. I was delighted, thinking I was going to get free sunbeds. The girl wanted to take some photos for their advert in the programme, and told me to go and take my clothes off, and I was like: 'Eh?' She said: 'No, I want you to wrap a towel round you and stand and pose for photographs.' So, I said, 'aye okay then, as long as I get 10 free sunbed sessions'. Johnny was along at reception getting more dignified photos with his clothes on while I was round the corner standing with nothing but a towel on, looking like a right bampot! The boys were giving me pelters, accusing me of being more interested in the sunbeds than the fitba, but my response was 'well, you've got to look the business, haven't you?'"

Huge respect to the Hibs supporter who resurrected the Torto Towel advert during lockdown by blasting it on to one of the giant cardboard cut-outs that filled the East Stand while the fans were absent. Fittingly, this was shown to Joe and Alex Miller when they were doing their turn on Hibs TV and even Alex Miller was grinning from ear to ear at the sight of topless Joe T, striking a Zoolander pose and wearing nothing but a flimsy wee white towel!

Chatting away to the wise-cracking Torto, it's clear that while he is a joker, he is also incredibly self-deprecating. It's hard not to feel sympathy for him, as to me, it always appeared that confidence not ability was the main reason he didn't become one of the mainstays in the team. Some supporters – the 'boo boys' as the tabloids say – did not take much persuasion to get on his case. When I put this to him, he says: "Listen, when you are playing well consistently every week, and you're scoring goals or making goals, then you are a favourite. But there were times I felt people had it in for me. When I first went there it was Ally Brazil who was getting it in the neck, then Alan Sneddon, and I was next on the list.

"To begin with, I was playing well, enjoying my football and playing regularly and I was really proud to have got into the Scotland Under-21 squad. Then Alex Miller came on board and I remember his first match in charge against Rangers, and I was on the bench. I just knew there and then that he didn't fancy me. I had been playing regularly for the previous 18 months so I felt the writing was on the wall and it affected me and my confidence started to slip. I was feeling low, playing shite when I did get the chance, and it got to the stage where I used to hate Saturdays. I was starting to dread them and I knew that if I didn't start the game well, or didn't get a good tackle in, or made a bad pass, the same punters would be on my case.

"It started to affect me big time and there were times I felt it would be better to go away to another club just to give myself a break from the abuse. But I thought 'no, I'm going to stay and try and go through this'. My confidence had gone and I wasn't wanting the ball, was feared to touch it, and I more or less knew the first-choice full-backs were going to be Graham Mitchell – who was my best mate – Snoddy, and later Willie Miller on the right. I was going to struggle to get into the team.

"I thought seriously about moving, but decided to stick it out and did extra training myself at night, doing road runs and getting myself into tip-top condition. And when my time came I just had to be ready to be called upon. You know as a player that if you are playing well, giving 100 per cent, making the right runs and setting up goals, then the supporters will back you all the way, but when your form dips it can be different."

John Campbell, author of a number of books on Hibs, says: "Joe Tortolano was a fine player but sadly attracted the attention of the boo boys. You could see how much that affected him and he himself confirmed many years later that he suffered as a result of that booing. Joe was apparently a real character in the dressing room and I recall being told by another player that Joe's impersonation of Alex Miller was legendary."

As it transpired, Tortolano stuck around for 11 seasons at Hibs and a testimonial was under consideration to reward his loyalty. Whether it was the Restraining Order filed by a Mr G Strachan, or something else, it didn't happen – and Joe is sad he didn't get a day in the sun, rather than another day under the sunbeds at Electric Beach. "The vibe I heard was that someone at the club said it wasn't worth their while and that bugged me big time because you don't see many guys, apart from the likes of Lewis Stevenson and Paul Hanlon, who do 10-years-plus at a club. It was a wee bit sad. But they put on a wee dinner for me, Kano helped organise it, an unofficial night and it was great. Kano and the Former Players' Association do a great job of keeping us all together. I always want to bring back the past and remember those days, it was a huge part of my life and I am a big Hibs supporter."

Given that this chapter already contains an element of slapstick (Joe in his towel) and violence (Joe's slide-tackle assault on Strachan), it seems the right place to tell the strange but apparently true story of faux terrorism perpetrated by a couple of Hibs players during one of the late-80s tours to British Army bases in Germany, which became a part of Alex Miller's pre-season preparations.

"Aye that was myself and wee Danny Lennon," Mickey Weir admits. "There was a heightened alert that the IRA might be targeting army bases in Europe, so just to break the ice, because it was so tense among all the lads, wee Danny and me came up with this idea: 'Why don't we wind a few of them up?' Wee Danny had cousins or someone he knew among the regiment that were staying there, so we came up with a plan to pull on balaclavas and all the combat gear in the middle of the night and then jump through the windaes into their rooms to terrorise them all. We had them all lined up against the wall, shouting at them in Irish accents. You wouldn't believe what we got away with! But the best thing of all was that the two of us are about 5ft 3ins – we must have been the smallest terrorists you would ever see in your life!

"We had a few of them screaming for their lives. We got Miller at the end too, him and Stuart Collie the physio. Alex Miller claimed that he knew all along that it was us, and was just going along with it, but we had him tied to the wall saying to us 'Dinnae be stupid!' The soldier boys thought it was hilarious. It seemed like a good idea at the time, but if we'd gone outside in the yard dressed like that they probably would have mistaken us for real terrorists and shot us!"

I was tipped off about this tale of nocturnal nonsense, again by the friend of the Weir family, Paul Clark, who used to holiday with Mickey and his brother. To have Mickey confirm it was true was a godsend in terms of this book, but I needed to get it corroborated before committing it to print.

I tried Graham Mitchell. "Oh aye, the IRA thing," he laughs. "I never knew anything about it at the time, I must have been sleeping, but they were all talking about it the next day. Wee Danny was hilarious though – what a character, I could probably tell you a million stories about him. The next again day we found out they had dressed up in the balaclavas and given some of them the fright of their lives. The base was on its highest alert because the IRA were bombing places in Europe. If you went out of the barracks with a car, you would have armed protection."

Given that Mitch was in his kip, why not ask the boss himself? "Aye, that happened," Alex Miller confirms. "There had been a group of soldiers who were Hibs supporters who had helped to get us to come out there for our pre-season. Whenever they bought something in the NAFFI in the months beforehand there was a collection jug to put spare change in to try and club together to bring Hibs there for a training camp. They provided us with the accommodation and food and we just had to get the money together for flights. They gave us the sergeants' mess to stay in and looked after us really well. Mickey Weir spent half his time in the jail because there was a boy from Edinburgh he knew that had been sentenced to a month by court martial – so he would go down there for a blether with him.

"We played a German second division team and then the Army team, and they were really good to us. But the night that we got warned that the Army was on a high state of alert because of the carry on in Europe, wee Mickey and Danny decided to burst in to a few rooms, all dressed up in the combat gear and balaclavas. They burst into Steven Tweed's room and I believe he was terrified. Big Tweedy was only 15 or 16 at the time, but he was out there to get some experience. We were in twin rooms and Peter Cormack was rooming with me, and the two of us got up about 1 in the morning to find out what was going on. All you could hear was this big commotion, people with their faces blacked, and big Tweedy close to tears!"

Tweed, understandably, denies that he was close to crying, and scoffs at an incident he says has "grown arms and legs" since it first happened. "We were on red alert in the camp, and the Army guys had big mirrors going under the cars to check for bombs and so on. I think there had actually been someone seen on the perimeter fence not long before we arrived, so what they did wasn't the best timing! They were going up and down the corridor, and I could hear it all happening, and they opened the door and had balaclavas on – I think one of them had a knife. They had already done every room by the time they got to me. I was still at school and had to go back for my O Grades!"

CHAPTER 13

BLOND BOMBSHELL

"We knew there were potential difficulties, but you're talking about a world-class player. I thought it was an incredible statement to bring a player like Steve to Hibs" – David Duff

I t requires something a little bit special to occur in order to draw a straight line connecting Diego Maradona, Barcelona, Johan Cruyff and Hibs – and there's no doubt Steve Archibald falls emphatically into the 'special' category! It might seem a bit tenuous to link these names, but they all contributed in some way to the sensational arrival at Easter Road in 1988 of the man dubbed 'Archigoles' at the Nou Camp.

To join the dots for you. Maradona left Barca for Napoli in the summer of 1984, and with Terry Venables installed as the new manager of the Catalan giants, it was his new signing Archibald who pulled on the No 10 shirt the world's greatest footballer had left behind. Fast forward four years, and with Venables gone and Cruyff now in charge at Barca, the legendary Dutchman received an enquiry from Edinburgh from Hibernian chairman David Duff, asking: "Is Archie for sale?" Ja... have him, was the response. And so, Duff delivered what he promised, a headline-grabbing signing that would send out shockwaves and announce that Hibs held ambitions to become big-time operators. A blond bombshell was coming our way!

What Duff and Hibs manager Alex Miller knew from the start was that they were taking on a controversial, complex character, and there would doubtless be challenges ahead in managing him. In the two years that followed, Archie would indeed test their patience to the max, and while he drove his pay-masters mad and ended up falling out completely with the manager, he had no such problems in winning over his team-mates or the Hibs support. To this day, fans remember his stellar displays in a green and white shirt with great affection, especially his famous goal against Hearts at Tynecastle in November 1988.

Archie's exploits are the stuff of legend, from breezing into training in his gleaming Rolls Royce, to ordering a taxi to take him home from Motherwell on a match-day after Miller had left him out of his team – the final straw in a strained relationship.

I would have loved to get Archibald's perspective first-hand and reached out to him through one of his friends in football, Alan Sneddon, but he politely declined and asked Snoddy to pass on his good wishes for the book project. That leaves me to base this important chapter on the memories of the others who worked alongside him during his two years in Edinburgh, Duff and Miller, but there is enough material to confirm that there was never a dull moment when Archie was around.

Duff begins the story with that pivotal call he made to Barcelona. "I spoke to Johan Cruyff and I asked him if Archibald was available. He said: 'I don't want him any more, you can have him any time you like. He is free to go – we pay his wages, but he owns his transfer fee, just do whatever you like, he's not coming in here. He's a great player, but a word of warning – you tell your manager that he's going to need a seat in his office with the name ARCHIBALD on it because he's going to be coming in to see him every day.' So, right away, we knew there were potential difficulties, but you're talking about a world-class player here. He had gone from Tottenham to Barcelona and was playing with top-class players."

Archibald's impact at Barcelona had been significant, especially with the weight he bore on his sleek shoulders when Venables bought him from Tottenham for more than £1 million in 1984. Archibald had a good pedigree, including two FA Cup winner's medals and a UEFA Cup medal to his name, to add to the league title he had clinched with Aberdeen at Easter Road in 1980, but this was literally another level. The Scottish championship Archibald had won early in his career had been under the tutelage of Alex Ferguson, and even Fergie had his moments with the maverick forward. Archibald has told the story about the time he was ordered by Ferguson to return a match ball he had taken home (without permission) after scoring a hat-trick, then complied by launching it into the manager's office the next morning accompanied by the words "here's your fucking ball!"

Venables was up for the challenge of working with Archibald from day one, and in his autobiography, *Football Heroes*, he says: "I was told Steve Archibald could be a problem, so best not buy him. Steve is his own man, and that is something people cannot come to terms with. But it doesn't make him a bad footballer and that was my first concern. Steve, on the other hand, will take any situation and try to make it work for him – and you can't ask for more from any man. As a result, he loved his time in Barcelona, took to the life, learned to speak Spanish fluently and his game flourished."

Archibald was still only 27 and at the peak of his powers when he flew out to Spain to join Venables, and expectations were high, especially among fans nervous about the gaping void their hero Maradona had left. Further pressure was applied when the front of *El Mundo Deportivo* quoted the Barcelona president in its front-page headline, saying: "Este es el hombre". This is the man. The man to replace Maradona.

The Scot, who had also played in the 1982 World Cup, did not see it that way, and has revealed that he did not even want the No 10 shirt he was eventually given. No 8 had always been on his back before the move to Barcelona, and that is what he had written into his contract. But when German Bernd Schuster pleaded to keep the No 8 shirt, preferring to shield himself from the added burden of inheriting Maradona's No 10, Archibald relented and took on that extra responsibility – even if he made it clear he was his own man. "I would have to be a lunatic to think that I could come in and do what Maradona had been doing," Archibald said in a rare interview with *The Scotsman's* Alan Pattullo when the pair met up in Barcelona. "It never entered my head. That is what I told the press when they asked me: how does it feel to be coming in to replace Maradona? I said I am sorry to disappoint you. I am not here to substitute Maradona. Maradona has gone and I have arrived. That's it. I am coming in to play the way I can play and that's it. They wanted to tag it as me coming in to replace Maradona and that was never going to happen. My play was totally different."

Archibald became an instant hit with the notoriously hard-to-please Barcelona fans, helping his side to a monumental win in their opening game of the season against foes Real Madrid in the Bernabéu, and propelling them to their first La Liga title in 11 years. A European Cup final followed in 1986, but a bitter defeat on penalties to Steaua Bucharest had ramifications and led to the departure of El Tel. He was replaced with Luis Aragonés, and then in came Cruyff. The club legend had his own plans as manager, and Archibald did not figure in them.

Duff reveals that getting Cruyff's approval was infinitely easier than convincing Alex Miller. From the moment they took over from Kenny Waugh, the ambitious Hibs chairman and his managing director Jim Gray wanted to think big and sprinkle some star-dust around Easter Road. In the pragmatic Miller, however, they found a man who could be stubborn and resistant – if he was not completely sold on a player's ability, worth, or where they featured in his plans, then he had a habit of digging his heels in. David Platt was famously at the centre of one such difference of opinion. While still an unheralded striker at Crewe Alexandra, Hibs dithered and debated, before Platt was instead snapped up by Aston Villa. Then, far away from Easter Road, he went on to establish himself as one of the finest England forwards of his generation. Platt was not the only 'one that got away'.

"Pete (Cormack, Hibs assistant manager at the time) wanted David Platt badly, and now we know why, but Alex didn't. It got to the stage that if I had taken David Platt then I would have had to sack Alex, and I didn't want to do that," remembers Duff. "It got to the stage where Pete was saying 'You have to do this chairman' and Alex was saying 'over my dead body'. It was my decision, and I didn't want to see our manager undermined, so in the end I had to side with Alex. When I spoke to Jim and said 'The only way we can get Platt is to go against Alex', Jim said 'well you can't sack Alex'. I didn't of course, although I must admit I got close a few other times!

"We were going for all sorts of players," Duff adds. "We even went for Justin Fashanu. As well as Platt we also thought about Ronny Rosenthal and Nigel Jemson – they were all on our radar. None of those came about and with Archibald we just did it on spec. We just phoned up Cruyff and asked, 'if he's not coming in to train or play at Barcelona, is he available?'

"We did most of the negotiations with his accountant, and finally with Steve at the end. I thought it was an incredible statement to bring a player like that to Hibs, and we said to Alex: 'Look, we've got the negotiations to the stage where we can make this happen and bring Steve Archibald to the club.' But Alex said 'I don't want him!' I remember saying to Alex, 'Look Alex, by this afternoon give me a list of five forwards that you want.' He said: 'I can't do that, it doesn't work like that chairman.' That was as much as I could take, so I said to him: 'Okay then, you're having Archie!' I had spent the whole fucking summer working on this deal, and if he wasn't going to come up with something better, then I was damned if I was going to let a transfer like that fall through.

"On a day-to-day basis it was Jim who worked closest with Alex. They could be with each other five or six times a day. For me, I would come in for the games. We demarked that pretty well. I think Alex was great on many levels, but he was a shit negotiator. With one player, we were thinking of getting Jim to negotiate on players' contracts, and Alex said 'oh no, no, no... I'm the manager, I've got to do that.' And I respected that, so we let him do it. We told Alex, 'here's what we are giving him for a signing-on fee, that's his wages, and that's it – as much as we are prepared to go to.' So Alex said 'great, that's very generous, leave it to me.' He met Bill McMurdo, the agent, along with the player in question and told them: 'They are giving you this... what do you think?' When the player said he would just have a quick word with Bill, Alex's response was: 'Have a word with Bill? This is the best fuckin deal you'll ever get' ... and he walked out. That was his style. It was a scream to watch, so after that, Jim became a little more involved in the negotiations.

"Alex didn't have a say in the purchase of Steve, and I don't think he ever got over that. I understood that – that it couldn't be easy for a manager to have the board intervene in such a way and go above his head. But the reason for that was that we badly needed to have a headline signing. We were getting dog's abuse, supporters telling us to get the cheque book out, and they were right. We had to start delivering on what we had promised. We could see we were not making the progress we wanted, so we needed to produce something special – someone top class."

Journalist Simon Pia, who developed a close working relationship with Duff, reveals how the Hibs chairman confided in him and, exasperated with Miller's defiance, told him: "I don't know what to do with Alex! He tells me he doesn't think David Platt has an engine!" Pia adds: "When a similar situation cropped up with Steve Archibald, and Miller told him 'Put away your cheque-book Mr Chairman, you're wasting your money', he decided to overrule him. A while later I was speaking to Duff, he told me: 'Maybe Alex had a point about Archie... what a great player, but Stevie! He's like a jailhouse lawyer. He's got all the boys down the stairs looking at their contracts and trying to rewrite them.' He had them all marching upstairs to Miller's office demanding better terms and a pay rise. Despite that, he was still bigging up the fact that we had signed Steve Archibald. But, however you look at it, it was a good move for Hibs because Archibald scored these important goals that took us into Europe for the first time in 11 years. He also helped end that miserable spell against Hearts."

Miller says the ego Archibald was well known for in the game rose to the surface the moment the parties started to discuss wages. "Archie right away said: 'I need to be the highest paid.' At that time John Collins was on £600 a week, but I didn't want to disclose any amounts, so I went back to Archie and told him that Collins was the highest paid, but I would make him the top earner. He asked 'how much are you giving me?' and when I told him '£601' he said 'fine'. That was enough for him – just to know that he was the highest paid, even if it was a pound more. I don't know the amounts involved, but I know that he also got a signing-on fee paid to him in instalments, so he was on more than the bare weekly wage."

Miller may have had reservations about the character of Archibald and his reputation as a rebel-rouser, but when he saw the professionalism, skill and ability of his new signing at close quarters, he was hugely impressed. "Archie was a great player," says Miller. "I didn't realise how good he was, particularly at receiving possession – one of the best I have ever seen. He was always side on, so he couldn't be tackled. He could always play a pass round the corner. He was a great finisher too. He used to stay behind at the end of training, and he would have a bet with Goram that he could score so many goals and Andy would always take the bet. I'm not joking, you had to see it to believe it. He was pinging them into the net with pin-point precision and there would be Andy getting angrier and angrier. He would do everything bar save it!"

The rest of the squad were wide-eyed at this prince among footballers in their midst. Sneddon, who would become a long-term friend of Archibald, said: "When you saw the teams he had been with and what he had done in the game, and then saw him come in and how he trained, it was something else – you could not fail to be impressed. People had their perceptions about Archibald, based on what they had seen on TV. Before he came to Hibs, I had fallen into that same trap. I had always thought he was a bit of a poacher, didn't link in much, but could finish. But when you played with him, trained with him and watched up close how hard he worked, his movement off the ball, his first touch, it gave you a completely different opinion of him. He had a very quick and nimble football mind."

Like Sneddon, Graham Mitchell had pre-conceived ideas about Archibald, which quickly evaporated when he saw him in action. "See when I used to watch Steve Archibald play for Tottenham, or in his even earlier days with Aberdeen or for Scotland, I didn't really see a great deal to be impressed with," says Mitch. "But when he came and trained and played next to you, I was like: 'What a player this guy is!' He didn't waste the ball a lot and Stevie could always play the ball and be off into the box, very clever. He was a great player to find from the back as well. He was one of these guys who somehow could always create space for himself. It is always hard as a defender to pick up players like that – very intelligent. Having those qualities was obviously the reason he got to the heights he did, with Barcelona. But what a signing: bringing a player from Barcelona to Hibs, which surprised everyone. An amazing player. It just goes to show you can maybe watch a player on TV and think you know them, and that you are in a position to judge him, thinking that he doesn't do that much, but then you see them up close and it's a completely different story. He was a brilliant player."

Captain Gordon Rae says: "I'd known a little about him when he played for Clyde, before he went to Aberdeen, but by the time he came to Hibs his career had gone stellar, into orbit, after what he had done at Tottenham and Barcelona. Right away you could see what a good player he was. You didn't realise just how good he was until you played with him. He was real quality."

Joe Tortolano says the entire squad were part of the Archie appreciation society. "What a signing," he says. "I remember him coming to training in the big brown Rolls Royce. We could see him arriving in the car park. We were just standing there stretching and one of the lads said: 'Is that the Queen that's just come into the car park in a Rolls Royce?' Out of the car stepped Steve Archibald and gave us a big regal wave. He was brilliant, absolutely in a different league. See his touch in training, oh my word. He wasn't the biggest physically, but he was tall and lean, and his touch was out of this world. You could not get the ball off him, he was that good. He always received it side-on so you couldn't get it. Alex Miller used to use him as the prime example of how to play the game and who to learn from. He was a brilliant boy too."

As a young striker, Gareth Evans learned more than most. "I played up front with Stevie Archibald that season, which was an absolute masterclass in how to play football, and he is probably the best football player I ever played with. I really enjoyed playing with him, he was so helpful and so caring – probably a side that not everybody gets to see in him. But he was a good man and great with the boys in the dressing room and fantastic with me. He would keep you right during a game. You wanted to listen. You would hang on every word he said and his first touch, I have never seen anything like it. Archie was just way above anything I'd seen or played with in the past."

Evans, from the less glamorous side of the football planet to Archibald, actually arrived at Hibs round about the same time they were being linked with Platt and a string of other strikers. While Archie was still registered as a Barca player, the unheralded Evans was beginning to make his way in the game with Rotherham United. He wasn't initially on Hibs' radar, but when Peter Cormack travelled down to take a look at an opposing player, he caught the eye.

Evans recalls: "I was at Rotherham and Peter came down to watch a match between Darlington and Rotherham because there was a boy playing for Darlington called David Currie and he was scoring a lot of goals. They noticed me in the game and signed me instead. I think contrary to what everybody thought at the time they (the Hibs fans) were expecting a David Platt or a Nico Clausen – it was nice to be associated with names like that if I'm being honest! I remember coming up and it was a bit of a whirlwind. I signed on the Friday and didn't have a chance to train with the players, and we played Dundee on the Saturday. After 20 minutes, someone went off injured and I went on and scored a diving header. Looking back on it now, Keith Wright was playing up front for Dundee alongside Tommy Coyne that day, and Keith would become a big mucker of mine. It was the perfect start to my Hibs career.

"I didn't know a huge amount about Scottish football, but it became more prominent because of the England players who had been moving up to Rangers at that time – Chris Woods, Terry Butcher, Graeme Roberts, Trevor Steven, Gary Stevens and so on. It was becoming much more in the spotlight at that time. English clubs couldn't compete in Europe at that time, so that was a big factor in English players coming up here to play. When the chance came, I thought why not? They were saying that European football was a possibility at that time, and that appealed to me too. I was the only Englishman in the team at first until big Houchy arrived. It was probably a brave decision at the time but one I'm very glad I took. I was a wee bit homesick to begin with if I'm being honest. I remember when I first arrived, in February 1988, and all the hotels were full because the Five Nations rugby was on, and there wasn't a room to be found anywhere. So, I stayed at Peter Cormack's house that night instead and old Peter threw his son, young Peter, out of his bed to give me somewhere to sleep that night! I was with them on the Friday and Saturday night, and they managed to get me into a hotel on the Sunday night. Peter was the man who brought me up here and was a big influence on me."

Archibald and Evans formed a great understanding up front for Hibs, and the Englishman immediately warmed to his strike partner, on and off the pitch. Evans is also tickled by the memory of Archie's grand entrance at one of Hibs' decrepit training venues in his gleaming Roller. Archibald had a fascination with cars stemming from his days as a teenager, when he had been an apprentice motor mechanic at Rolls Royce. From the time he had been playing part-time with Clyde, it had been a long-held dream of Archibald to splash out and treat himself to a Roller, if or when he made it in professional football. Evans says: "We were training at Jock's Lodge, the old Royal High primary school, with the grass inches high so the ball wouldn't roll, no showers and with the windows boarded up, and then Archie turns up in his Rolls Royce. You couldn't make it up."

Neil Orr laughs at the memory of Archibald, rolling up in his Roller. "That was typical Steve," he says. "But these training venues were beyond basic. There was the time Keith Houchen turned up for his first day's training at Easter Road, and we all headed to Jock's Lodge in our cars. When we got there, we started heading down to the pitch. The grass had actually been cut for once, but it was lying around in clumps. Keith had come from Coventry, who had state-of-the-art training facilities, and when he saw where we had taken him, he refused to get out his car. He thought it was a wind-up, that we were all in on a joke, and there was no way that this is where we trained."

Orr, who had played in the top division in England with West Ham, says Archibald was a great addition to the squad, and Paul Kane agrees: "He was the best I ever played with," says Paul. "In the season-and-a-half I had alongside him, I could see why he had played at the highest level. Johnny Collins and Andy Goram were still developing and would go on to great things, but Archie had already played at that very top level and you could see why. He was great for us – on and off the pitch. He used to do his own pre-season and really looked after himself. I used to watch him training and he was at least five years ahead of his time. He was also brilliant with the young guys – just a great lad. If he liked you, he liked you!"

Callum Milne agrees: "You had to know how to take him. Archie was a really nice guy but you had to get to know him first, although he never spoke a lot, he just kept himself to himself. He liked me for some reason, don't know why! I used to go in his Rolls Royce to training with him sometimes."

Steven Tweed, in the youth ranks at the time, says: "I remember Archie playing cards and he would go £100 blind immediately without even picking up his hand. Archie was a different breed from them all. He was a good example to us all though, and he probably gave John Collins an insight into what he wanted to become, with his professionalism and the way he looked after himself. Archie was the first real superstar I had encountered. Us young boys were all groundstaff, so we were pretty starstruck. He had the Rolls Royce and would park it in front of the big green gates next to the stand at Easter Road. One day, it was blocking our minibus and the youth team couldn't get out, so we found him and asked him: 'Archie, any chance of moving the car?' He chucked the keys to Davie Nicholls and said: 'You move it!' Davie's face was a picture."

Archibald wasted no time in showing that he had substance as well as style, proving that he could deliver in matches as well as on the training ground. He deftly scored a double on his debut in the League Cup against Stranraer and got off the mark in the league, again scoring twice in an exhilarating 3-1 win at Easter Road against the 1988 double winners Celtic. The goals kept coming, but one strike stands the test of time more than any other – the sublime winner he supremely executed against Hearts in November to give Hibs their first triumph at Tynecastle in almost ten long years. Sean Allan, former co-editor of *Hibs Monthly/Mass Hibsteria*, sums up what it meant to us: "We were in the Gorgie Road end, and it was heaving. We all went mental when that went in, and I ended up about 30 feet and ten rows away from where I started celebrating. It was wild. I don't think many Hibbies saw Stevie's celebration at the time because of our own celebrations. Once we saw the papers though we were treated to one of the best fitba photos ever. Stevie standing, arm aloft, Henry Smith on his knees, the ball in the net, thousands of Hibees behind the goal going bonkers! That ended up on the front cover of the fanzine."

David Duff was understandably delighted as he watched the game from the directors' box, yards from Mercer & Co, particularly as his star striker had delivered on a personal promise. "Before that win at Tynecastle, I was actually chatting to Archie and told him how much it would mean to me, and us as a club, to finally win there and he said: 'Mr Chairman, if I have to do it single-handed then I will win you this game.' He scored a goal of such individual brilliance. Boy, he showed his class that day! I almost felt like it was a present after what he had said to me."

Archibald was motoring in his Rolls Royce, motoring in front of goal, and motoring Hibs up the league. European qualification was within touching distance. Even the elusive Scottish Cup was entering the realms of possibility!

Defeat to Celtic, a game covered later in this book, put that pipedream to bed for another 27 years, but Hibs finished in front of Hearts to claim fifth spot in the league and a place in the UEFA Cup. The Archibald signing was starting to pay off it seemed.

There were a couple of comings and goings in the transfer market as Archibald's first season at Hibs came towards an end. Out went Eddie May to Brentford, to make way for the arrival of Brian Hamilton from St Mirren, and in came another big name to bolster the forward line, Keith Houchen.

"Scottish football hadn't even entered my mind before that to be honest, and I was on the verge of signing for other clubs in England," says Houchy. "I got very close to signing for QPR on the English deadline and I thought that was my chance gone and I would be staying put at Coventry. But then I got this phone call out of the blue from Alex Miller. When I heard the Scottish accent, I thought it was wind-up from one of the lads, I really did. I wasn't prepared for any of it.

"I drove to East Midlands airport, got on a plane to Edinburgh, stayed in a hotel near the museum, got picked up by the chairman the next morning and was then shown round the ground and did a bit of training. Then the next day I made my debut against Hearts! I got on the bus on match-day and the streets were mobbed, it was just absolutely crazy everywhere. Getting to the ground at Tynecastle, I was saying to myself, 'Dearie me, this is on another level.' It just so happened that on the Friday, we had quickly worked on a free-kick session for me to get on the end of a free-kick. I was in the game 20 years, and even though you worked on these type of things, it maybe worked once or twice in a match. But that was the day it all worked like clockwork! The reaction was just unbelievable. I had scored and was preparing just to walk back to the half-way line, but everyone went mental, and the lads were jumping up on the railings and running round the pitch. That's when it dawned on me: 'This really means something!' We ended up losing 2-1 that day but it was a fantastic atmosphere, it was like nothing I had experienced, other than perhaps cup finals. It was that fervour; I hadn't seen anything like that. And it used to get like that at Easter Road too, when we were playing well and the crowd got going, it was amazing. They were so close to the pitch, which was great, but also a reason why it was so easy to fall out with people for someone like me because you could hear what was being said. Some of the stuff that could get fired at me, it wouldn't be allowed now, you'd get sent to jail now! My younger self couldn't take it and sometimes I would react to it.

"But overall, I loved it. If I had my more mature 60-year-old head on, looking back on it now, I should have stayed at Hibs far longer. I should have sorted everything out, settled my differences, and stopped trying to fight the world, like I did at the time. Even though it didn't end the way I would have liked, it was great. I loved the club, the fans, the city, all the lads in the dressing room – it was a good time in my career."

Eddie May also has regrets about the manner of his exit from Hibs. "The only disappointment I have is how I left Easter Road. I didn't enjoy how I got treated," he says. "One day I turned up at training and got told I was leaving. I had just signed a three-year contract but that didn't matter – they wanted Brian Hamilton in the door, and I had to get sold to make way for the finance of that transfer. I don't think that was the right way of going about it, but if you've basically been told either go or you will be playing in the reserves, then what is the point of being there? It was not the way I wanted to leave, but that's just the way it was then. Although that was an abrupt end, I played in some very memorable games and loved my time. It was just a little unfortunate I didn't get the chance to stay longer and fulfil what I think I could have done for the football club over a longer period. When I went to Brentford, if I ever needed to come back up the road, Alex would still let me train with the club, which was good of him, and it was always nice to go back. I have no ill feelings towards Alex at all, he was just doing his job and what he thought was best for the football club."

As Miller looked to recalibrate his squad, Archibald was starting to get restless. A battle of wills emerged between the manager and his star striker and within weeks of the 1989-90 season starting, there was unbearable tension between the pair. "He wanted to be different and at that time it was a real struggle," says Miller. "It could be silly stuff he was difficult about. To give you an example, if we went down to stay somewhere overnight before a game I would go to the hotel and speak to them. Remember, in those days, as manager you were doing everything – you didn't have staff to do that for you. I would go there and try and negotiate a deal to save the club a few quid. I worked out we could get a cheaper deal if you knew in advance what you wanted for your tea: chicken or fish, that kind of thing. I would usually go round the squad on the Wednesday and ask them what they all wanted, so the order was done in advance, and it made it easier on the night. But when you asked Archie, he would say 'Don't know, it's only Wednesday'. I would say, if you tell me it's going to make it easier for me, but he would be stubborn and say he didn't know what he wanted. It got to the point where I said, 'okay just order what you want, but you can buy it yourself'. And that's what happened. There was one time he went and got a fillet steak, while we all ate the stuff that had been pre-ordered. The only reason he got a fillet steak was the guy in the kitchen was Spanish and happened to be a Barcelona fan, so he had got him the steak and he hadn't even had to pay for it! I was then left to deal with all the boys arguing, 'how can he get a fillet steak and we can't?' All before a game... it was infuriating!"

The disharmony between the pair was obvious to the other players, and it often manifested itself on the training ground. "It got to the stage where Archie hated Alex Miller – he detested him," says Callum Milne. "Archie had a lot of influence. Sometimes you would think Steve Archibald was taking training not Alex Miller." Gordon Rae says: "Yes, he had a personality clash with the manager, but it wasn't difficult to clash with Alex. He was like that."

The deteriorating relationship even played out in front of the youth team. "Archie and Alex soon fell out," recalls Steven Tweed. "I remember there was a spell that Archie had to train with us in the afternoon and was having another argument with Alex Miller. He was telling him: 'I have a siesta at 1 o'clock, I don't train at 1 o'clock.' You would see him sleeping on the physio bed. This went on for days. We were going down to train in the afternoon and Archie was having to train with us for fitness, when they started bickering on the bus, I'll never forget it. I think Winker Watson, who had played with Archie at Aberdeen, was driving, and Alex Miller was in the front with him. Archie was at the back and Alex was at the front and they were properly shouting at each other. Eventually, Archie went: 'Look, will you just shut the fuck up!' Archie then followed that up by telling Miller: "I mind at Aberdeen if I was tired in a game, Alex Ferguson used to say to me just go and stand on Alex Miller and you'll get a rest for ten minutes!' All of us didn't know where to look, we were thinking 'Holy shit, this is unbelievable'. And I don't think it ever got better than that between the pair of them from that point on. They didn't have a good relationship."

Hibs initially did a good job of keeping these squabbles out of the press, but Scotland is a small football pond, Edinburgh even smaller, and football writers soon suspected that there was trouble brewing. Their hunch was corroborated when Archibald first turned up late for pre-season training, then slapped in an unexpected transfer request, which was denied. Miller's patience had been exhausted, and he started to take action against the belligerent star, notably when he left him at home rather than taking him to the crucial second leg of Hibs' UEFA Cup tie in Liege.

The winter of discontent between the two rumbled on, and the inevitable outcome arrived in the first days of 1990 at Fir Park, Motherwell, when Archibald famously called for a taxi to take him away from the ground, rather than watch the game, after he had been told he had been left out the squad. Paul Kane recalls: "Basically we were all just sitting there. Archie had his own routine and he would do his stretching session himself, he would do it in the shower room or wherever. He went and did his normal thing, and then came out the shower room and started to get his gear on, ready to play, when Miller asked him: 'What are you doing? You're no playing.' It was like a red rag to a bull with Archie. He said: 'What do you mean I'm not playing?' He got his shirt, tie, shoes, blazer on and away. Taxi for Archibald! And that was him, that was the type of guy he was."

David Duff winces at the memory. "Oh yes, there was the game he wanted a taxi home because Alex wouldn't play him! A lot of the senior pros really respected him and liked him at Easter Road, but there was always a bit of personal baggage with Steve. He could be a nightmare."

Miller reveals there was far more to the Motherwell meltdown, and that he felt well justified in standing up to Archibald and behaviour he felt he could no longer tolerate. "I left him out at Motherwell because he was getting very disruptive," Miller explains. "There had been one problem too many. What happened was that he had a slight detachment in his retina, and I spoke to the medical people, including our club doctor. I asked him who the best eye surgeon was in Scotland at that time. They said it was a Dr Chawla based at Ninewells Hospital in Dundee. I phoned him up and I said: 'Thanks for taking my call, I'm the manager at Hibernian Football Club in Edinburgh. We have a top player who is ex-Barcelona who has slightly detached the retina in his eye. He is a major player for us, and we need him back as quick as possible. Could you possibly fit him in and operate on him?' He said he had no appointments, but then said he would squeeze him in a few days later, so I was hugely appreciative and reassured him that the bill would come to Hibernian Football Club. I stressed to Steve that he should be there in plenty of time to have the operation and told him beforehand to give himself plenty of time to get up to Dundee. My phone went about half an hour before the op was scheduled. 'Boss, it's Archie.' 'Where are you, Dundee?' 'No, I'm not going to bother.' So I was left so embarrassed and had to phone the surgeon – he had put someone off a list to squeeze him in. I was really raging at him for putting me in that position.

"Another day, he was in my office complaining to me about something. I left him in my office, gave him my contacts book, and said 'Here, take your pick, phone someone up, and I'll speak to them and agree a fee with them, but I'm off – I have players to see.' He said I was disrespecting him by leaving him in the office, but by that stage he was driving me daft. I don't for a minute regret taking him, because he was such a good player, but there were limits."

CHAPTER 14

HIBEES are BACK... in EUROPE!

"We were brought up watching Pat Stanton playing in Europe. Myself, Johnny and Kano – we all yearned to be back there, and we wanted to make Hibs a big club again." – Mickey Weir

Bring on the Hibees! Bring on the Hibees! More than 2,000 Hibs supporters demanded this loudly as they stood on the sweeping concrete terrace of the Stade Vélodrome de Rocourt, home to RFC Liege, a mixture of pride and disappointment the overriding emotions. Hibs, in their first European campaign for 11 years, had just been denied by a strike of such outrageous freakishness that it was hard to determine whether it had been witnessed through a prism of reality or strong Belgian beer.

After almost 200 tense minutes had failed to produce a goal, and with penalties looming to settle this UEFA Cup second-round tie, Hibs did well to clear their lines from a corner. Workhorse Gareth Evans, in that typical selfless manner of his, scurried over to close down the Liege captain Jean-François De Sart, who was running towards the loose ball some 40 yards from goal. It was the right thing to do, to try to force the central defender back and let Hibs regroup and get their shape back. But rather than play it safe, De Sart instead gambled on an outrageous first-time attempt, without breaking his stride, and struck a shot with such ferocity and accuracy that no-one could quite believe what they were seeing when it arrowed into the top left-hand corner of the net.

As he came crashing down to earth next to his goalpost, a bewildered Andy Goram, wearing the captain's armband for Hibs, saw the ball still bouncing up and down, and for a moment seemed to think it had hit the crossbar and come down on the line. Only when he saw the home players engulfing De Sart, did the keeper realise he had been beaten by either a moment of sheer brilliance or downright luck. As Paul Kane puts it: "Goram thought he had saved it. It bounced back up and he tried to grab it and we shouted to him, 'What are you doing you bam, it's hit the back of the net!'" Goram grabbed the ball in frustration and then punched it up the pitch. Hibs were 1-0 down and had only the second half of extra-time to try to win the tie with an away goal.

Liege stubbornly held firm, then – and despite the defeat – the loud and loyal Hibs following also held firm inside the stadium. We were going nowhere. We shall not be moved – not by the Hearts, the Celtic, or the Rangers... and certainly not on this October night by Liege. Not, at least, until the Hibs players – and manager Alex Miller – answered our call and returned to the pitch to take a bow in front of us, before we headed back into the city centre en masse to drown our sorrows in Jupiler.

Some of the fans present that night had also been lucky enough to join the club on their travels in the previous round, which had been won emphatically with a 1-0 win at Easter Road against Videoton, followed with a spectacular 3-0 win in the return leg in Hungary. It was quite the way to signal an end to our European exile, having returned to the UEFA Cup for the first time since 1978. But with a flash of De Sart's devastating boot, the continental adventures were over, for now at least.

David Duff, having taken over as chairman from Kenny Waugh in 1987, was realising a personal dream of restoring European football to Easter Road. Excitement rose another notch when Hibs were drawn against Videoton, a well-regarded team with a strong European pedigree who had beaten Paris Saint-Germain and Manchester United on their way to the 1985 UEFA Cup final, losing 3-1 on aggregate to Real Madrid, but winning the second leg 1-0 in the Bernabéu. It was beyond our wildest dreams that we would record an even bigger aggregate victory over the Hungarians than the mighty Spaniards had managed.

"It was brilliant for Hibs to be back in Europe and to get a taste of it," says lifelong Hibbie Mickey Weir. "I had always wanted to play in European ties. You just can't buy those European nights, nothing touches them. We had a decent side at the time who could compete with some top European sides like Videoton, Liege and Anderlecht. We also had younger players all champing at the bit to play in Europe. The club had been starved of playing in Europe, which would have been unthinkable to fans who had watched them from the 1950s onwards playing regularly in European competition, so it was a big thing and a sign of the progress we had made to finally make our return to playing in Europe. Myself, Johnny and Kano – we all yearned for that, and wanted to make Hibs a big club again. We had been brought up watching Pat Stanton and so on playing in Europe so that's what we wanted. It's something me and the other guys are very proud of, that we were part of the team that brought European football back after a long time out. My Dad used to always say that to me: 'You'll not realise that until you get a bit older, that you should be proud of getting back to Europe.'"

Pipers led out the teams on that first electric night at Easter Road on 12 September 1989 and Keith Houchen recalls: "I remember the pipe band leading us on to the pitch and the hairs on the back of your neck would be standing up. It was amazing." With Hibs fans on all four sides of the ground, an extra special atmosphere was generated, and the decibel level soared when Hibs took a first-half lead with an unconventional goal scored by Graham Mitchell of all people in front of the Dunbar End. When the Videoton keeper punched Gareth Evans' cross well clear, Neil Orr was first to the ball to loft it back towards the edge of the box, where Mitch was lurking to intelligently loop a header over their stranded keeper and into the net.

"It was Hibs' first European goal at Easter Road in ten years, so I felt a lot of pride in that," says Mitchell, who has become an HGV truck driver since hanging up his boots. "I remember Neil Orr hit it back towards me and I just tried to get as much purchase as I could to divert it in the direction of the goal – I was a bit surprised to see it loop in over the keeper, who was off his line. The stadium was full that night and the roar that went up when that goal went in, it was deafening. It was just about the busiest that I ever saw the Easter Road stadium of old. There were Hibs fans in each end and the whole place was rocking. Willie Haughey, who went on to become a Celtic director, is a good friend of mine, and he was there that night with some other Celtic fans – I remember they said it was one of the best atmospheres they had experienced. They were obviously used to Celtic Park and watching them all over Europe and yet Easter Road was one of the best they had ever seen. I think Easter Road at that time was just built for European games and midweek games – it just seemed to generate a real cup atmosphere, it was great to be on the pitch playing in front of the fans in these games."

Mitchell's magical moment proved to be the winner, and Hibs' only regret was that they had not won more handsomely, because they had looked the better team throughout the contest, and the Hungarians were reduced to committing a string of petty fouls in a crude attempt to try to disrupt our rhythm. "Videoton at home was a tough match," recalls Neil Orr. "It was the first European game for the club in years, and when Alex briefed us he was adamant that we couldn't concede at home, because he was looking at how crucial away goals were in Europe. In other words, he didn't want us going gung-ho and he knew how well foreign teams could play on the counter-attack. It wasn't a great game but we managed to win 1-0, it was a good win considering Videoton had gone to Old Trafford and won not so long before."

It was a good win, but would it be enough? "Before the return leg, I think Derek Johnstone was the pundit at the time, and he said on STV news: 'I think

Hibs could be struggling, having won only 1-0,'" says Mitchell. "But I thought 1-0 was a brilliant result to be getting at home in Europe in a first leg. Having not conceded was a big thing in our favour. We were confident we could go over there and finish the job." Gareth Evans adds: "I was surprised they weren't as good as people were making them out to be, but we played very well that night and the fans were fantastic. They hadn't seen European football for years and they savoured the occasion."

Ever the professional, Hibs' fastidious manager Miller demonstrated his eye to detail by flying out to Hungary in advance of the second leg, to ensure that Hibs had a comfortable hotel and facilities to settle into. However, Miller reveals that this reconnaissance mission led to him being accused of mixing with an altogether different type of 'pro'!

With a smile, he recalls the awkward mix-up: "I flew to Budapest and I went into the hotel, which wasn't in the area where Videoton played, it was about 45 minutes away. I was in the lift, and this dolly bird came in. I didn't think anything of it at the time. But then this guy came in said: 'Can I have a word with you?' She was seemingly a prostitute and he started accusing me of being involved with her. I got a bit angry for him judging me, and I told him who I was – the manager of Hibernian Football Club in Edinburgh – and that we had been drawn against Videoton in the UEFA Cup and that I had come to inspect the facilities because I was going to bring our whole party there. 'I can tell you one thing we won't be staying here,' I told him! We moved to another hotel nearer the ground."

Miller might have been experiencing flashbacks when he saw another 'dolly bird' on the flight over to Hungary for the second leg. This time, it was all in good humour though – it was none other than captain Andy Goram! In an interview with *The Scotsman*, team-mate Alan Sneddon laughed: "Andy disappeared up the aisle of the plane and behind the wee curtain. Next thing he was pushing the drinks trolley in full stewardess gear, skirt, high heels and even some lipstick, swinging his hips as he went." In his book, Goram confirmed: "On the trip, I decided to get the boys relaxed and give them a laugh by dressing up as an air hostess with lipstick, blusher and the full gear on. It went down a treat and set the buoyant mood that stayed with us throughout the trip. We were quietly confident and determined to get everything out of the experience."

Miller's preparations were done to the nth degree as usual, even if he was at the mercy of some local quirks. "I would always go to the hotel to check it out first, and the opposition too," he says. "I went on a two-hour journey in a cab to go and watch Videoton at their training camp, because their season hadn't started at the time. The driver waited for me while I went to watch the game. On the way back I asked him if we could stop for some food, which we did, but we got offered wine in this tavern. It wasn't for me, but the next thing I know he's sinking the wine. I was sitting in the back of the taxi after that thinking 'Oh no, what I have done here, I hope I get back safely!' The players knew I always had to see a team first. No disrespect to anyone else going to scout a team, but I liked to see them for myself and size them up so we could get our tactics spot-on when we faced them."

Miller came up trumps from his Hungarian spying mission, employing a tactical masterclass in the second leg. "In that first Videoton game I thought we were unfortunate in that I felt we could have had a bigger lead," he says. "Having watched them in the first tie, I knew we could exploit them over there. They had an old, experienced player at left-back, and if their manager had been strong he might have left him out of the team, but he was too established at the club and he played. I thought he was a weakness, and we worked on exposing him by overloading on that side and leaving space in front of us for us to take him on and we exploited all that space and won 3-0."

Hungary was still part of the old Eastern Bloc at the time, and I did not have the know-how or the student grant that would stretch to organising a trip 'behind the Iron curtain', but the Hibbies that made the trip to the city of Székesfehérvár, about an hour south-west of Budapest, will testify that it was an incredible night on and off the pitch. The players involved react with pride and satisfaction at what they achieved that evening.

"I always say that Videoton away was my game – the game of my career, cup finals aside," says Houchen, best remembered for his FA Cup-winning diving header for Coventry City in the 1987 FA Cup final... until he joined Hibs of course! "Hungary was a strange place to be at that time because it was still Communist-run. I remember one or two of us going into the shops and there was nothing in them, they were really old-fashioned and bare. Their fans would be outside our hotel with drums trying to keep us awake on the night before the game. It was all exciting and new – an amazing experience.

"You start as a kid, then an apprentice and young pro and move through the leagues and you build towards something. That 'something' for me was that game against Videoton. Like in golf, when you are trying to hit the perfect round. I just think that night was the game where everything just clicked into place for me – that everything I had learned as a pro came off perfectly. Everything I tried to do worked that night. We were worthy winners – even Gareth got on the scoresheet that night! We just played outstandingly well. I remember how amazing the Hibs supporters were on these nights – they wouldn't go away until we came back out of the dressing room, so we all went back out and took a bow in front of them and joined in their songs. I've still got the old Videoton flag that was thrown to me by one of the Hibs supporters, who was insistent that I have it. It was a fantastic experience. I loved those matches in Europe and I appreciated that Hibs had a rich history of these occasions and had played a lot of top teams over the years. It was great for the fans."

Thanks to Houchen's headed opening goal, Hibs went into the interval 1-0 up and 2-0 up on aggregate, and realised they were on the brink of achieving something special. "At half-time there was chaos in the dressing room," said Goram. "Everyone was shouting and yelling at the same time, we were so high. We were almost verging on hysteria. The boss quietened us down and told us to make sure we kept it tight and we would get another."

Of more concern was the damage done in the first half to Graham Mitchell. Videoton were no shrinking violets and, just as they had been in the first leg, they were guilty of a few dirty tricks off the ball. He remembers: "The boy just about snapped me because I came off just after half-time. He caught me on the calf which was agony in itself, but as I landed I damaged my shoulder as well, so I was in double the pain. I think I missed a few weeks after that. It didn't spoil my enjoyment because I had a few beers after the game, which acted nicely as painkillers, but the next day it was hurting, and I can remember being in a lot of discomfort on the plane. I had to go and see the physio Stuart because my calf was about twice the size it should have been with the swelling. It was black and blue. He went for me deliberately. I think Pat McGinlay came on for me, he was starting to make a name for himself as an attacking midfielder. I should have come off at half-time, and went out to try it, but I knew early in the second half my game was over, seconds after we kicked off."

There were more cynical, and downright violent, tactics to come from the Hungarians, especially when they sensed they were beaten. First Tamas Petres was red carded for a backhand punch on Neil Cooper early in the second half, and another Videoton player, Mirsad Sprecak, should have quickly followed after lashing out at Paul Kane. John Collins found himself booked for retaliation against Lajos Takacs, who had deliberately ripped a gold chain from the Hibs midfielder's neck – which he was at least able to recover after the match. The remaining memories of that night, just like JC's jewellery, proved to be golden!

Miller's half-time team talk and confidence that Hibs would score again was soon proved right, Gareth Evans pouncing when Houchen's header rebounded off the upright. "The game over in Hungary was down to Alex Miller," Evans insists, "he really set us up to counter-attack them. I played in a strange position wide on the right and he spent a lot of time with me beforehand, talking through how to play that game. I think that was an Alex Miller masterclass that night, tactically."

The icing was on the cake, and a cherry was put on top when John Collins reacted quickest to a Brian Hamilton shot that had thundered off the bar and tucked away goal number three. "That was my first European goal," JC recalls fondly. "It was an outstanding result and performance and a memorable night for the club. It was a great experience, something new and exciting, heading to the airport and then going to a new country and a new stadium. It was quite an adventure for us."

Neil Orr says: "We felt good from the start that night. Even in the changing room before you went out, and again at half-time, all you could hear was the Hibs fans. The travelling support was brilliant and gave us such a lift. When we scored quite early, the mentality changed even further. We were thinking that's us 2-0 up, they need three to win. And then we got another one, and one of them got sent off. It ended up as a really convincing win."

The celebrations began the moment Hibs set foot back in the dressing room, and continued on the team bus, and then at the post-match dinner. "As we were leaving the stadium, I asked the boss if we could have a few beers on the bus," Goram says in his autobiography. "Normally he never allowed it, but as this was a special occasion, he permitted it. I spotted Billy Erskine, a Powderhall bookie, and I asked him to get some bevvy. The singing continued and the bus set off for the hotel. I caught sight of a little figure, arms full of wine bottles running after the bus screaming at us. Of course it was Billy who we had clean forgotten about in the euphoria! We sang Hibs songs all the way back. Alan Sneddon, who had played in Europe, said this was a night to top them all. All credit to Videoton, as their full team turned up for the dinner afterwards in the hotel and stayed while we were singing, laughing and joking throughout the meal."

Paul Kane also recalls this incident. He says: "You look at our team and just about everyone had never played in Europe. We had no prior experience of it, so it was all fresh, exciting and new. You were just going into it with a fresh outlook and lapping it up. I can remember Billy coming on to the bus with a crate of champagne. He said it was like heaven to him. All the guys were delighted. That's what it meant to people. We hammered them and there was a good Hibs support that night. For him, watching Hibs away in Europe, it was a dream come true." Houchen adds: "I remember the atmosphere among the lads on the bus. We used to put The Proclaimers on so loud the bus was shaking, people used to look at us and think we were crazy."

Mitchell agrees: "It was absolutely brilliant to be involved in. I remember we were on the team bus and there were all these Hibs fans marching along the street before and after the game and Mickey Weir and Kano knew half of them! There must have been at least 400 or 500 fans in Hungary, it was brilliant for them, especially when we went over there and gave them something to celebrate by giving Videoton a bit of a doing."

David Duff visibly wells up with emotion when I ask him about his memories of that first sojourn on to European soil in 11 years. "The Hungarian trip was one of the great adventures in Hibs' history," he says. "That was the first time we played Sunshine on Leith. The players had it on the bus and we were all belting it out, like gladiators. It was really one for the club's history – we were fantastic that night. We had to be, because they were a fine team – they had knocked Manchester United out of Europe the previous season."

Belgian side RFC Liege were next up for Hibs, and again the first leg would be at Easter Road. Again, we should have won 1-0, only for big Houchy to fluff his lines by missing the penalty kick that came his way after he had been bundled over in the box. There is a story that has long done the rounds, confirmed to me by a couple of Hibs players involved that night, that Kano – who normally took the penalties – was bumped in favour of Houchen on the say-so of one member of the team (I'll leave you to work that one out!), who allegedly stood to make a few quid at the bookies on the centre-forward scoring the first goal of the evening. Houchen, who did not collude in any of these reported she-nanigans, still can't believe he missed from the spot. "I honestly thought it was a great penalty," he says. "I didn't miss many penalties and I took a really good one that night, and I thought it was an amazing save. I hit it sweet but their keeper got a fingertip to it. I hit it so hard that it flew past me on the rebound before I even realised that I had missed it. I just never expected to miss."

The chance of the night was gone, and Hibs had to settle for a hard-fought 0-0 draw against Liege, who had a certain Jean-Marc Bosman in their starting XI that evening – still an obscure and relatively anonymous player, before his contract dispute in 1990 and the intervention of the European Court of Justice made him a world-famous name in football.

While I had been forced to admit defeat and let the Videoton trip slide, there was no chance I was going to pass up on the opportunity to join a huge Hibs support in making the trip to Liege. I had just turned 18 and had the latest instalment of my student grant burning a hole in my pocket, so what better way to blow it than following the Hibbies to Europe?

Me and my pal Burnsy were regulars on the Whelahan Bus at this time, and we signed up to their trip of madness and mayhem, which started with an afternoon sesh in the Robin's Nest on Gilmerton Road and continued on to the ferry to Zeebrugge and beyond. The craic in Liege was just out of this world – Hibees here, Hibees there, Hibees fuckin everywhere! Dundee United sup-porters would doubtless have experienced the same when they faced Antwerp in the same competition that very month, but there was an added edge within the ranks of the Belgian polis – a hangover from events in Heysel no doubt, considering we were from the UK – and they treated our presence warily, as we did them, especially those with firearms, who were herding us into the ground.

The atmosphere was great throughout, with Hibs flags, Saltires and Lion

Rampants draped over the steep velodrome walls, and the assembled Hibees in full voice as we willed on our team to defy the odds and record another big win in Europe. Whatever vantage point you had, the split second the ball left De Sart's boot, it was one of those moments where time seemed to stand still. For Mickey Weir, he saw the drama unfold from behind the goal – he was a substitute that night, devastated not to be out there on the pitch trying to influence the game. "I was warming up behind the goal when the ball flew into the net," Mickey explains. "It was an amazing atmosphere, but it was one of the worst nights of my career for me personally. I remember he (Miller) dropped me for the second game, in Belgium, and I was absolutely devastated – I had never been so low. It was a good time for Hibs, but a bad time for me. It didn't help our relationship. I was gutted to the bottom of my stomach to be on the bench. I felt distraught because you don't get many chances to play in games like that. People talk to me about that game, and I have mixed emotions."

Also rendered a spectator at that stage of the tie was Houchen. "I think I pulled my hamstring in that game and had to come off (for Pat McGinlay). The lad smashed it from about 40 yards, just hit it with everything he had. We didn't deserve to lose that way, but we had two great nights away in Europe that season and the atmosphere was just amazing."

Although the casuals did what the casuals did at that time and got a bit naughty after the game, the rest of us swapped scarves with the Liege fans and enjoyed a carnival atmosphere. During some recent reminiscing about these scenes on Twitter, I had a good laugh at the story shared on social media by Simon Tracey, who recalled: "I swapped my treasured Hibs scarf through a gap in the fence. Fellow supporters were getting some beauties. A Belgian hand grabbed my scarf and gave me theirs. Much later in the night I unfurled it, and it read 'DEF LEOPARD!'" Poor Simon. I got myself one of the 'beauties' he missed out on, and I took a tidy 'Royal Football Club de Liège' red and blue scarf back to Scotland with me, as well as some amazing memories, and – in the short-term – a raging hangover. De Sart's bolt from the blue was never going to stop us having a party.

One highlight while out drinking that night in Liege was to see the majority of the Hibs players wander into town and mingle with the fans. I remember slavering some platitudes to Mitch and Snoddy, while Goram was visibly crestfallen at losing the goal. The players were understandably a bit downbeat and didn't have the volumes of alcohol inside them that we did, but it said a lot for their character that they had made the effort to come and say thank you face to face with the fans. It meant a lot to us.

Sneddon acknowledges: "The European games are always special but it's nice when the fans appreciate that you have made the effort – and the same goes the other way, for the players to appreciate that fans have travelled a long way to support them, it makes it so worthwhile and special. I can understand why Andy Goram felt so upset – he had played brilliantly in Liege and it took a wonder strike to beat him. It was a corner to the front-post and it was me that cleared it, and Gareth Evans ran at the guy and closed him down, and all he could do was smack it, and it flew into the top corner. It was a total worldy! It was the only way he was going to get beat that night because he had pulled off some incredible saves."

Evans says: "We all remember when De Sart scored his wonder goal. It was some strike. After the game, a few days later, Andy Goram came up and said to me: 'It's your fault that goal.' I said, 'what do you mean? He's banged it in from 40 yards,' and Goram says: 'If you had never pressed him, he would never have hit it.' We actually went out for a couple of drinks in Liege and there were loads of Hibs fans out in the centre."

Mitchell says the players felt it was the least they could do to recognise the backing the Hibs fans had given them throughout the 120 minutes that night, and the three earlier European ties in the campaign. "We should have definitely beaten them, and we only went out to a goal that was out of this world," says Mitch. "Any shot that beats Andy Goram from 40 yards has to be a pretty incredible strike. He would have been disappointed getting beaten from that distance, but nobody would have saved that, it was unstoppable. I can remember being out with the fans after the game. The Hibs support was just unbelievable. I always had a great relationship with the Hibs fans, but they were great on those European nights. Unfortunately, we didn't get into Europe as much as we would have liked, but these games and the following ones that we had home and away were just absolutely brilliant."

Mickey Weir agrees: "The European nights were something to behold, you could really feel the excitement coursing through the fans. I remember going over to Liege and being shocked to see how many Hibs supporters had made the journey over, by whatever way they could, to cheer us on. I saw loads of my friends while we were there. They just booked up and didn't worry about accommodation, they were quite happy to sleep rough if that's what it took to get to Belgium and watch Hibs. That's what the European ties are all about. Getting into Europe felt like a bit of a celebration, and you would see Hibs supporters from all over the world at some of these games."

Hands up to sleeping rough. For me and my pal Burnsy, young and stupid was our default position back then, and we had neither the common-sense or wherewithal to think ahead and book ourselves accommodation... although reading some older fans' memories of that trip on forums like the Hibees Bounce or Hibs.net, maybe as young impressionable chaps we dodged a moral bullet by not staying in some of the fleshpots they ended up in!

We were rendered street urchins for the night, and although we made a good go at trying to drink all the way through until the morning, we fell asleep in one of the many cheesy, neon-lit disco-type bars in the city playing Technotronic's *Pump Up The Jam* on a seemingly endless loop, and were promptly poured back into the cold, dark outdoors. Time to get the head down and sleep rough, we thought, and we were dreaming sweet Hibbie dreams in the shelter of a shop doorway within the train station, when big Burnsy was awoken about 6am with a blow to the ribs delivered from the boot of a humpty and muscular cleaning woman, with an even fiercer shot on her than De Sart! Or maybe we had the wrong end of the stick... was she merely paying tribute to the numerous renditions of the 'Houchy Houchy' from the night before, putting her left leg in, her left leg out?

Houchen laughs at the memory of this tribute song, which was belted out from the terracing in Hungary and in Belgium. He also tells an amusing story about how the chant re-appeared in more recent times, closer to home. "My son and his friends were visiting Edinburgh. He got to the end of Princes Street and kept walking, and he didn't really know where he was. He had obviously wandered down to Leith and when he went into a pub on Leith Walk to play pool with his mates, there were a few hard-looking lads in there and they started to get a bit edgy. He was worried they were going to start a fight, but then he saw green and white everywhere, and Hibs pictures on the wall. He asked the lads in the bar if they were Hibee supporters, and when they said yes, he casually mentioned 'Oh, my Dad is Keith Houchen'. He told me when he got back: 'Dad, they started doing the strangest thing... they started putting their hands in the air and singing 'Oh Houchy, Houchy Houchy!' I never realised you were that popular when you were playing.' I said to him I was like Bovril: sometimes I was popular and sometimes I wasn't. I think I had both worlds at Hibs! The European adventure was brilliant for the players and the supporters, and I don't think we let them down. Maybe we did in the 1989 semi-final v Celtic, but in Europe we gave it our all and played as well as we possibly could, sometimes it's just circumstances that go against you.

"You'd have gone through a brick wall for those fans. I loved the 'Houchy Houchy' song and I think because I did have a good rapport with supporters that when it turned sour, it turned a lot more sour than it should have been. It went from all love to hate. One extreme to the other. But I didn't handle it as well as I could have done and maybe Alex Miller could have done more for me, but I was just trying to fight too many battles on too many fronts."

It wasn't just Houchy who had his battles to fight when we got back. As we neared the conclusion of our mammoth minibus trip back from Belgium, one of our number on the Whelahan Branch requested to be dropped off on the doorstep of Haddington Sheriff Court where, with impeccable timing, he was due to be sentenced that morning for a breach of the peace. I can just imagine him addressing the Sheriff and asking for a De Sart goal to be taken into consideration!

CHAPTER 15

SATURN for the WORSE

"Becoming chairman of Hibs was a total ego trip. When I took over, I was 33 – it was a dream come true. I'm totally aware of what a privilege it was to lead my club." – David Duff

Ambition was at the heart of everything Hibs chairman David Duff did during his time in charge of the club. A new marquee signing from Barcelona, a return to European football, a new club crest, a share flotation and place on the Stock Exchange and... err... the acquisition of a string of hotels and bars 500 miles away from Easter Road. It's fair to say that ambition was also Duff's downfall.

When Duff walked through the door at Easter Road with his managing director and brother-in-law Jim Gray, Hibs supporters were promised a change for the better, following years of under-investment and under-achievement. At surface level, the pair were true to their word, and the arrival of Steve Archibald, quickly followed by those heady European nights in Hungary and Belgium, signalled that Hibs were back for a shot at the big time.

The club became more forward-thinking, improving its corporate offering, introducing a match magazine instead of traditional programme, and rebranding the club badge with an odd continental creation resembling the Planet Saturn. However, it was Hibs' place on Planet Earth that would soon be in jeopardy and the razzamatazz days of Duff and Gray came screeching to a sickening halt in the summer of 1990 when the club's vulnerability as a PLC was laid bare in the most sinister of ways, as Hearts chairman Wallace Mercer moved in and fronted a hostile takeover bid which threatened the very existence of our beloved club.

The emotion-charged battle to save the club was ultimately won and the predatory Mercer was sent packing, thanks to the heroes steering the steadfast

Hands Off Hibs campaign, our spirited supporters, and the thousands of well-wishers from across the football world who rallied sportingly to our cause. That pivotal episode in Hibernian Football Club's history has been chronicled elsewhere, and as this book is focused on the 1980s, I have deliberately refrained from retelling the whole story chapter and verse. It is fascinating, however, to look back on the state of the club as the decade drew to a close, and I have always been curious to meet Duff and learn how he now views the extraordinary chain of events, with the benefit of hindsight.

After years of silence, Duff was persuaded in June 2020 to finally give his side of the story, and gave a candid interview to Alan Pattullo of *The Scotsman*, coinciding with the 30th anniversary of Mercer's £6 million takeover attempt. Whatever your take is on Duff's moral compass, it is widely recognised that the former solicitor did play an instrumental role in saving Hibs from Mercer's clutches, and he was keen to emphasise this in the confessions of a football chairman piece he did with *The Scotsman*.

The egomaniac Hearts chairman and his consortium were a wafer-thin margin away from securing the majority shareholding they needed to take control of Hibs. When he was summoned to a London hotel at the behest of majority shareholder David Rowland, to discuss a 'mystery' bid for the club, not only did Duff flatly refuse to cave and sell his shares, he then did his level best to right a wrong and pulled whatever strings he could to ensure that the Hands Off Hibs campaign emerged victorious.

"If I had agreed to what was offered that night in London it would have been game, set and match – the matter settled before it was even announced," Duff explained to Pattullo. "It was not a merger, it was a destruction of Hibs for nothing more than money. Be sure, if I had agreed to that proposition Hibs would not exist today or at least not in the form and position they are now. (Rowland) told me that if I were to win, nobody would recognise or remember what I did. My legacy would be that it was all my fault and I would be the villain of the piece. I would never be involved in football again and would be ruined."

Certainly, Duff has never been considered some kind of a noble, heroic figure in the tug-of-war for Hibs. Far from it. And Rowland's prediction that he would be "ruined" also proved accurate. When Duff was subsequently jailed and discredited in 1993 for two years for an unrelated mortgage fraud at Winchester Crown Court, Bill Alcorn – secretary of the Hibs Supporters Association – probably spoke for the majority of fans when he said: "He has got his just desserts. We know it is not connected with what Duff did at Hibs but at least he has got some punishment."

Duff did a year of that sentence in Ford open prison and, until he resurfaced on the sports pages of *The Scotsman* in 2020, existed in relative obscurity, his name only sporadically popping up in threads on the Hibs fans forums, recalling those crazy days from 1987-1990.

Although he had already answered many lingering questions in *The Scotsman* exclusive, Duff remained uppermost on my list of intended interviewees for this book, and I am indebted to my old colleague Alan for making the introductions and securing me an audience with the man who doubtless gave us older Hibs fans some uplifting memories during his colourful time in charge, but then tarnished his legacy by leaving the club so exposed to potential catastrophe.

As I enter the latter stages of this project, it transpires that Duff is back in Edinburgh, and that he has written an explosive book of his own on the takeover battle. The memoirs are complete, but the manuscript must first navigate its way past the scrutiny of lawyers before it is cleared for publication. A meeting is set up for the Café Royal, and before long I am sitting in a booth in the ornate old West Register Street bar in the convivial company of our old chairman. Now 67, the black curly hair and thick moustache which made him instantly recognisable in his Hibs heyday, have given way to a more anonymous look, and we have no problems having a chat in privacy.

He greets me with genuine warmth, and it is clear that he has lost none of the gregarious charm he was known for in the late 1980s when he walked the walk and certainly talked the talk as a big shot around town. He also tells me if I had met him at the same venue 24 hours earlier, I would have had the added bonus of meeting Andy Goram, 'The Goalie' having paid a visit to what seems to have become Duff's temporary office while he is back in Edinburgh. "Goram was telling me he's never been invited back to Easter Road, which I find a little bit sad," says Duff in defence of the former Scotland No 1, whose career is now defined by his time at Rangers rather than Hibs. "I get it that he's made a living out of talking at Rangers functions, but even yesterday he was as enthusiastic about our club as he was about Rangers. It would be a lovely act of reconciliation if Hibs welcomed him back."

It is clear from this comment that the hopeless romantic lives on in Duff, and that he too would love to confine his stormy waters under the bridge and return to Easter Road, then be forgiven – at least partly – for his role in the chaos of 1990. He hopes his forthcoming book will go some way to doing that and appeasing fans still wary of him and his motives. "For me, it was utter hell for me and my family what we went through," he says. "But time is a healer and when I talk to people now they kind of get the fact that not selling the shares helped to save the club. I was a Hibbie... I would never have done that! It's a terrible shame that I haven't been back (since 1990). I have stuff I would like to gift back to the club, including John Collins' first ever Scotland shirt from the game against Saudi Arabia when he scored. My heart was always with Hibs. I really regret that I am now 67 and I have never been invited back to Easter Road – I'm not moaning about it, but it's such a shame because I still love the club."

Perhaps not too many people would readily shake hands on a deal with David Duff, given his track record, but I am happy to do so – promising him that to avoid over-exposing the bulk of the content he has shared in his own memoirs, we don't do too many 'spoilers'. So, most of our conversation is restricted to the 1980s portion of his chairmanship and we tackle some of the minor issues first. Let's start with that wretched Planet Saturn crest! "Yes, we changed the badge. That was a bad move, but we had to because we were ordered by the Lord Lyon to change the old one, because it featured the Crown without permission," says Duff. "So, we decided to have a competition. The winning entry was based on one of the Milan clubs. But when I look back at it, it was shit! We should have kept the tradition, and we got that one wrong – you win some, you lose some."

Duff is also delighted to hear that the record *Hibs Heroes*, released during his regime, still gets an airing at Easter Road. This catchy song was released on 'Duff Records' label, and sung by Colin Chisholm (a well-kent Edinburgh musician, and Jambo of all things), and I must admit it has stood the test of time and remains a toe-tapper to this day!

It doesn't take us long to stray into weightier matters though, and referring to the summer of 90, he does wish something to be put on the record. "As far as the bid is concerned, I was under so much pressure – I was 33 years old. I remember our professional advisors saying to me: 'You cannot say that you are not going to sell. You have a duty under Stock Exchange rules not to say that.' I said: 'yes, I can!' There were hundreds of Hibs fans outside Easter Road and I got up on a chair and I started saying what they wanted me to say – I'm telling you all now I will never sell my shares. I got into trouble for that, but that to me was the only thing they wanted to hear, and I had to make damn sure I stuck to that."

I'm also interested to hear if the rumours are true that after the Mercer merger saga, he and brother-in-law Jim Gray fell out for good and never spoke. "Absolutely not true," insists Duff. "I love him, because he's part of my family, but what we didn't do for many years was discuss Hibs. What happened which was really, really strange, was… it was just left there. He didn't know what I went through, and I don't know what he went through and until I wrote this book, that didn't change. I said to Jim: 'I'm going on this 30-year memory trip and I need you to read it – you are the best person to do that.' He was very touched by the book and said it brought back some great memories. It opened up a dialogue where we came to a massive understanding on what we had both experienced, and that all happened in the last year. There is truth that we didn't speak of Hibs for years and years, but because we were family we didn't fall out. Indeed, there was nothing to fall out about. As they say biblically, what brought us together was stronger than what divided us.

"I'm going to tell you, in all honesty, all is forgiven, it's all forgotten and it's in the past. I've let it go a long time ago. Did Jim do me wrong? I don't know, but it doesn't matter, I love him and that's the end of it."

It may or may not be the end of it, but let's look back on the start of it. Entrusting David Rowland to finance his purchase of Hibs was perhaps the biggest mistake of all for Duff. The wide-eyed innocence of putting his trust in a multi-millionaire businessman once described by the *Evening Standard* as having the "emotions of an ashtray" would, in the fullness of time, backfire spectacularly. Rowland did not give a flying fuck about Hibs. He just wanted his money back, a return on his investment, and Duff and his fanciful dreams of greatness for his boyhood football club, did not feature prominently in that equation.

Rowland is from another planet, indeed maybe another species, when compared to the average Hibs fan. He is a hardy annual on Britain's rich list, was a tax exile for many years in Monte Carlo, and now resides in Havilland Hall, the largest privately-owned estate in Guernsey, where in 2005 Prince Andrew unveiled a life-size bronze statue of Rowland smoking a cigar in a "vaguely Churchillian pose". You can see how he bonded with Wallace Mercer. Rowland was and is a private man, but he showed enough to Duff to have the Hibs chairman entranced and willing to let him bankroll his masterplan for Hibs.

While Rowland saw Hibs as a pawn on his lavish chess board, his soon-to-be ex-wife Sheila did not. Holding the honour of becoming the first woman football director when she was voted on to Hibs' board in 1987, this admirable woman quickly grew to love the Easter Road club. Cometh the hour, cometh the woman, and when the time came she stood up to her estranged husband and the Mercer camp to ensure Hibs survived.

Duff certainly rues his involvement with David Rowland, and back then it quickly became apparent where the power really lay after the club's ill-fated share issue in October 1988 and flotation on the Stock Exchange. The prospectus is still a fascinating document to digest, providing a snapshot of where Hibs were financially at the time, and – reading between the lines – casting major doubt on their suitability to pursue this plan to become Edinburgh Hibernian plc. The opening page of the document reports: "At the close of business on 16 September 1988 the Group had outstanding secured bank overdrafts of £912,000, secured loans of £917,000 (of which £500,000 will be repaid immediately following the Offer), hire purchase commitments of £30,000 and outstanding mortgages of £24,000." It showed that Hibs' turnover had in 1988 surpassed £1 million for the first time in its history, but had made a £549,000 loss, inclusive of transfer fees, that year. The year before Duff and Gray arrived, a more frugal Hibs had balanced the books, and operated at a turnover of £789,000 a year.

The minimum investment for a piece of the action was £198, and the share offer was heavily oversubscribed – more than 1,700 supporters helped to surpass the target figure of £1.6 million. Given that Steve Archibald had joined the club, most fans probably thought that there would be more stars heading to Easter Road now that Hibs were seemingly in an enviable position to flex new-found financial muscle.

After Edinburgh Hibernian was listed on the Stock Exchange, a bullish Jim Gray told the Scottish media: "I could present a healthy balance sheet at the end of every financial year if that is what the directors of Hibs wanted, but football is an uncomfortable game if you are known only as the nearly team. We have got an overdraft, but we are fighting back against the investments we have made."

The club was divided into three sections: parent company Edinburgh Hibernian PLC, Hibernian Leisure and Hibernian Land and Property. But instead of players' names popping on to Hibs' radar, it was the names of obscure pubs and hotels in Devon that were being bandied about. Alarm bells started ringing as early as February 1989 when Hibs set their sights on an altogether different transfer market.

"Supporters of Hibernian Football Club who helped to finance a £2 million shares flotation four months ago are to be asked to provide more money for the purchase of a £5 million hotel, restaurant, and public house group (Avon Inns) based in Bath," reported *The Herald* at the time. "Mr Duff said he regarded the proposed purchase as 'probably the most important and exciting event' since he and his brother-in-law, Hibs managing director Mr Jim Gray, took over the reins. The chairman and managing director both believed the only way to the top for Hibs was to have a 'strong financial company with good assets and good income'."

This time, only 220 of the original Edinburgh Hibernian plc shareholders took up the offer, but £3 million was raised. By 23 December 1989, the company accounts showed that the original 55p shares offered in October 1988 had lost more than £500,000 of their value in the first year of trading. Shares had dipped as low as 11p as a result of the Avon Inns rights issue, before climbing back up to 33p. The company's turnover was £1,782,000 but produced an operating loss of £501,000. A statement issued on behalf of the board, with heads appearing to be buried firmly in the sand, claimed: "The directors are confident in the future development of the group."

The overwhelming majority of Hibs supporters had bought the shares with the best of intentions, to feel a sense of ownership, no matter how small fry it was in the grand scheme of things – not to make a profit or speculate to accumulate. It already looked to all and sundry that Hibs' business interests were getting far removed from the targets of a traditional Scottish football club, ie: wishing to be judged first and foremost for their success on the pitch. The club was looking vulnerable on all fronts. Even the future of Easter Road was in serious doubt.

Business and news journalists, as well as sports writers, were beginning to ask awkward – but wholly justified – questions about the overall strategy and direction of the club. As a pre-emptive strike, ahead of a BBC *Focal Point* investigative documentary, Jim Gray confirmed that Hibs had made a speculative enquiry about Meadowbank Stadium as a potential new home, but reassured fans they had nothing to worry about. Aye right! "There is nothing new in any of this," Gray told *The Scotsman* in November 1989. "The requirements of FIFA and UEFA mean that all leading clubs will have to move towards all-seated grounds, and there will come a time when we will have to decide whether that means staying at Easter Road or going elsewhere. That decision will be made by Hibs shareholders. But there is nothing imminent and we have no plans to leave Easter Road. Indeed, the fact we have just spent £1 million on improving Easter Road tells its own story."

With Duff said to be down in the South-West of England most of the time, running the opaque Avon Inns arm of the operation, it was increasingly being left to Gray to explain the wisdom of wheeling and dealing in Avon and Somerset, and how exactly it correlated with the desires of the supporters – namely to have a secure, well-run football club, with a team challenging for honours.

In 1987, not long after he was appointed managing director, Gray had vowed in *The Scotsman*: "We want to make Hibs great again. There is a new enthusiasm at Easter Road and we need to channel that constructively. I firmly believe that a football club is a business and should be run like one. Our mutual aim is the future wellbeing of the club. Suggestions that Hibs are now run from London are nonsense. Our base is at Easter Road and business interests in the south are being pursued to the benefit of the club in Edinburgh. We have to decide at what level we want Hibs to operate. The chairman and myself would rather Hibs pinned themselves on to the pack of who will be successful in the Premier Division. It cannot, with respect, be solely done off the money that comes in at the gate. I would like to think the supporters know we are Hibs fans, first and foremost. Now that we have control of the club, we will not sell it either."

Three years on, those words had a hollow ring to them when the Big Bad Wolf Wallace, and his cronies, came to the door.

Journalist Simon Pia was among those who were completely unsurprised when the shit finally hit the fan and Hibs' financial fragility was brutally exposed. "There were already some financial bad smells around Easter Road even before Duff came in," he says. "I was at *The Herald* at the time and I remember writing something along the lines of he'd bought Hibs for the cost of a semi-detached house in Corstorphine – meaning he got the club for a really easy price. I remember asking who was this guy? Nobody knew anything about him. I wrote a piece saying Hibs supporters ought to be wary of this guy. It was more to do with where the money had come from rather than Duff himself – namely it was David Rowland I was trying to put under the microscope.

"I remember doing a bit of research into David Rowland, and I didn't like what I had found. I thought it had the smell about it that something wasn't right. But in saying that, as a person David Duff was a very affable guy. I remember after one game, him inviting me up to Charlie Parkers in George Street. He gave me a lift up the road and he wasn't put off by the fact I had written pieces that were asking some difficult questions – he remained charming and friendly as he always was. He would be going round buying everyone cigars and drinks. You could tell that he loved the limelight, he loved being the big guy. I would say to his face: 'Nobody knows anything about you, even the boys you were at Trinity with.' He would just laugh and say: 'I was a quiet living boy.' He was a likeable guy, a loveable rogue, and much warmer than Jim Gray. We used to have this funny relationship. He always wanted to have you on his side and wanted to be your pal.

"The players also really liked Duff. When they came in at the end of that game where they beat Hearts at Easter Road (in October 1987), Duff and Gray had got down the stairs and were waiting for them with champagne. As they came into the dressing room they popped the corks and started spraying the players with champagne. Duff had that sense of rock 'n' roll about football.

"But when they went public in 1988 I was against that. I remember being very critical of it. I warned that Hibs weren't a big enough football club to be a public limited company. It was a bad move. I never bought shares because of that, although I did end up buying them in 1990 when Wallace Mercer came along. When the launch came along in 1988, I asked him outright what his plans were. He had these grand plans to develop Hibs, but they never added up. Although, he was always very accessible to the media and very open and willing to talk, he was a mixture of being a bit of a wide boy but at the same time quite naive and innocent."

Fellow writer Mike Aitken had also been around long enough to know that there was an element of the Walter Mitty surrounding the new Hibs boardroom. "Duff and Gray were an entirely different kettle of fish to what had gone before! It always stunk. I never thought it rang true," says Aitken, looking back. "I remember the first time they came into the room at the press conference to tell us about all their grand plans and I remember looking at Duff's shoes and seeing that they were scuffed and cheap looking. I thought they are not the shoes of someone who is a millionaire businessman and who is going to transform the fortunes of this football club. I might have been doing him an injustice in thinking that, but at the time I just felt uneasy about the whole situation, and it just didn't add up for me. And so it proved. In the history of the club, that whole saga was damaging. What Wallace Mercer tried to do was terrible but I think Duff and Gray have to take a lot of the responsibility for putting Hibs in that situation, because there was desire on both sides of the city to see both clubs continue. Duff and Gray were only part of the problem, but more so the guys in the background like Rowland. When you are a sports-writer you have your job to do and that is mainly covering sport, not business, but we never had the resources or the time to find out exactly what was going on in the background. It was a fascinating time as a journalist to be covering it, but it was a terrible time for the football club."

Hibs could even have created a smokescreen for all the financial shit that was about to hit the fan – by winning the Scottish Cup in 1989. Following low-key wins against Motherwell, Brechin and Alloa, Hibs faced Celtic in the semi-finals of the Scottish Cup at Hampden, less than 24 hours after the horrors of Hillsborough had unfolded at the FA Cup semi-final between Liverpool and Nottingham Forest.

The mood was sombre, with a minute's silence observed and both teams wearing black armbands, and the occasion seemed to get to Hibs. Gareth Evans says: "It was a strange weekend. We stayed in the Erskine Bridge Hotel and we were all watching the TV when Hillsborough happened and saw the news coming in on the Saturday afternoon while we were resting up in our rooms. It was devastating. It was kind of bizarre the game was allowed to take place the next day, and it was played in subdued circumstances. It was horrific watching all the ambulance staff using advertising hoardings to carry people away, it was sickening, and to think that we had to go out and play the next day in those circumstances was kind of strange. But we did and it probably did affect us. In saying that, it was the same for Celtic, and they had a very good team at that time and Stevie Fulton had the game of his life. We were behind early and by the time Archie scored it was too little too late."

Neil Orr recalls: "We never got going. They came out really quick and finished the tie before we even got settled. I felt sorry for Tommy McIntyre because he got subbed in the first half, but we were at sixes and sevens. Celtic had obviously said, these guys are not used to Hampden, or to semi-finals, so let's go for the throat – and they did, with three goals in the first half. I don't know whether it was down to stage fright, but Celtic certainly came out of the blocks."

Graham Mitchell, left out of the starting XI that day but sent on as a first-half sub to stem the flow of Celtic goals, says: "The game should likely have been called off. I remember that game not just for the fact it took place 24 hours after Hillsborough but also because Alex Miller dropped me for the game. It was due to a bit of an argument in training about a goal we had conceded the previous week. I still thought I'd be playing to be honest, because at that time I thought I was playing well, but after something like 28 minutes he brought me on for Tam McIntyre – who had started in my place. We actually played really well in that second half but 3-0 down and there was not a lot you could do. The media made it out like it was Steve Fulton's game, his semi-final, and the media were building him as Baggio, which wasn't fair on him."

Keith Houchen, who started up front alongside Hibs' goalscorer Steve Archibald that day, also has bad memories of that opportunity spurned. "I look back on that with regret because I think there was a big chance for us. But it got away from us before we could even settle into the match properly. We were chasing it from early on. I remember falling out with Ian St John who blamed me on TV for the loss of our first goal. There weren't many people who got away from me when I was given the job defensively of picking people up at set-pieces. It was a live match on TV and when big Mick McCarthy lost Gazza, I instinctively left my man to try and cover, but big Mick headed it into the top corner. Ian St John was the analyst and picked on me as the player who had left McCarthy to score, so I fell out with him because that was far from the truth."

Duff, who must have pictured himself astride an open-top bus, cigar in hand, waving to thousands of Hibs supporters on a victory parade from City Chambers to Easter Road, ruefully admits: "We thought that was going to be our year. The boys had been playing so well and we really fancied our chances, and Hillsborough happened, and it was hard for everyone to focus. Credit to Celtic mind you, they had a great team, and they deserved their victory. It was the same for them. Alex had fallen out with Graham Mitchell and left him out of the starting XI... would it have made a difference? I don't know. Celtic in the first half were something special."

Duff and the team boarded the bus back to Edinburgh with heads bowed. He would soon be remembered for something other than Scottish Cup glory. So what about the players and manager... how do they remember their extravagant chairman? "With Duff and Gray it was showbiz for a while," says John Collins. "They came in and sounded very ambitious. They wanted to take the club forward and sign new players. They gave me a good new contract extension and wanted to keep me at a time when Chelsea had been on the phone and wanted to buy me from Hibs. I think the fee being talked about was £750,000, which was fortunes at the time, but they turned that down so it proved that they wanted to build – or that's certainly the impression they gave us, and they brought in Stevie from Barcelona to Easter Road. Obviously, it didn't turn out the way they had hoped but they came in with some bold plans and came in with a bang that's for sure."

Joe Tortolano laughs: "We used to have a few nicknames for those two! But they spent money and they wanted Hibs to be the best team in Scotland. They were really ambitious and gave Alex Miller money to spend on players like Goram and Archibald."

Alex Miller's closest working relationship was with Jim Gray rather than Duff, and his assessment reflects this dynamic. "Jim Gray was hands-on, worked hard, and was at Easter Road all the time, Duff wasn't – he was closer to Rowland," says Miller. "To be honest with you, they used to come up on a Saturday and stay in the Hilton, four or five of them at a time, and we didn't have the finances for that. They made some bad business decisions. Personally, I didn't think Jim Gray was involved. It was all through London connections, buying and selling pubs, and you did used to wonder how that could possibly work. I still occasionally see Jim Gray and he recognises that they made mistakes, but they did it to try and get the club to the next level."

 Mitchell, another player still at the club when the takeover turmoil was unleashed in 1990, reflects: "They had ambition, but see all this walking about the park and standing in the terracing with the fans, it's as if it was all about them. I don't think anyone had a mobile phone back then, but they did – it was like the big brick you used to see Del Boy waving about in *Only Fools and Horses*! It was all about them getting in the media – it was right up his street, cigars and all the flash stuff. They had ambition for the club, but by the same token, they near enough lost everyone the club."

One can only wonder now whether David Duff slept soundly when he went to bed on the last day of 1989, getting ready to lead Hibs into the next decade. Was he already lying awake at night, feeling the sixth sense, that the club was spiralling out of control? Probably not. In his head, he was still living the dream – as the champagne-swilling chairman of the club he had always wanted to own.

"Becoming chairman of Hibs was a total ego trip," he admits. "When I took over, I was 33 years old – it was a dream come true. I'm totally aware of what a privilege it was to lead my club at that time, a really important time. Bosman happened at that time, Hillsborough happened at that time, football changed dramatically at that time. It was an immense privilege to be chairman of Hibs and I'm so glad I did it at that age, rather than an older age. It was the age to really enjoy it.

"And despite all that happened, I'm always pleased that I had the opportunity to steer Hibs for a while – it really was worth all the pain that came afterwards."

The Eighties was also worth the pain, for what eventually transpired – first with the Skol Cup win in 1991 and then the Holy Grail itself, the Scottish Cup in 2016. Glory-hunters we are not, but Glory Glory to the Hibees is sometimes worth the wait and the grey hairs!

SOURCES/BIBLIOGRAPHY

- iHibs: https://www.fitbastats.com/hibs/

- *In Colours Green and White: a post-war history of Hibs* by John Campbell

- *Scotland's For Me* by Andy Goram, with Simon Pia

- *Hibernian Greats* by Stewart Brown

- *Eddie Turnbull, Having A Ball,* with Martin Hannan

- *Hibernian, The Complete Story* by John R Mackay

- *The Hibees* by John R Mackay

- *Sunshine on Leith, Hibernian's Finest Sons* by Simon Pia

- *Pat Stanton, The Quiet Man* as told to Simon Pia

- *When George Came to Edinburgh* by John Neil Munro

- *Where Do I Go From Here,* George Best – an autobiography

- Hibernian official match programmes, 1980-1989

- Hibslog: https://thehiblog.wordpress.com/

- *Football Heroes* by Terry Venables

- London Hearts website: https://www.londonhearts.com/hibs.htm